Teacher's Edition
STRUCTURES IN SPELLING

Words with Prefixes, Roots, and Suffixes

Tim Brown & Deborah F. Knight

New Readers Press

About the Authors

Deborah F. Knight began her teaching career in the early 1970s and has taught both reading and English in urban, suburban, and rural settings. Since 1984, Ms. Knight has served as Coordinator of the Learning Disabilities Assistance Program at Onondaga Community College in Syracuse, New York. Working closely with the students there, she has helped them to develop strategies for improving their reading, writing, spelling, and study skills.

Tim Brown has worked with developing and remedial readers and writers since 1978. He teaches courses in spelling as well as freshman composition and literature at Onondaga Community College. He also serves as Senior Professional Tutor at the college's Writing Skills Center, where he has a special interest in teaching spelling to developing and remedial writers and ESL students.

Knight and Brown are also the authors of the *Patterns in Spelling* series published by New Readers Press.

ISBN 0-88336-134-5

Copyright © 1992
New Readers Press
Publishing Division of Laubach Literacy International
Box 131, Syracuse, New York 13210-0131

Printed in the United States of America

Sponsoring Editor: Christina M. Jagger
Editors: Mary Hutchison and Mary Mackay
Design: Kathleen T. Bates
Production: Sharon Naftal
Cover Design: The WD Burdick Company

9 8 7 6 5 4 3 2 1

Table of Contents

Terms and Symbols Used in This Book 5

Introduction 6
   The Structural Approach · The Rationale for This Program

Features of the Program 7
   Three Modes of Learning to Spell Morphemes
   Using Patterns and Probabilities
   Related-Word Strategies · Using Meaning

An Overview of the Program 8
   Introductory Unit
   Suffixes · Prefixes · Roots · Greek Morphemes
   The Unit and Book Reviews · Lesson Notes and Answer Key

The Lesson Formats 9
   Exercise 1 · Remaining Exercises
   Sentences for Dictation · Quizzes

Introducing Students to _Structures in Spelling_ 10
   Previewing the Book · Practice in Using the Dictionary

Suggestions for Teaching the Lessons 11
   Session 1 · Session 2 · Session 3

Free Writing 12
   Errors in Words That Have Been Studied
   Errors in Words Not Studied

Final Considerations 13

Lesson Notes and Student Text

Unit 1:   An Introduction to Structures in Spelling
   Lesson 1   Some Basic Concepts 14
   Lesson 2   Using Morphemes 18
   Lesson 3   Patterns for Adding Suffixes 23

Unit 2:   Common Suffixes
   Lesson 4   -ful, -less, -ly, -ward 28
   Lesson 5   -hood, -ness, -ment, -ship 31
   Lesson 6   -er/-or, -er, -est, -en, -ery/-ary/-ory/-ry 34
   Lesson 7   -ion, -ian 38
   Lesson 8   -ant, -ance/-ancy, -ent, -ence/-ency 42
   Unit 2 Review 46

Unit 3: **Common Prefixes**

Lesson 9   a-, ad-/ac-/ap-/as-, in-/im-, in-/im-/il-/ir-, un-.................................. 50

Lesson 10   con-/col-/com-/cor-, de-, dis-/dif-, di-, ex-/ef-/e-, per-.................. 54

Lesson 11   pre-, post-, re-, pro-, mis-.. 57

Unit 3 Review 61

Unit 4: **Latin Roots**

Lesson 12   act, cent, cord, cure, fact/fect/fit/fic(t).. 65

Lesson 13   file, fine, found/fund, fuse 68

Lesson 14   mand/mend, merge/merse, muse, pass/pat, ply 71

Lesson 15   pone/pose/post/pound, port, prove.. 74

Lesson 16   tend/tent/tense, quest/quer/quire, sane, sect, serve, side 77

Lesson 17   ten/tain, sign, sort, stance/stant, test, tail 80

Lesson 18   vert/verge/verse, text, tour, vent, verb...................................... 84

Unit 4 Review 88

Unit 5: **Greek Roots**

Lesson 19   graph, gram, photo, phono/phone/phon, tele, thermo/therm 92

Lesson 20   bio, crat/cracy, cyclo/cycle, log(ue)/logy, gen, astro/ast, geo.................... 95

Lesson 21   aero/aer, techno/techn, mechan, metro/metr/meter,

                   psycho/psych, chrono/chron 98

Unit 5 Review 102

Unit 6: **More Suffixes**

Lesson 22   -ic, -al, -ial, -ous, -ious 106

Lesson 23   -age, -ate, -ite, -able, -ible 110

Lesson 24   -ist, -ism, -ive, -ize, -ine 114

Lesson 25   -ure, -y, -ty/-ity, -ice 117

Unit 6 Review 121

Unit 7: **More Prefixes**

Lesson 26   ob-/oc-/of-/op-, anti-, contra-, inter-... 125

Lesson 27   auto-/aut-, sub-/sup-/suc-/suf-, super-/sur-, trans-.................. 128

Lesson 28   multi-, poly-, mono-/mon-, uni-, bi-, tri-................................... 131

Unit 7 Review 134

Unit 8: **More Roots**

Lesson 29   ceed/cede/cess, ceive/cept, cide/cise, clude/clus...................... 138

Lesson 30   cur, dict, duce/duct, fer 142

Lesson 31   gress, ject, lect, mit/miss, mote 146

Lesson 32   form, pel/pulse, pend/pense, plore, pute 149

Lesson 33   reg/rect, rupt, scribe/script, sist, spire 152

Lesson 34   sume/sumpt, tract, turb, vide/vise 155

Unit 8 Review 158

Text Review 162

Sentences for Dictation 166

Glossary of Morphemes 174

Terms and Symbols Used in This Book

adjective
A describing word. Example: *hot*

affix
A prefix or suffix; a part that is added to a root to change its meaning. Examples: *pre-* and *-ion* in *prediction*

combining form
A word part that may be used as either a root or an affix. Example: *photo* in *photograph* and *telephoto*

homophone
One of two or more words that sound the same but have different meanings, spellings, and origins. Example: *patience* and *patients*

morpheme
A group of letters with meaning. Prefixes, roots, suffixes, and combining forms are all morphemes.

noun
A word that names a person, place, thing, quality, or action. Example: *prediction*

prefix
A part added to the beginning of a root to change its meaning. Example: *pre-* in *predict*

root
The base of a word, to which other parts are added. Example: *dict* in *predict*

schwa
A vowel sound that usually occurs in unstressed syllables in English as heard in the first syllable of *against;* also the symbol /ə/ often used to represent the sound

suffix
A part added to the end of a root to change its meaning. Example: *-ion* in *prediction*

variant forms
Morphemes that are similar in spelling, origin, and meaning. Examples: the prefixes *in-* and *im-;* the roots *scribe* and *script;* the suffixes *-able* and *-ible;* and the combining forms *thermo* and *therm*

verb
A word that expresses action, occurrence, or existence. Example: *predict*

/k/
A letter between slashes indicates a sound rather than a spelling. Example: /k/ is the sound produced by the letter *k*

/ə/
This indicates the schwa sound.

/ā/
A straight line (macron) over a vowel indicates the long vowel sound.

Introduction

Structures in Spelling provides a systematic method of learning to spell English words of more than one syllable. Unlike a purely phonics-based approach, the structural approach stresses the regularity of spelling in the English language. Many spellings that seem irregular are actually revealed to be regular when the structure of words is examined.

This program is designed for students who have a good grasp of English phonetic patterns but who have difficulty spelling words of more than one syllable. It is also valuable for students with spelling disabilities who depend heavily on phonetic spelling and who have difficulty remembering what words look like. The program emphasizes both the look and the sound of words, as well as meaning and context, and is an excellent follow-up to a more basic spelling program such as *Patterns in Spelling*. Since *Structures in Spelling* incorporates many sophisticated words, students using it should have well-developed oral and reading vocabularies. The program can be used successfully in large group, small group, and tutorial settings.

The Structural Approach

With the structural approach, students learn that many English words are constructed by combining standard parts called morphemes. A morpheme is a group of letters that has meaning. Prefixes, roots, and suffixes are all morphemes. Students learn to recognize prefixes, roots, and suffixes and to understand how they function in the building of words. As the building blocks of language, morphemes usually retain their spellings from word to word even though their pronunciations may change. Most of the more than 200 morphemes included in this program are phonetically regular. When students learn how to spell and combine these morphemes, they can spell thousands of words, even words that contain schwas or have more than one phonetically possible spelling.

The Rationale for This Program

This program is based on an understanding of how people spell, coupled with an understanding of the regularity of the English language. People often learn to spell by associating a sound with a letter. While this is a perfectly logical way to learn, the proficient speller clearly uses several types of knowledge to spell correctly. Recent research into how people spell indicates that good spellers frequently retrieve entire words from memory. When unable to do this, they retrieve parts of words. Only if these two approaches fail do they resort to spelling words by sounding them out. It has become clear that proficient spellers rely on information about how a word sounds, how a word looks, what a word means, and how a word is used in context in order to spell correctly. The purpose of this program is to help less proficient spellers learn to use the morphemic and visual information that good spellers use.

Computer-based research indicates that when only sound/letter correspondence is used, the correct spelling can be predicted for about half of English words. When other factors are used as well, spelling regularity increases to about 90 percent. These other factors include word structure, syllable stress, and the position of sounds in words. It is therefore important to understand these other factors that can help to determine how a word is spelled. The results of an informal survey may help to illustrate this concept. Sixty teachers were asked to spell the nonwords *translection* and *ingression*. All but one spelled the final syllables *-tion* and *-sion* respectively. The overwhelming agreement on how to spell the final syllable demonstrates the use of structural regularity in predicting spelling.

Features of the Program

Three Modes of Learning to Spell Morphemes

This program integrates three ways of learning to spell morphemes: hearing, seeing, and writing them in words. As students use these three modes, they are simultaneously developing three memories for the spelling and three ways to access it: their memory for how it sounds, their memory for how it looks, and their memory for how it feels to write the morpheme in a word. By using three modes, they learn the spelling more thoroughly, and they have three ways to access the correct spelling when they need it. So although the primary emphasis is on the way words look, students also hear and write them.

Using Patterns and Probabilities

Certain rules for adding suffixes, such as dropping a silent *e* or doubling a final consonant, are presented as patterns to emphasize the regularity of the language. Students are also taught to use patterns to predict the spelling of endings such as *-ance* and *-ence* that sound alike. When there are alternative spellings for the same sound combination, if one spelling is far more common than the other, students are taught to use the more probable spelling if they do not have access to a dictionary.

Related-Word Strategies

In order to promote linguistic awareness, it is important to point out to students that they know more than they realize. Sometimes they can predict the spelling of a word by associating it with a related word. For instance, they can predict the spelling of /shən/ in *direction* if they recognize that the root is *direct*. Practice with related-word strategies is included when these strategies can help to predict correct spelling.

Using Meaning

Morphemes are based on meaning, and some strategies for determining spelling are also based on meaning. The definition of each morpheme is therefore given when it is introduced. Exercises involving meaning are included when knowing the meaning assists in predicting the spelling of the word.

Since this is a spelling text, vocabulary development is beyond the scope of this book, and definitions are not included for most of the words in exercises. Students, however, should know the meanings of the words they learn to spell. It can seem pointless or frustrating for students to practice spelling words they cannot use in their own writing. When going over exercises, ask if there are any unfamiliar words, and if so, define them or use them in simple sentences. Help students to form the habit of looking up the meaning of unfamiliar words. This will also give them practice in using the dictionary.

An Overview of the Program

Structures in Spelling is divided into eight units. Unit 1 introduces basic concepts and terminology necessary to understand the structural approach to spelling. Suffixes are presented in Units 2 and 6, prefixes in Units 3 and 7, Latin roots in Units 4 and 8, and Greek morphemes in Unit 5. Reviews are provided for Units 2–8 as well as for the entire book. Most morphemes included in the program are common. A few less common morphemes have been included because they are difficult to spell.

Introductory Unit

This unit introduces the concept of using morphemes to determine spelling. Terms are defined and the processes of building words by combining morphemes and dividing words into their component morphemes are introduced and practiced. In addition, basic rules for adding suffixes to roots are reviewed and practiced.

Suffixes

Suffixes are morphemes that are added to the end of roots to change their meaning. For instance, the suffixes *-ful* and *-less* create opposites, as in *thoughtful* and *thoughtless.* Suffixes can also change the way words are used in context. For example, the suffix *-ly* is commonly used to change an adjective to an adverb.

Although suffixes themselves are usually spelled the same way in every word, when they are added to roots that end in certain letters, the spelling of the root may change. For example, a silent *e* may be dropped or a final consonant may be doubled. These changes are generally predictable because they follow regular patterns. The pronunciation of a word may also change when a suffix is added.

Some common suffixes included in Unit 2, such as *-ion, -ance,* and *-ence,* are among those that create the most spelling problems. They are introduced early in order to provide practice and review throughout the rest of the book.

Prefixes

Prefixes are morphemes that are added to the beginning of roots to qualify or change their meaning. For example, adding *in-* and *un-* to *complete* and *necessary* creates the negative words *incomplete* and *unnecessary.* Like suffixes, the spelling of most prefixes does not change from word to word. Assimilative prefixes, however, are exceptions to this general rule. An assimilative prefix is one in which the final consonant changes before roots that begin with certain consonants. These changes often result in double consonants near the beginning of words. For example, the prefix *ad-* changes to *as-* before the root beginning with *s* in *assimilative.*

Roots

While a prefix may qualify meaning and a suffix may determine the part of speech a word will be, roots provide words with their core of meaning. A single root can lend its meaning to many words. Lesson 1 contains a word web that illustrates this concept visually with the root *dict.* When students learn to spell a root, they should also learn the meaning so that they can more easily recognize and accurately spell words containing that root.

Greek Morphemes

Greek and Latin morphemes differ in significant ways. Many Greek morphemes can have more than one function in word building. For instance, *phono* functions as a prefix in *phonograph* and as a root in *telephone*. For this reason, these morphemes are often called combining forms. Words derived from Greek also have special spellings for certain sounds, such as *ch* for /k/ and *ph* for /f/.

The representative selection of Greek morphemes is designed to acquaint students with the particular concepts related to spelling words of Greek origin. It is not exhaustive.

The Unit and Book Reviews

Unit reviews provide additional practice and reinforcement of the material presented in each unit. A suggested word list for the unit test is included in the notes for each review. You may want to adapt these lists to emphasize words your students find particularly troublesome. Correctly spelling 90 percent of the words on each test should be considered mastery.

The review of the book provides an opportunity to determine how well students have mastered the material. If you choose to give a final test, include words that contain the morphemes your students have found most difficult.

Lesson Notes and Answer Key

This teacher's edition contains lesson notes that give suggestions for teaching the lessons as well as reduced replicas of the student pages with the answers filled in. For many exercises, the answers given are examples of possible student responses. Examples of original phrases or sentences are given only when they might help to clarify what students should aim for in their writing. Some answers provided in the answer key are based on information from *The American Heritage Dictionary,* which is the primary reference dictionary for this program. Answers to those exercises may vary if students use different dictionaries. Accept all answers that form correctly spelled words and that make sense.

The Lesson Formats

Except for the three introductory lessons, each lesson in this book introduces several morphemes of one specific type: prefixes, roots, or suffixes.

Exercise 1

The format for the first exercise is the same in each lesson. The individual morphemes are listed with their definitions and representative words that contain them. This exercise is designed to be presented orally, with students underlining the target morpheme in each word as you pronounce it. Sometimes the pronunciation of a morpheme changes from word to word. For instance, the long *i* in *final* becomes a short *i* in *finish.* It is important that students hear these changes and recognize that the morpheme's spelling doesn't change even though the pronunciation does.

In Exercise 1, students identify morphemes by sight and sound. This exercise is crucial because successfully completing the rest of the lesson depends on students giving careful attention to the look and the sound of the morphemes in that lesson. It is important to draw students' attention to the way a morpheme looks so that they can visualize it in a whole word.

Remaining Exercises

Exercise 2 in each lesson is a simple word-building exercise in which students combine given morphemes to build whole words.

The remaining exercises vary according to specific features of, or strategies relating to, the individual morphemes being presented in a lesson. These exercises are designed to give students practice in combining or changing morphemes, in dividing words into their component morphemes, in building many words from a group of morphemes, and in using words in context. Students also discover patterns and practice strategies for predicting the spelling of morphemes that sound alike. In addition, students have the opportunity to write original sentences in most lessons.

Apart from Exercise 1, which you lead, all exercises are designed to be completed by students working independently or in small groups.

Sentences for Dictation

Pages 166–173 of this teacher's edition contain sentences for dictation that can be used at the end of each lesson for review and to help you to determine if students have mastered the material. These sentences have words that contain the morphemes from the lesson as well as some from previous lessons. When dictating sentences, encourage students to listen to an entire sentence and repeat it to themselves before beginning to write. You may need to dictate longer sentences twice.

Quizzes

As an additional check on whether students have mastered the lesson material, you will probably want to give a quiz on words from the lesson. Select 10 to 20 words for the quiz. If students have had difficulty with words in the lesson, you may want to choose only words they are likely to use in their everyday writing. For students who are doing well, you might include words that contain the target morphemes but were not used in the lesson. In giving the spelling quiz, say each word, use it in a simple sentence, and then say the word again. Students should be able to spell 90 percent of the words correctly.

Introducing Students to *Structures in Spelling*

Before students begin using *Structures in Spelling,* you should preview the program with them. Explain that they will be learning and practicing techniques and strategies that are used by proficient spellers to spell many words.

Previewing the Book

As you are introducing students to the book, draw their attention to the reference material at the front and the back of the book. On page 5, there is an explanation of the terms and symbols used in the book. Discuss the terms as students encounter them in the lessons. The Glossary of Morphemes at the back of the book lists all of the morphemes presented in this program, their variants, and their definitions. Note that variant forms of a morpheme are listed after the original form rather than as separate entries.

Point out that Unit 1 is an introduction to the program and that the first three lessons present some basic concepts and review some spelling rules that students probably already know.

As students glance through the rest of the book, they should notice that the first two exercises in each lesson are alike, while the remaining exercises follow varying formats. This variety makes the program more challenging and interesting.

Practice in Using the Dictionary

To be successful in this program, students must be able to use a dictionary efficiently. You may want to develop supplemental activities for students with weak dictionary skills. Encourage them to develop the habit of looking up a word when they are unsure of the spelling.

We recommend that a good-sized dictionary that has reasonably complete information on word origins be available to students. Students should also have their own dictionaries.

Before students begin the program, make sure that they are familiar with the various sections and features of their dictionaries. They should know how to find a main entry and how to interpret the pronunciation guide. Point out listings of related forms of a main entry. Help students to find and interpret information on word origins in their own dictionaries. Also help them to find the section that tells them the abbreviations that are used and what they stand for. Keep in mind that dictionaries differ in what information they include, as well as in the format and abbreviations they use.

Suggestions for Teaching the Lessons

When preparing to teach a lesson, you should read the lesson notes and pay particular attention to the morphemes presented and the representative words that contain those morphemes.

Because students need to learn both to recognize and to remember the spelling of words and word parts, we recommend that each lesson be taught over two or three sessions. Normally a session should take up only part of a regular 45–60 minute tutorial or class period. Here is a suggested three-session format.

Session 1

1. Introduce the morphemes in Exercise 1 and pronounce the representative words while students underline the target morpheme in each word. Note words in which the pronunciation of the morpheme changes and words that have undergone spelling changes when affixes were added.
2. Introduce the remaining exercises and make sure students understand how to do them.
3. For homework, have students complete those exercises.

Session 2

1. Review Exercise 1.
2. Go over students' answers to the homework exercises.
3. Dictate the sentences for that lesson, which are on pages 166–173 of this book.
4. For homework, have students prepare for a spelling quiz on words containing the morphemes in the lesson.

Session 3

1. Review any parts of the lesson that students request.
2. Give a graded spelling quiz on selected words containing the morphemes presented in the lesson.

Lessons vary in length and in the difficulty of morphemes being introduced. You may want to have two sessions on some lessons and four on a few others. For lessons that require only two sessions, you may not need to give both the dictation sentences and a quiz to determine mastery.

Free Writing

When students study spelling, it is helpful to concentrate on words in isolation. Thus many exercises deal only with the correct spelling of words. But spelling is generally only one element of a more complex writing task, so most lessons provide opportunities for students to use some of the words in free writing.

We urge you whenever possible to provide additional opportunities for your students to use the words they learn to spell in their own sentences. Have them keep notebooks for free-writing activities. As they progress, encourage students to be increasingly adventurous in their writing. Their sentences should become longer, include more of the target words, and use varying forms of those words. For example, if an exercise calls for using two of the words in sentences, they might use the plural form of a noun or the past tense of a verb.

Errors in free writing can be divided into two broad categories: those in words that students have studied and those in other words. Each group can be informative.

Errors in Words That Have Been Studied

Try to determine the source of the errors in words that have been studied. Does the evidence suggest that the student has misunderstood something, has failed to make a connection between spelling and meaning, has not studied enough, or has a poor visual memory for words?

Help students to develop a sense of their personal spelling strengths and weaknesses. Look for recurring patterns of strength and weakness in students' spelling. Examine their free writing. Does a student spell phonetically and thus correctly spell words that follow phonic principles but misspell those that do not? Do errors involve specific morphemes or specific combinations?

Help students to correct errors by using what they already know. For example, a student who had written *awfly* quickly corrected her spelling when asked to write the word without the *-ly* ending.

As students become aware of their strengths, they begin to feel confident about their spelling and are better able to focus their learning attention on areas of weakness. Students who know their weaknesses can develop a healthy sense of doubt when writing words that fall into those areas. Encourage students to proofread their work for those words and to check a dictionary when in doubt.

Errors in Words Not Studied

Misspelled words that have not been studied can be handled in a variety of ways. If a student has misspelled many words in a piece of writing, pointing out all of them can be discouraging. We suggest again that you look for patterns. If you find a pattern and address it, you will be teaching the student to spell a number of words correctly rather than just one.

Errors in words that have not been studied should not be treated negatively. Point out the correctly spelled portions of a word, and try to discover the cause of any errors in the remainder of the word.

Consider asking students which misspelled words they most want to learn to spell. Suggest that they keep a pocket-sized notebook in which one page is devoted to each letter of the alphabet. Thus they can create their own personal dictionaries of words they find difficult to spell.

Final Considerations

As students work through *Structures in Spelling,* they should develop a sense of the logic of language. Be sure that they pay attention to the consistent spelling of morphemes.

Students' success in spelling is related to their understanding and appreciation of English as a whole. This program also attempts to instill in students an understanding, appreciation, and enjoyment of language. No text, however, can hope to be responsive to all the questions students have. You can greatly enhance the learning experience by encouraging questions about the language and relating what students are learning about spelling to what they are learning in other areas of study.

Lesson 1 _____

Some Basic Concepts

Objectives

- **Concepts:** Learn that many English words are built from parts and that the parts have meaning.
  Learn that being able to recognize and spell word parts makes spelling whole words easier.
- **Word Origins:** Learn to find information on word origins in a dictionary.
  Learn that many English words come from Latin and Greek.
  Learn that knowing the origin of a word can help in predicting its spelling.
- **Terms:** Learn some necessary terms and their definitions.
- **Word Building:** Join morphemes to build whole words.
  Select and combine morphemes to build as many words as possible.

1 What Are the Structures in Spelling?

Explain to students that "structures" refers to word parts that can be combined and rearranged to form many words. Many of the common word parts are included in this book.

Many students rely primarily on phonetic information when approaching the task of spelling. For longer words, the structural approach is valid. Tell students that if they learn to recognize and spell common word parts, they will be able to spell many English words more easily.

2 Word Parts Have Meaning

The word web based on the root *dict* is a graphic presentation of the interrelationships of many words. All of these words contain the element *dict,* and they also carry the meaning *to tell.* Although this book concentrates on spelling, morphemes are meaning based. In many cases, meaning is an important clue to the correct spelling of a word.

Pick some of these words and ask students to explain how the meaning *to tell* is contained in the meaning of the whole word. For instance, given *dictator,* a student might respond that a dictator is a person who tells other people what to do and how to live.

Lesson **1** _____ **Basics**

Some Basic Concepts

1 What Are the Structures in Spelling?
Many English words are formed by putting parts of words together. Some parts get used over and over again to spell thousands of different words. Learning to recognize and spell the word parts is easier than learning the spelling of each individual word.

The lessons in this book will help you to recognize and spell word parts. They will also help you to review and practice some patterns for putting parts together. If you know how to spell the common word parts and how to put them together, the building and spelling of many words becomes automatic.

2 Word Parts Have Meaning
Most words are built from parts that have meanings. For example, *dict* means *to tell,* and *pre-* means *before. Predict* means *to tell before,* or to tell about something before it happens.

Look at the following group of words. All of these words are built using the word part *dict,* meaning *to tell.*

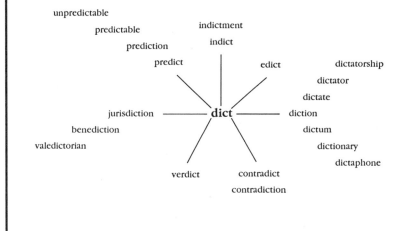

This diagram does not include every word with the part *dict,* but it gives you an idea of how many different words can be formed using one part.

Our minds can organize and remember more words when we understand the relationships among them. If you know the meanings and spellings of word parts, many new words will be easier to learn. Some words you may have heard but never written will be easier to spell.

3 Word Origins

The English we use is based mostly on older languages. Most English words come from Latin, Greek, or Old English. Many dictionaries give information about word origins. Usually this information is abbreviated. It may follow the pronunciation guide that appears after a word in the dictionary, or it may come after all the definitions.

All dictionaries do not give the same information about word origins. Here are three examples of how the origin of *predict* may be given, depending on which dictionary you use.

Example 1: [L. *praedictus,* pp. of *praedicere,* fr. *prae-* pre- + *dicere* to say]

Example 2: [Lat. *praedicere: prae-,* before + *dicere,* to say]

Example 3: [*pre* before + *dict* tell <Latin]

Now look up *predict* in your dictionary. Copy what it gives about the origin of *predict* on the line below.

predict: _[Lat. praedicere, praedict-: prae-, before + dicere, to say.]_

Look up the following words. Does your dictionary show the parts of each word? Copy what the dictionary gives about the origin and parts on the line following each word.

impart _[Lat. impartire: in-, in + partire, to share < pars, part.]_

pretend _[ME pretenden < Lat. praetendere: prae-, in front + tendere, to extend.]_

suppose _[ME supposen < OFr. supposer < Med. Lat. supponere < Lat., to put under: sub-, under + ponere, to place.]_

triceratops _[NLat. Triceratops, genus name: tri-, tri- + Gk. keras, horn + ops, face.]_

Ask students if there are any words in the word web that they don't know. Discuss the meanings of unfamiliar words.

3 Word Origins

In this exercise, students practice finding information in their dictionaries about the origins of words. Study the example entries with students. Point out that dictionaries differ in what information they include, where they include it, and the format and abbreviations they use.

Before they begin to work, help students to find and interpret the information on word origins in their own dictionaries. Also help them to find the section that tells them the abbreviations that are used and what they stand for.

Some dictionaries give only the language from which a word came into English. Other dictionaries may indicate only the language in which a word originated. Still others trace the path a word took to get from the original language into English. If a student's dictionary gives the complete etymology, students may be confused by an entry such as the one for *suppose:*

[ME *supposen* <OFr, *supposer* < Med. Lat. *supponere* < Lat., to put under: *sub-,* under + *ponere,* to place.]

Explain that this indicates that *suppose* went from Latin into Medieval Latin, then into Old French, then into Middle English, and finally into modern English. Point out that the last language listed is the language of origin, while the first language is the one from which the word came directly into English.

If students' dictionaries give more information than will fit on the lines in the text, tell them to use their notebooks to complete this exercise.

The answers given on the replica of the student page are based on *The American Heritage Dictionary.* Answers from other dictionaries may differ. You may want students to compare answers from various dictionaries.

The boxed student page

4 **Using the Dictionary**

Most English words built from parts come from Latin and Greek. Knowing the language of origin may help you to understand or to spell a word. For example, words from Greek usually spell /f/ as *ph*. If you know that *graph* is from Greek, you may find it easier to spell *telegraph*, *geography*, or *photograph*.

Use a dictionary to find out the language of origin of each of the following words. Write the answers on the lines provided.

1.	adapt	Latin	6.	tycoon	Japanese/Chinese
2.	border	Middle English/Germanic	7.	graphic	Latin/Greek
3.	dictate	Latin	8.	neighbor	Middle/Old English
4.	emerge	Latin	9.	technology	Greek
5.	bludgeon	origin unknown	10.	microscope	New Latin

Notice how many of these words come from Latin or Greek.

5 **The Names of Word Parts**

In order to talk about words that are built from parts, you need some terms for the parts of words. You may know these already.

Prefix: a part added to the beginning of a root to change its meaning.
 Example: *pre-* in *predict*

Root: the base of a word, to which other parts are added.
 Example: *dict* in *predict*

Suffix: a part added to the end of a root to change its meaning.
 Example: *-ion* in *prediction*

Affix: a prefix or suffix; a part that is added to a root to change its meaning.
 Examples: *pre-* and *-ion*

Combining form: a word part that may be used as either a root or an affix.
 Example: *photo* in *photograph* and *telephoto*

Morpheme: a group of letters with meaning. Prefixes, roots, suffixes, and combining forms are all morphemes.

Variant forms: morphemes that are similar in origin, spelling, and meaning.
 Examples: the prefixes *in-* and *im-*, the roots *scribe* and *script*, the suffixes *-able* and *-ible*, and the combining forms *thermo* and *therm*.

8   Lesson 1

Teacher's-edition columns

4 **Using the Dictionary**

This exercise gives students more practice in using the dictionary and in finding information on word origins. It also illustrates the fact that many English words have Latin and Greek origins. This book concentrates on Latin and Greek morphemes, although individual words in some exercises may have other origins.

Remind students that different dictionaries may have different information. Remind them also that the first language listed is the one from which the word came directly into English. You may accept either the first or the last, the original language.

Tell students to read the definitions of any words that are unfamiliar.

The answers on the replica of the student page are from *The American Heritage Dictionary.* Accept answers from any dictionary a student may use.

It is very important for students to know how to use the dictionary. Notice whether your students have any trouble completing these exercises. You may want to develop supplemental activities for students who have weak dictionary skills.

5 **The Names of Word Parts**

To the extent possible, technical terminology has been avoided in this book. The terms introduced and defined in this exercise, however, are essential for discussing and understanding the structural approach to spelling. If students have trouble remembering the definitions of any of these terms, review and reinforce them until the meanings become familiar.

6 **Word Building**

This exercise introduces students to the concept of word building. In it they combine prefixes, roots, and suffixes to build words. There are many exercises of this type in this book.

Explain to students that the process of word building is a straightforward one. Point out that English spelling is mostly regular. The "rules" of spelling deal with

6 Word Building

In this book, the plus sign (+) indicates the process of word building: *re + spect* indicates that *respect* is to be built.

Join the morphemes as indicated below to make words. Write the words on the lines provided. Do not add, drop, or change any letters.

Prefixes	Roots	Suffixes	Whole words
1. dis	+ ease		disease
2.	press	+ ure	pressure
3. re	+ spect	+ ful	respectful
4. pre	+ dict	+ able	predictable
5. intro	+ duct	+ ion	introduction

Although you do sometimes add, drop, or change letters, the process of word building is generally as simple as in the above examples.

7 Challenge Word Building

On a separate piece of paper, combine the morphemes below to build as many words as you can. Use as few or as many parts as you need for each word. Use a dictionary if you are unsure of a word.

Prefixes	Roots	Suffixes
con-	tent	-al
in-	vent	-ly
un-		-ion
		-ious
		-ive

How many words did you build? _____

---

exceptions to basic patterns. Point out also that by combining morphemes, students have spelled some two- and three-syllable words.

Make sure students know the meanings of all these words. Encourage students to look up the meanings of unfamiliar words. This will also give them practice in using the dictionary.

7 Challenge Word Building

This less-structured word-building exercise helps students to realize that there are many ways to combine morphemes. Before they begin, make sure they have completed and understood Exercise 6. Depending on their vocabulary levels, students may find this exercise challenging and may eagerly supply non-word answers. Remind them that using a dictionary is a necessary and ongoing strategy for good spelling. When doing this kind of word building, they will need to check to be sure that the words they form are actual words.

Emphasize that students can use as few or as many morphemes as needed for particular words. For instance, the roots *tent* and *vent* function as whole words. More than one affix can be added to build some of the words.

Note that we present the morpheme *-ion* rather than the syllable *-tion* as a suffix. This is because the *t* is part of the root. Explain to students that morphemes are units of meaning, while syllables are units of sound. If students are used to dividing words into syllables, it may take them a while to get used to this distinction.

You may want to build one or two words with students before they begin to work on their own. You may also want to have them work in pairs or small groups for this first Challenge Word Building.

Possible responses are listed here. There may be others. Accept all correctly spelled words.

content	invent
contention	invention
contentious	inventive
convent	tent
convention	unconventional
conventional	unconventionally
conventionally	unintentional
intent	unintentionally
intention	uninventive
intentional	vent
intentionally	

Lesson 2

Using Morphemes

Objectives

- **Terms:** Review terminology used in this book.
- **Word Building:** Join morphemes to build whole words. Select and combine morphemes to build 10 words.
- **Definitions:** Learn to use the Glossary of Morphemes to find definitions.
  Learn definitions of given morphemes.
- **Taking Words Apart:** Divide words into morphemes.
- **Categorizing:** Recognize and categorize morphemes by their type.

1 Reviewing Terms

In this exercise, students match terms presented in Lesson 1 with their definitions. Students who have difficulty with these terms should be given occasional reviews. Point out that they can refer to Exercise 5 in Lesson 1 if they are unsure of any meanings. These terms are used frequently enough in the coming lessons that students should eventually learn them.

2 Word Building

In this exercise, students combine morphemes to build words. Emphasize that students should add one morpheme at a time to

minimize the chance of making errors. Encourage students to make a habit of pronouncing the new words before writing them and of proofreading their work.

Additional activity:

Have students use one or two of these words in sentences.

3 Discovering How Words Are Built

Part A: Point out the following to students:

Only the morphemes presented in Exercise 1 of each lesson in this text are included in the glossary. Some words in individual exercises may include other morphemes. Most morphemes can usually be found in dictionaries.

In the glossary, variant forms of morphemes are listed with the main form. They do not have separate listings. For example, students will find *im-* and *sup-* listed after *in-* and *sub-*, respectively.

Using Morphemes

Lesson 1 described morphemes, the building blocks of language. If you learn about morphemes and how to combine them, you can spell thousands of words. In this lesson you will practice using morphemes in various ways.

1 Reviewing Terms

Write one of the following terms in each blank below, beside the appropriate definition.

affix   morphemes   suffix   root

combining form   prefix   variant forms

1. Word parts that have meaning: ___morphemes___
2. A word part added to the beginning of a word: ___prefix___
3. A word part added to the end of a word: ___suffix___
4. The part of a word to which other parts are added: ___root___
5. A prefix or suffix: ___affix___
6. Morphemes that are similar in spelling and meaning: ___variant forms___
7. A word part that can be both a root and an affix: ___combining form___

2 Word Building

Join the morphemes that follow to build whole words. Write the words on the lines provided.

1. re + fer ___refer___
2. sub + mit ___submit___
3. re + ceive ___receive___
4. sub + scribe ___subscribe___
5. re + cept + ion ___reception___
6. re + fer + ence ___reference___
7. sub + script + ion ___subscription___
8. ex + cept + ion + al ___exceptional___

3 Discovering How Words Are Built

Part A. The Glossary of Morphemes at the back of this book gives the meanings of all the morphemes presented in this text. Look up each morpheme below and write the meaning on the line provided.

de- <u>reverse, remove, reduce</u>   sup- <u>under, lesser</u>

ex- <u>out of, from</u>   trans- <u>across</u>

im- <u>in, not</u>   port- <u>carry</u>

re- <u>back, again, anew</u>

Part B. Now write a definition for each of the following words, using the definitions of the morphemes above.

1. report   <u>carry back</u>

2. export   <u>carry out of</u>

3. import   <u>carry in</u>

4. transport   <u>carry across</u>

Part C. On a separate piece of paper, add the prefixes and suffixes below to the root *port* to build as many words as you can. Use a dictionary if you are unsure of a word.

Prefixes	Root	Suffixes
de-	port	-able
ex-		-er
im-		-ive
re-		-ment
sup-		
trans-		

Lesson 2   11

The definitions are also given in Exercise 1 of Lessons 4–34. For the purposes of this book, the most common or useful definitions are given. Some dictionaries may give additional or different meanings.

Part B: Discuss students' definitions with them to be sure that students can relate the definitions they derived from the morphemes to the actual meanings of the words. The definitions may vary.

Note that the modern meanings of many English words are not this closely related to the definitions of the morphemes from which they are built. In many words, the definitions of the morphemes have become obscured. For instance, the root *tail* means *to cut.* This meaning is still fairly obvious in *tailor,* but it is obscure in *detail* and *retail.*

Part C: Emphasize that students can use as few or as many morphemes as needed for a particular word. For instance, *port* is a whole word. More than one affix can be added to build some of the words.

Remind students to use a dictionary for checking both spelling and words of which they are uncertain.

Point out that related words are often listed after the main entry word, rather than as main entries themselves. For example, *supportable, supporter,* and *supportive* may all be listed at the end of the entry for *support.*

Possible responses are listed here. There may be others. Accept all correctly spelled words that students can find in a dictionary.

deport	report
deportment	reporter
export	support
exportable	supportable
exporter	supporter
import	supportive
importer	transport
port	transportable
portable	transporter
porter	

Additional activities:

Have students compare their lists and develop a master list of all the words they form.

Have students use some of the words they build in sentences.

Lesson 2   19

4 Taking Words Apart

In this exercise, students divide words into their component morphemes. This will help them to recognize individual morphemes in whole words. Remind students that this is not the same as dividing words into syllables. Syllables are units of sound, while morphemes are units of meaning.

Refer students to the glossary or a dictionary if they are unsure of individual morphemes. Remember that only morphemes presented in Exercise 1 of Lessons 4–34 in the student text are included in the glossary.

You may want to discuss the example with students before they begin. Note that although the examples in this book look printed, students are not expected to print their answers unless they prefer to do so. Legible cursive writing should be acceptable.

In number 3, make sure students have an *s* both on the end of *trans* and at the beginning of *scribe*.

Numbers 4, 6, 7, and 8 all contain variant forms of morphemes. The roots *cept, clus,* and *script* are variants of *ceive, clude,* and *scribe* respectively. You may have to help students find these forms in the glossary. Variant forms are treated more fully in Exercise 6.

Remember that *-ion* rather than *-tion* is the suffix in numbers 4, 7, and 8. The *t* is part of the root. Spelling /shən/ is addressed in Lesson 7.

5 Recognizing Morphemes

In this exercise, students must recognize and categorize prefixes, roots, and suffixes in a group of mixed morphemes. When going over this exercise, you may want to point out that when morphemes appear in isolation in this book, prefixes are followed by hyphens and suffixes are preceded by hyphens. No hyphens are used with roots.

Recognizing Variant Forms

Some words have forms that are spelled differently. For instance, *take* and *took* are different forms of the same word. The spelling changes depending on how the word is used in phrases or sentences.

As you learned in Lesson 1, morphemes that are similar in spelling and meaning are called variant forms. Variant forms of the same morpheme are listed together in this book. *Scribe* and *script* are examples of variant forms. Look at these sentences:

>   I sub*scribe* to the local newspaper.
>   My sub*script*ion runs out soon.

Usually the variant forms are alike enough in spelling that their relationship is fairly obvious. List A below contains several morphemes that have variant forms. List B has one variant form for each morpheme in List A. Match the variant forms in Lists A and B and write the pairs on the lines provided. Use the glossary if you need to.

List A	List B	Pairs of variant forms
-ance	merse	-ance, -ant
cede	im-	cede, cess
fact	miss	fact, fect
-ery	-ant	-ery, -ary
in-	tense	in-, im-
merge	ef-	merge, merse
sub-	-ary	sub-, sup-
tend	cess	tend, tense
ex-	fect	ex-, ef-
mit	sup-	mit, miss

 Recognizing Variant Forms

Before students begin this exercise, discuss with them the relationship between *subscribe* and *subscription*. Help them to see that the words are very close in meaning but that they are used in different ways in the sentences.

You may want to introduce the terms noun and verb, if students do not already know what they mean. These terms are used throughout this book.

If students have trouble completing this exercise, remind them that variant forms are listed together with the main form in the glossary.

7 Creating and Using Words

Add a prefix, suffix, or both to each root below to create a word. Then use the words in original phrases or short sentences. You may use affixes from this lesson, from the glossary, or any others that you know. The first one is started for you.

		Whole words	Phrases or sentences
1.	sist	resist	I couldn't resist eating some cake.
2.	port	portable	a portable radio
3.	vent	prevention	Prevention is better than cure.
4.	clude	include	Did you include Ralph on the list?

8 Taking Apart and Rebuilding Words

Part A. Divide the following words into prefixes and roots and write each part under the correct heading. Check individual morphemes in the glossary if necessary.

		Prefixes	Roots			Prefixes	Roots
1.	infuse	in	fuse	4.	import	im	port
2.	resign	re	sign	5.	expose	ex	pose
3.	deduct	de	duct	6.	conceive	con	ceive

Part B. Now combine the prefixes and roots above in different ways to form 10 new words. Write them on the lines provided. Check a dictionary if you are unsure of any combination. The first one is done for you.

confuse	refuse
design	report
depose	receive
deceive	export
impose	conduct

14   Lesson 2

---

7 Creating and Using Words

In this exercise, students add affixes of their choice to the given roots. Then they use the words they build in short phrases or sentences.

Before students begin, you may want to review the silent *e* pattern for number 4. Point out that they can use more than one affix if they wish. Encourage them to use the glossary to find a variety of affixes. Instruct students to add one affix at a time to avoid errors.

Answers given on the replica of the student page are examples. Accept all correctly spelled words.

Having students write phrases or sentences allows you to see if they are able to transfer their skills from doing exercises to writing words in context. Spelling words in context differs from spelling them in exercises. In exercises, attention is focused on the spelling task. In phrases or sentences, attention is divided among the many tasks involved in writing. Using words in context is an important additional activity that should be included at any appropriate opportunity.

Students should not be held responsible for correctly spelling words they have not yet studied. If students make errors in such words, point out any parts of the word that are spelled correctly and praise their effort. Refer to pages 12–13 in the introduction to this teacher's edition for ways to deal with misspelled words in free-writing exercises.

8 Taking Apart and Rebuilding Words

Part A: Students first divide words into their component prefixes and roots. Encourage students to refer to the glossary to check individual morphemes if necessary.

Part B: In this part, students are asked to build 10 different words from the morphemes they listed in Part A. They will need to use some morphemes more than once. Suggest that they start with the roots and see what other prefixes can be used with each root.

Possible responses appear on the replica of the student page. There are others. Accept any answer that forms a correctly spelled word.

Additional activities:

Have students build as many other words as they can using these morphemes.

Have students compare their lists and build a master list.

Lesson 3

Patterns for Adding Suffixes

Objectives

- **Pattern Review:** Review and practice the following patterns for adding suffixes to words:
  The *y* to *i* Pattern
  The Silent *e* Pattern
  Doubling Pattern 1
  Doubling Pattern 2
- **Pattern Recognition:** Identify patterns that were used when suffixes were added to given words.

Four common patterns for adding endings to words are reviewed in this lesson. It is assumed that students are somewhat familiar with these patterns. If a student has particular difficulty with any of these patterns, you may want to design additional exercises for practice and reinforcement.

1 The *y* to *i* Pattern

In this exercise, students review and practice the *y* to *i* conversion pattern. Make sure students understand that the *y* is changed to *i* only when it is preceded by a consonant.

(Exceptions to this are a few words that end in *ay*, such as *daily* and *gaily*.)

Part A: Remind students to check their answers in a dictionary if they are unsure of any spellings.

Make sure they retain the *y* in number 3.

Part B: Point out that the number of blanks after a word indicates the number of morphemes in that word. This should help students to recognize the suffix *-ly* in number 2 and the suffix *-y* in number 4.

In all exercises where students divide words into their component morphemes, they should write the original form of a root or suffix. They should restore the *y* to the roots in numbers 3 and 5 and to the suffixes in numbers 2 and 4.

The roots *lone, happy,* and *greed* are not in the glossary, but they are words with which students should be familiar.

Lesson 3

Suffixes

Patterns for Adding Suffixes

The spelling of a root sometimes changes when a suffix is added. This lesson reviews four common patterns in which this happens. You will be using these patterns often.

1 The *y* to *i* Pattern
Study the pattern below.

> When adding a suffix to a word that ends in a consonant plus *y*, change the *y* to *i*, unless the suffix begins with *i*.

Part A. Combine the following roots and suffixes following the *y* to *i* pattern. Write the new words on the lines provided, and answer the question in the last column.

	New words	Was *y* changed to *i*?
1. supply + er	supplier	yes
2. crazy + ness	craziness	yes
3. imply + ing	implying	no
4. merry + ly	merrily	yes
5. happy + ness	happiness	yes

Part B. Divide the following words into morphemes and write each one under the correct heading. The first one is done for you.

	Prefixes	Roots	Suffixes	
1. replying	re	ply	ing	
2. loneliness		lone	ly	ness
3. unhappily	un	happy	ly	
4. greediness		greed	y	ness
5. compliance	com	ply	ance	

Lesson 3   15

The silent *e* at the end of a root is usually dropped when a suffix that starts with a vowel is added. The silent *e* is not dropped if the suffix starts with a consonant.

Part A. Combine the following root words and suffixes following the silent *e* pattern. Write the new words on the lines provided.

1. advise + er ___adviser___
2. taste + less ___tasteless___
3. diverse + ity ___diversity___
4. ignore + ant ___ignorant___
5. repute + able ___reputable___
6. reverse + ible ___reversible___
7. compose + er ___composer___
8. confuse + ion ___confusion___
9. emerge + ency ___emergency___
10. require + ment ___requirement___

Part B. Divide the following words into morphemes and write each one under the correct heading. If you are unsure of the spelling of a morpheme, look it up in the glossary at the back of this book. Then write the answer to the question in the final column. The first one is done for you.

	Prefixes	Roots	Suffixes	Was *e* dropped?
1. service		serve	ice	yes
2. careful		care	ful	no
3. definite	de	fine	ite	yes
4. receiver	re	ceive	er	yes
5. incurable	in	cure	able	yes
6. approval	ap	prove	al	yes
7. universal	uni	verse	al	yes
8. improvement	im	prove	ment	no

2 The Silent *e* Pattern

Part A: Make sure students retain the *e* in numbers 2 and 10. When going over their answers, ask them to explain why the *e* is not dropped when building these two words.

Note that the pronunciation of *ignore* and *repute* changes when the suffixes are added. Changes in pronunciation are common when suffixes are added to roots. Here, the stress on syllables changes. Point out to students that even though *repute* and *reputable* are pronounced differently, they share the same root and are related in meaning.

Part B: Remind students to write the original form of a root. If a silent *e* has been dropped, they should restore it. Make sure students restore the *e* to the roots in numbers 3–7.

Remind students that if they use the glossary to verify their spellings, some of these morphemes are variant forms that will be listed after the main form of the morpheme. The root *care* is not included in the glossary, but students should not have trouble dividing *careful* into its two morphemes.

3 Doubling Pattern 1

Study the pattern below.

If a word has one syllable, one vowel, and ends in one consonant, double the final consonant before adding an ending that begins with a vowel. Do not double a final *w* or *x*.

Part A. Look at the chart below. If a word has one syllable, one vowel, or one final consonant, check the appropriate column. If you check all three columns and the suffix begins with a vowel, double the final consonant before adding the suffix. Write the whole word in the last column. The first one is done for you. Remember: Don't double *w* or *x*.

	One syllable?	One vowel?	One final consonant?		Whole words
1. rig	✓	✓	✓	+ ing	**rigging**
2. hot	√	√	√	+ est	hottest
3. finish				+ ing	finishing
4. box	√	√	√	+ er	boxer
5. drug	√	√	√	+ ist	druggist

Part B. Combine the following roots and suffixes following Doubling Pattern 1. Write the words on the lines provided.

1. slip + er __slipper__
2. fix + ed __fixed__
3. tip + ed __tipped__
4. rub + ery __rubbery__
5. bow + ing __bowing__

6. shut + er __shutter__
7. drum + er __drummer__
8. fish + ing __fishing__
9. jump + ing __jumping__
10. design + ed __designed__

Lesson 3   17

3 Doubling Pattern 1

Tell students that this pattern is sometimes referred to as the one-one-one pattern. This may help them to remember it. Remind them that the final consonant is doubled only before an ending that begins with a vowel and that *w* and *x* are not doubled.

Part A: This exercise is presented in chart form to serve as an easy reference for students if they need to review this pattern as they work in later lessons.

Make sure students do not double the final consonant in numbers 3 and 4.

Part B: When going over students' responses to this part, ask them to explain why they should not double the final consonants in numbers 2, 5, and 8–10.

If students have trouble with this exercise, try to determine which part of the pattern is causing them difficulty, and give them extra practice. They should not go on to Exercise 4 until they understand this pattern.

Doubling Pattern 2
Study the pattern below.

If a word has more than one syllable, look at the last syllable. If the last syllable has one vowel, ends in one consonant, and is accented, double the final consonant before adding a suffix that begins with a vowel. Do not double a final *w* or *x*.

Part A. Look at the words below. If the last syllable has one vowel, one final consonant, or is accented, check the appropriate column. If you check all three columns and the suffix begins with a vowel, double the final consonant before adding the suffix. Write the whole word in the last column. The first one is done for you.

Last syllable:	Has one vowel?	One final consonant?	Is accented?		Whole words
1. transmit	✓	✓	✓	+ al	transmittal
2. propel	√	√	√	+ er	propeller
3. admit	√	√	√	+ ance	admittance
4. profit	√	√		+ able	profitable
5. occur	√	√	√	+ ence	occurrence

Part B. Join the root words and suffixes below following Doubling Pattern 2, and write the new words on the lines provided.

1. expel + ed __expelled__   6. collect + ion __collection__
2. begin + ing __beginning__   7. repair + able __repairable__
3. forbid + en __forbidden__   8. avoid + ance __avoidance__
4. forgot + en __forgotten__   9. commit + ee __committee__
5. control + er __controller__   10. prosper + ous __prosperous__

4 **Doubling Pattern 2**

This pattern is an extension of the one reviewed in Exercise 3 and is the pattern that usually causes the most difficulty. Make sure students understand it before they begin Part A. Explain that it is built on Doubling Pattern 1, so they are already familiar with most of the pattern. The only new step is to determine whether or not the last syllable of a word is accented.

Part A: Go over number 1 with students. Have them first identify the final syllable. Then ask them to identify the vowel and final consonant in *mit*. Ask if they can hear the stress on *mit* when *transmit* is pronounced. You may want to pronounce it with the accent on the first syllable to see if students can hear the difference. Make sure they do not double the final *t* in number 4.

Part B: Go over students' responses to this part of the exercise carefully. Make sure they do not double the final consonants in numbers 6–8 and 10. Ask students to explain why they did not do so.

Some students have a great deal of difficulty identifying the accented syllable in words. If you discover students who cannot hear the stress, recommend that they develop the habit of checking the dictionary to determine which syllable is stressed. Most dictionaries will also list the spellings of related forms when a final consonant is doubled.

5 Reviewing Patterns for Adding Suffixes

Below are the patterns reviewed in this lesson.

1. **Changing *y* to *i*:** When adding a suffix to a word that ends in a consonant plus *y*, change the *y* to *i* unless the ending begins with *i*.

2. **Silent *e* Pattern:** Drop the final *e* if the suffix begins with a vowel.

3. **Doubling Pattern 1:** Double the final consonant if the word has one syllable, one vowel, one final consonant, and the suffix begins with a vowel. Do not double *w* or *x*.

4. **Doubling Pattern 2:** With words of more than one syllable, double the final consonant if the last syllable has one vowel, one final consonant, and is accented and if the suffix starts with a vowel.

Remove the ending from each word listed below. Then write the number of the pattern above that had been followed when the ending was added. The first one is done for you.

		Root words	Patterns
1.	fitting	fit	3
2.	pliable	ply	1
3.	refusal	refuse	2
4.	refinery	refine	2
5.	variance	vary	1
6.	recurring	recur	4
7.	beginning	begin	4
8.	happiness	happy	1
9.	supervisor	supervise	2
10.	transmitter	transmit	4

Lesson 3   19

5 Reviewing Patterns for Adding Suffixes

This exercise reviews the four patterns presented and practiced in Exercises 1–4. Before students begin, make sure they understand that they are to write root words on the lines, removing only the endings. In this exercise, prefixes remain part of the root words.

Remind students to write the original form of the root word. If a *y* has been changed to *i*, the *y* should be restored. If a silent *e* has been dropped, they should restore it. If a final consonant has been doubled, the added consonant should be dropped.

Check to be sure that the *y* is restored in numbers 2, 5, and 8; that the silent *e* is restored in numbers 3, 4, and 9; and that numbers 6, 7, and 10 end in a single consonant.

If a student is having trouble with any of these patterns, try to discover which part of the pattern is causing the difficulty and provide reinforcement and review. Students will be applying these patterns regularly throughout the rest of this book.

Lesson 4

The Suffixes *-ful, -less, -ly,* and *-ward*

Objectives

- **Suffixes:** Learn to recognize and spell words with *-ful, -less, -ly,* and *-ward.*
- **Word Building:** Join morphemes to build whole words.
- **Terms:** Review terminology used in this text.
- **Taking Words Apart:** Divide words into morphemes.
- **Pattern:** Practice the *y* to *i* pattern when adding suffixes.
- **Creating and Using Words:** Create words and use them in context.

For general information on suffixes, refer to page 8 in the introduction.

1 Recognizing Suffixes

The purpose of this exercise is to help students learn to isolate morphemes in words.

Read aloud the representative words listed for each suffix. Read the words in a normal speaking voice without stressing the suffix. Instruct students to underline the suffix as you pronounce each word. If you present the first exercise of each lesson orally, students are able to process each word both visually and aurally. The rest of the lesson depends on students having given careful attention to both the look and the sound of the morphemes presented in the lesson. In order to become better spellers, students need to learn both to associate sounds with letters and to be able to visualize words or word parts.

Sometimes the pronunciation of a morpheme changes from one word to another, even if the spelling does not. An example is the suffix *-ward* as it occurs in *backward* and *toward.* It is important for students to recognize the morphemes in words regardless of how they are pronounced. In most cases, the spelling of a suffix does not change from word to word.

Point out that the definition is listed beside each suffix. Definitions are given when a morpheme is first introduced and in the Glossary of Morphemes at the back of the book. This book emphasizes the spelling of morphemes, but exercises dealing with meanings or usage are included as well.

Use *helplessly* and *thankfully* as examples of words that have more

---

Lesson 4

Suffixes
-ful, -less, -ly, and *-ward*

1 Recognizing Suffixes
In each group of words below, underline the suffixes listed on the left.

-ful	*full of*		
	useful	careful	faithful
	helpful	thankful	cheerful

-less	*without, lacking*		
	useless	careless	lifeless
	helpless	thankless	hopeless

-ly	*in the manner of*		
	usefully	carelessly	happily
	helplessly	thankfully	willingly

-ward	*direction*		
	eastward	afterward	toward
	backward	homeward	upwardly

2 Word Building
Join the morphemes that follow to build whole words. Write the words on the lines provided.

1. like + ly __likely__
2. lone + ly __lonely__
3. play + ful __playful__
4. awk + ward __awkward__
5. speech + less __speechless__
6. fear + less + ly __fearlessly__
7. grate + ful + ly __gratefully__
8. out + ward + ly __outwardly__
9. breath + less + ly __breathlessly__
10. thought + ful + ly __thoughtfully__

20   Lesson 4

Emphasize that the process of building words is generally straightforward.

3 **Reviewing Terms**

It is important for you to be sure that students know and understand these terms before continuing to work in this book. You may want to require students to memorize the terms or to give a quiz on them.

Accept either *affixes* or *morphemes* for number 6.

4 **Taking Words Apart**

In this exercise, students divide words into their component morphemes. All of these words follow regular patterns. Encourage students to refer to the glossary or a dictionary to check individual morphemes if necessary.

Remind students that they should write the original form of a root. Note whether they restore the *y* in numbers 1, 3, and 7. For number 7, accept either *hurry ed ly* or *hurried ly*. Review the pattern if necessary.

Note whether students separate the suffixes from one another in numbers 5, 6, and 8–10. Review those suffixes if necessary.

Students who have difficulty should begin by identifying only the suffixes.

than one suffix. Have students draw a vertical line between the suffixes.

Note that *-wards* is a common variant form of *-ward*. Students may use the *-wards* form in such words as *backwards* and *afterwards* if they wish.

2 **Word Building**

In this exercise, students combine roots and suffixes to build words.

Remind them that a silent *e* at the end of a root is retained when adding a suffix that begins with a consonant.

Emphasize that students should add one suffix at a time to minimize the chance of making errors. For example, when spelling *gratefully,* they shouldn't have trouble with the two *l*'s because there is one in each of the two suffixes. After they have written *grateful,* they simply add *-ly*. Remind students to proofread their words.

5 Adding Suffixes to Words That End in a Consonant Plus *y*

Add the suffix to each word below, and write the new word on the line provided. Remember to change the *y* to *i* if necessary.

1. lazy + ly __lazily__
2. easy + ly __easily__
3. penny + less __penniless__
4. sleepy + ly __sleepily__
5. beauty + ful __beautiful__
6. way + ward __wayward__

6 Creating and Using Words

From each word listed below, create two new words by adding one or more of the following suffixes. Then use the new words in phrases or short sentences. The first one is started for you.

-ful   -less   -ly   -ward

	New words	Phrases or sentences
1. law	lawless	a lawless gang
	lawfully	The arrest was made lawfully.
2. tact	tactful	Try to be tactful.
	tactlessly	Elizabeth criticized him tactlessly.
3. pain	painful	a painful procedure
	painfully	The injured man moaned painfully.
4. home	homeless	a shelter for the homeless
	homeward	homeward bound
5. thought	thoughtless	That was a thoughtless thing to say.
	thoughtfully	speaking thoughtfully

5 Adding Suffixes to Words That End in a Consonant Plus *y*

This exercise allows students to practice the *y* to *i* conversion pattern. Review the pattern before they begin.

Note whether students incorrectly change the *y* to *i* in *wayward*.

6 Creating and Using Words

In this exercise, students add selected suffixes to the given roots. Then they use the words they build in phrases or short sentences.

Encourage them to use the glossary if necessary and to use more than one affix for some of the words.

Creating two words for each root emphasizes the consistency of the spelling of morphemes as well as their function.

Having students write phrases or sentences allows you to see if they are transferring their skills from doing exercises to writing words in context. In exercises, attention is focused on the spelling task. In phrases or sentences, attention is divided among the many tasks involved in writing.

Remember that errors in words not yet studied should not be treated negatively. If students make errors in such words, point out any parts of the word that are spelled correctly and praise their effort. Help them to correct misspellings by using what they already know.

The answers on the replica of the student page are examples. Accept all correctly spelled words.

Quizzes

Give a graded spelling quiz on the words in this lesson. Be sure to include the suffixes that your students need to practice. For advanced students, you may want to include other words that contain these suffixes.

Sentences

Sentences for dictation are available at the back of this book if you wish to use them.

Lesson 5

The Suffixes -hood, -ness, -ment, and -ship

Objectives

- **Suffixes:** Learn to recognize and spell words with -hood, -ness, -ment, and -ship.
- **Word Building:** Join morphemes to build whole words.
- **Taking Words Apart:** Divide words into morphemes.
- **Changing Meanings:** Add suffixes to roots to change the meaning of words.
- **Composing Sentences:** Write original sentences using selected words.
- **Completing Words in Sentences:** Build words to fit in context by adding suffixes to given roots.
- **Word Game:** Play a game to build words.

1 Recognizing Suffixes

Read aloud the representative words listed for each suffix. Read the words in a normal speaking voice without stressing the suffixes. Instruct students to underline the suffixes as you read each word. Do this exercise orally so that students can both see and hear the suffixes.

Remind students that the definitions of the suffixes are listed above the representative words.

It is more important that students recognize the function of words that end with these suffixes than that they learn the complex conceptual meanings of the suffixes.

When you come to such words as *likelihood* and *helpfulness*, ask students to identify both suffixes. They may also identify *-ion* as a suffix in *relationship* and *companionship*.

Point out the words in which the silent *e* is not dropped because the root is followed by a suffix beginning with a consonant. Note also that students are less likely to misspell *government* if they think of the word as the root and suffix.

2 Word Building

In this exercise, students combine morphemes to build words.

Note that *friendliness* requires the *y* to *i* conversion. Before students begin, you may want to review the pattern. Remind them that they can use Lesson 3 as a reference.

Lesson 5 — Suffixes
-hood, -ness, -ment, and -ship

1 Recognizing Suffixes
In each group of words below, underline the suffixes listed on the left.

-hood — *state, quality, or condition of*

adulthood	statehood	falsehood
motherhood	neighborhood	likelihood

-ness — *state, quality, condition, or degree of*

darkness	carelessness	uselessness
helpfulness	thankfulness	homelessness

-ment — *state, act, or process of*

movement	arrangement	government
measurement	development	involvement

-ship — *state, quality, or condition of; skill*

hardship	relationship	workmanship
friendship	companionship	apprenticeship

2 Word Building
Join the morphemes that follow to build whole words. Write the words on the lines provided. Remember to change *y* to *i* if necessary.

1. weak + ness __weakness__
2. child + hood __childhood__
3. state + ment __statement__
4. equip + ment __equipment__
5. father + hood __fatherhood__
6. own + er + ship __ownership__
7. champion + ship __championship__
8. re + fresh + ment __refreshment__
9. friend + ly + ness __friendliness__
10. shame + less + ness __shamelessness__

Lesson 5   23

Emphasize that students should add one morpheme at a time to minimize the chance of making errors. In early lessons such as this one, some words are not broken down into all their component morphemes. This allows students to concentrate on using the suffixes to build words rather than on learning new morphemes. Words will be more completely divided into morphemes in later lessons.

Remind students to pronounce the new words before writing them and to proofread their work.

3 Taking Words Apart

In this exercise, students divide words into their component morphemes. All of these words follow regular patterns. Encourage students to refer to the glossary or a dictionary if necessary. The number of blanks provided should also help students to divide the words correctly.

Remind students that they should write the original form of a morpheme. Thus the *y* should be restored in numbers 7 and 8. Note whether students divide the two suffixes in numbers 7 and 8. Review those suffixes if necessary.

Students who have difficulty should begin by identifying only the suffixes.

4 Changing the Meaning of Words

In this exercise, students change the meaning and function of given words by selecting and adding suffixes. Then they use two of the new words in original sentences.

Part A: Before students begin, you may want to review the *y* to *i* conversion pattern for *lazy,* and the silent *e* pattern. The silent *e* is retained when these suffixes beginning with consonants are added.

Remind students that knowing affixes greatly increases the number of words they can spell and use. You may want to discuss how

adding these suffixes affects the function of some of these words. Point out that all of the suffixes in this lesson are noun endings.

Throughout the book, writing whole words is required where appropriate. Make sure that students proofread the words they write.

Part B: Once students can spell words, they need practice in using them correctly. The exercise instructions are deliberately flexible about how many sentences should

---

3 Taking Words Apart

Divide the following words into morphemes and write each one under the correct heading. Check the suffixes in the glossary and remember to change letters if necessary.

		Roots	Suffixes	
1.	hardship	hard	ship	
2.	girlhood	girl	hood	
3.	fragment	frag	ment	
4.	township	town	ship	
5.	treatment	treat	ment	
6.	cheerfulness	cheer	ful	ness
7.	likelihood	like	ly	hood
8.	sleepiness	sleep	y	ness

4 Changing the Meaning of Words

Part A. Add one of the following suffixes to each word below to change its meaning. Write the new words on the lines provided. Remember to change *y* to *i* if necessary. The first one is done for you.

-hood   -ness   -ment   -ship

1. sister	sisterhood	5. refine	refinement
2. lazy	laziness	6. partner	partnership
3. priest	priesthood	7. require	requirement
4. gentle	gentleness	8. sportsman	sportsmanship

Part B. On the lines below, write original sentences using two of the new words.

My grandmother was loved for her gentleness.

Being a good loser is one aspect of sportsmanship.

5 Completing Words in Sentences

Add one or two of the following suffixes to the root word given under each blank below and write the completed word in the blank. The word you build must make sense in the sentence. The first one is started for you.

-hood	-ment	-ness	-ship
-ful	-less	-ly	-ward

1. What is the _____likelihood_____ of that dog being _____friendly_____?

like   friend

2. It is _____disgraceful_____ that there are so many _____homeless_____ people.

disgrace   home

3. I appreciated your _____thoughtfulness_____ during my son's _____illness_____.

thought   ill

4. The new _____ownership_____ resulted in a _____rearrangement_____ of our duties.

owner   rearrange

5. That dance is a complex series of _____backward_____ and _____forward_____ steps.

back   for

6 Missing Links

Add a word to link each pair of morphemes or words below. The missing link will form the end of the first word and the beginning of the second word. You can find all the second words in other exercises in this lesson. The number of blanks indicates how many letters are in each missing link. Study the example before you begin.

Example: down t o w n ship

1. inter s t a t e ment
2. grand c h i l d hood
3. girl f r i e n d ship
4. die h a r d ship
5. re t r e a t ment
6. foster f a t h e r hood

---

be written. Some students may write two sentences with one new word in each, while others may write one sentence using two new words. If students need more room to write, encourage them to use their notebooks. Make sure that they proofread their work.

Help them to correct misspellings by using what they already know. Errors in words not yet studied should not be treated negatively.

5 Completing Words in Sentences

In this exercise, students are required to add suffixes to roots to form words that are appropriate in the context of the sentences.

Tell students to read a whole sentence first to decide which suffixes to use. After they've written words in the blanks, they should reread the sentence to be sure that it makes sense.

Numbers 1 and 3 include words to which more than one suffix must be added.

6 Missing Links

In this word game, students form two unrelated words by writing a missing word in the blanks. The word that is filled in will form the end of the first word and the beginning of the second: *downtown* and *township*. The second word in each pair can be found in an exercise in this lesson. The number of blanks indicates the number of letters in the missing word.

There is more than one possible answer for some items. For instance, correct answers for number 5 include *restate/statement* and *retreat/treatment*. Accept any two words that make sense.

This and other word games included in this book are intended to be fun. You may want students to work in pairs or small groups when doing them. If students find the games confusing or frustrating, let them skip them.

Quizzes

Give a graded spelling quiz on the words in this lesson. For advanced students, you may want to include other words that contain these suffixes.

Sentences

Sentences for dictation are available at the back of this book if you wish to use them.

Lesson 6

The Suffixes -*er*, -*est*, -*en*, and -*ery*

Objectives

- **Suffixes:** Learn to recognize and spell words with -*er*, -*est*, -*en*, and -*ery*.
- **Word Building:** Join morphemes to build whole words.
- **Patterns:** Practice Doubling Patterns 1 and 2 for adding suffixes.
- **Variant Forms:** Practice spelling words containing variant forms of -*ery*.
- **Composing Sentences:** Write original sentences using selected words.
- **Strategies:** Learn strategies for spelling /ər/ at the end of words.
- **Completing Words in Sentences:** Build words to fit in context by adding suffixes to given roots.
- **Word Game:** Play a game to build words.

---

1 Recognizing Suffixes

In each group of words below, underline the suffixes listed on the left.

-*er*, -*or*	*someone who;*			*something that*
	driver	jogger	operator	folder
	teacher	reader	spectator	refrigerator

-*er*	*more*			
	bigger	nicer	colder	happier

-*est*	*most*			
	biggest	nicest	coldest	happiest

-*en*	*made of; cause to be or have; become*			
	golden	wooden	deafen	fatten

-*ery*, -*ary*, -*ory*, -*ry*	*place where; collection, condition, or practice of*			
	surgery	library	factory	ministry
	machinery	secondary	advisory	carpentry

2 Word Building

Join the morphemes that follow to build whole words. Write the words on the lines provided. Remember to change or drop letters if necessary.

1. sticky + er ___stickier___
2. loose + en ___loosen___
3. bribe + ery ___bribery___
4. dentist + ry ___dentistry___
5. strange + er ___stranger___
6. bright + en ___brighten___
7. simple + est ___simplest___
8. burgle + ary ___burglary___
9. satis + fact + ory ___satisfactory___
10. ad + ministrate + or ___administrator___

---

1 Recognizing Suffixes

Read aloud the representative words listed for each suffix. Read the words in a normal speaking voice without stressing the suffixes. Instruct students to underline the suffix as you read each word. Do this exercise orally so that students can both see and hear the suffixes.

Remind students that the definitions of the suffixes are listed above the representative words.

Point out that -*or* is a variant form of -*er*, and that -*ary*, -*ory*, and -*ry* are variants of -*ery*.

Additional activity:

Have students work in small groups to generate as many words as they can that end with these suffixes.

2 Word Building

In this exercise, students combine roots and suffixes to build words.

Remind students to pronounce the new words before writing them and to proofread their work.

Students should drop the silent *e* in numbers 2, 3, 5, 7, 8, and 10, and change the *y* to *i* in number 1. Review the patterns if necessary. Remind students that they can use Lesson 3 as a reference.

3 Practicing Doubling Patterns 1 and 2

Join the root words and suffixes below. Remember to double the final consonant of the root if necessary.

1. hid + en ___hidden___
2. can + ery ___cannery___
3. rub + ery ___rubbery___
4. pot + ery ___pottery___

5. drum + er ___drummer___
6. sharp + en ___sharpen___
7. control + er ___controller___
8. transmit + er ___transmitter___

4 Variant Forms of -ery

The suffix *-ery* has three variant forms: *-ary*, *-ory*, and *-ry*. Often you can determine the spelling of the suffix by the way the word is pronounced. For example, you can hear an *a* in *dictionary*. On the other hand, the suffix in *burglary* is pronounced /ərɪ/. The suffixes *-ery* and *-ory* are also pronounced /ərɪ/ in many words. If you are not sure which spelling to use, the best strategy is to look the word up in a dictionary.

Add a form of *-ery* to the roots below and write the new words under the appropriate heading. Add or drop letters if necessary. Use a dictionary to check your spelling.

access	contradict	honor	poet
arch	direct	launder	prime
brew	found	moment	slip

-ery	-ary	-ory	-ry
archery	honorary	accessory	foundry
brewery	momentary	contradictory	laundry
slippery	primary	directory	poetry

Use three of the new words in original sentences.

Maria had a momentary lapse of memory.

The laundry floor is dangerously slippery.

3 Practicing Doubling Patterns 1 and 2

In this exercise, students practice the doubling patterns presented in Lesson 3. You may want to review the patterns before they begin.

If students are not doubling correctly, check to see what aspect of the patterns they find confusing. Go back over the appropriate part of Lesson 3 if necessary. Have students explain why they do not double the *p* in *sharpen*.

4 Variant Forms of -ery

In this exercise, students select and add *-ery* or one of its variant forms to root words. They must also categorize these words by writing them under the correct heading. Have students check each word they are unsure of in the dictionary, since that is the only reliable strategy for spelling these words correctly.

Note whether students drop the silent *e* from prime. They should discover, if they don't already know, that *-er* is dropped from *launder* before the *-ry* suffix is added. Tell students that this is an exception that they should memorize.

Students are also asked to write sentences. Once they can spell words, they need practice in using them correctly. This allows you to see if they are transferring their skills from doing exercises to spelling the words in context.

The exercise instructions are deliberately flexible about how many sentences should be written in order to accommodate different student styles and abilities. Advanced students may enjoy trying to use three of their words in a single sentence. If students need more room to write, encourage them to use their notebooks. Make sure that they are proofreading their own sentences.

Help them to correct misspellings by using what they already know. Errors in words not yet studied should not be treated negatively.

Using words in context is an important additional activity that should be included at any appropriate opportunity.

5 Discovering Strategies

Wherever possible, strategies are presented to help students predict the spelling of morphemes in words they haven't studied. It is important to keep reminding students of the single most important strategy for spelling such words: looking them up in the dictionary. You may want to require students to memorize some strategies, such as probabilities and roots that take specific morphemes.

Strategy 1: Using probabilities is a useful spelling strategy, but students should not rely on it as a substitute for using a dictionary when one is available.

Strategy 2: Although this book deals with spelling rather than meaning, when the meaning of a morpheme can help to predict the spelling of a word, meaning is emphasized. Tell students that if they have trouble deciding when *-er* means more, they can try adding *-est* to the root.

Strategy 3: We believe that students will more easily remember strategies they discover for themselves, and we use the discovery approach whenever possible.

Note whether students drop the silent *e* in numbers 4, 5, and 6.

After students have added *-or* to the verbs, they should answer the

three questions that follow. Their answers will lead them to discover the pattern that is then stated.

6 Completing Words in Sentences

In this exercise, students add suffixes to roots to form words that are appropriate in the context of the sentences.

Remind students to read a whole sentence first to decide which suffixes to use. After they've written words in the blanks, they should

reread the sentence to be sure that it makes sense.

For number 3, accept *cleverer* or *cleverest*. For number 4, accept *bumpier* or *bumpiest*.

Note whether students drop the silent *e* in numbers 3 and 4, change the *y* to *i* in number 4, and double the final consonants in *robbery* and *biggest*. Review the patterns if necessary. If they do not capitalize the *S* in *Slavery*, remind them that completed sentences should be mechanically correct.

---

5 Discovering Strategies

At the end of a word, *-er* and *-or* sound the same. There are some strategies for choosing the correct spelling of /ər/, however.

Strategy 1: Probabilities. The most common spelling of /ər/ at the end of words is *-er*. There are more than five words with the suffix *-er* for every word with *-or*. If you can't use a dictionary and have to guess at the spelling of a word, you should usually use *-er* because that is the most probable spelling of /ər/.

Strategy 2: Meanings. The suffix *-er* has two meanings: *someone who or something that* and *more*. The suffix *–or* only means *someone who or something that*. When /ər/ means *more*, it is spelled *-er*.

Strategy 3: Looking at root words. The suffixes *-er* and *-or* are added to verbs to change them into nouns meaning *someone who or something that* does an action. The suffix *-or* is added to certain kinds of verbs. Add *-or* to the verbs below and answer the questions that follow.

1. visit ___visitor___   5. decorate ___decorator___
2. invent ___inventor___   6. operate ___operator___
3. conduct ___conductor___   7. profess ___professor___
4. elevate ___elevator___   8. process ___processor___

What is the last letter in the roots in numbers 1–3? ___t___

What are the last three letters in the roots in numbers 4–6? ___ate___

What are the last three letters in the roots in numbers 7 and 8? ___ess___

Pattern: The suffix *-or* is usually added to roots that end in *t*, *-ate*, or *ess*.

28   Lesson 6

---

6 **Completing Words in Sentences**

Add one of the following suffixes to the root given under each blank below, and write the completed word in the blank. The word you build must make sense in the sentence.

-er   -or   -est   -en   -ery   -ary   -ory   -ry

1. __Slavery__ was one cause of the Civil War.
     slave

2. The steel __industry__ provided some __temporary__ employment.
     indust   tempor

3. The __hijacker__ was caught by the __cleverest__ __investigator__ .
     hijack   clever   investigate

4. If they __widen__ the road, will they also fix the __bumpier__ parts?
     wide   bumpy

5. The __robbery__ was the __biggest__ in recent __history__ .
     rob   big   hist

7 **Missing Letters**

A pair of letters has been omitted twice from each word below. Using only the two-letter morphemes from this lesson, fill in the missing letters to make whole words. The first one is done for you.

1. cat **e r** e r
2. _e n_ light _e n_
3. _e r_ as _e r_
4. h _o r_ r _o r_
5. l _e n_ gth _e n_
6. dec _o r_ at _o r_
7. m _e r_ ri _e r_
8. che _e r_ lead _e r_
9. p _e r_ form _e r_
10. str _e n_ gth _e n_
11. co _o r_ dinat _o r_
12. conv _e r_ t _e r_

Lesson 6   29

7 **Missing Letters**

In this word game, students use the two-letter suffixes from this lesson, -er, -or, and -en, to build complete words. In each word, one of the pairs of letters is missing twice. Before they begin, make sure students understand that they must use the same pair in the same order twice in each word.

Word games are intended to be fun. Students may want to work in pairs or small groups. If they find this game confusing or frustrating, let them skip it.

Additional Exercise: Practicing the Comparative and the Superlative

Generally, students do not have difficulty understanding or using the comparative and superlative suffixes -er and -est. This supplemental exercise is suggested in case you have a student who needs some work on this.

Explain to students that -er and -est are used to show comparisons. When more than two things are compared, -est is used. The -er form is called the *comparative,* while the -est form is called the *superlative.* Have students write the two forms for the following words. Numbers 5–10 provide extra practice for Doubling Pattern 1 and the *y* to *i* conversion.

1. high   (higher, highest)
2. slow   (slower, slowest)
3. hard   (harder, hardest)
4. strong   (stronger, strongest)
5. big   (bigger, biggest)
6. sad   (sadder, saddest)
7. glad   (gladder, gladdest)
8. funny   (funnier, funniest)
9. happy   (happier, happiest)
10. lovely (lovelier, loveliest)

Quizzes

Give a graded spelling quiz on the words in this lesson or other words that contain these suffixes.

Sentences

Sentences for dictation are available at the back of this book if you wish to use them.

Lesson 7

The Suffixes
-ion and -ian

Objectives

- **Suffixes:** Learn to recognize and spell words with -ion and -ian.
- **Word Building:** Join morphemes to build whole words.
- **Strategies:** Learn and practice strategies for spelling /shən/ at the end of words.

The suffix -ion presents spelling problems when it follows t or s, because the ending syllables -tion and -sion are both pronounced /shən/.

When -ion follows other letters, as in champion or onion, it does not present particular problems.

When the suffix -ian follows c, the ending syllable is also pronounced /shən/, and the spelling can be confused with -ion. When -ian follows other letters, it is usually pronounced clearly as two syllables, /ē-an/.

Predicting the spelling of /shən/ is one of the most difficult spelling problems addressed in this book. It is introduced here in order to be able to provide practice throughout the book.

Several strategies are presented here to help students predict the various spellings of /shən/. All students will not retain all of the information, but they should remember that there are reasons for these spellings and that generally English is not arbitrary.

Lesson 7 — Suffixes — -ion and -ian

1 Recognizing Suffixes

In each group of words below, underline the suffixes listed on the left.

-ion — *act, result, state of*

direction	taxation	discussion
attraction	inspection	persuasion
association	contraption	transmission
participation	contamination	comprehension

-ian — *person who; of, relating to, belonging to*

musician	civilian	Asian
politician	vegetarian	Italian
technician	pedestrian	Christian

2 Word Building

Join the morphemes that follow to build whole words. Write the words on the lines provided. Remember to drop the silent e if necessary.

1. Paris + ian — Parisian
2. quest + ion — question
3. physic + ian — physician
4. remiss + ion — remission
5. convict + ion — conviction
6. process + ion — procession
7. relocate + ion — relocation
8. celebrate + ion — celebration
9. automate + ion — automation
10. immigrate + ion — immigration

Say the words you built. Notice that they end in the sound /shən/. Underline the letter that comes before the -ion or the -ian in these words.

When -ion follows t or s, it creates a spelling problem. Both -tion and -sion spell /shən/. When -ian follows c, it also spells /shən/. In the exercises that follow, you will practice some strategies for predicting the spelling of /shən/.

Tell your students that this lesson contains a great deal of information, so they should not feel discouraged if they don't remember it all at once. They will be practicing and reinforcing these strategies in later lessons. They can refer to this lesson whenever necessary.

1 Recognizing Suffixes

Read aloud the representative words listed for each suffix. Read the words in a normal speaking voice without stressing the suffixes. Instruct students to underline the suffix as you read each word.

Students may understand the definitions better when they see how words with these suffixes function in sentences.

Emphasize that usually a suffix is spelled the same way in every word. Explain that the suffix is -ion and that other letters in the final syllable belong to the root.

3 Words That End in *-tion*

Strategy 1: Probabilities. The most common spelling of /shən/ is *-tion*. There are more than seven words that end in *-tion* for every word that ends in *-sion*. If you don't know how to spell a word ending in /shən/ and you can't look it up in a dictionary, you should use *-tion* because that is the most probable spelling of /shən/.

Strategy 2: Looking at root words. Sometimes knowing the root word can help you to decide the correct spelling of /shən/. On the lines provided, write the root words for the words below and answer the question that follows.

1. direction __direct__   3. pollution __pollute__

2. adoption __adopt__   4. participation __participate__

What is the last consonant in each of these root words? __t__

Pattern: When a root word ends in *t* or *te,* the ending /shən/ will probably be spelled *-tion.*

Strategy 3: Extra letters. Sometimes when the suffix *-ion* is added to a root, other letters are also added. Write the root words for the words below.

1. taxation __tax__   3. addition __add__

2. continuation __continue__   4. definition __define__

Say the words ending in *-ion.* Listen for the other letters that were added to the root.

Pattern: When extra letters are added to the root before *-ion,* /shən/ will probably be spelled *-tion.*

Add *-ion* to the words below following these patterns. Say each new word before writing it.

1. react __reaction__   6. qualify __qualification__

2. apply __application__   7. protect __protection__

3. locate __location__   8. compete __competition__

4. satisfy __satisfaction__   9. transport __transportation__

5. correct __correction__   10. transform __transformation__

Point out that when *-ion* follows *t* or *s,* it is pronounced /shən/.

Ask students to point out what letter usually comes before *-ian* when it is pronounced /shən/. Then ask them to point out words in which *-ian* is pronounced as two syllables (/ē-an/).

Note that the pronunciation of *Italy* and *Christ* changes when the suffix is added.

2 Word Building

Since students should focus on adding the suffixes *-ion* and *-ian,* these words are not divided into all their component morphemes.

Note whether students drop the silent *e* in numbers 7–10. Review the pattern if necessary.

Students are asked to underline the last letter of each root after they add the suffix. Make sure they understand this. Tell them to pronounce the new words after writing them, listening to the sound of the endings.

Note: The next four exercises focus on strategies for predicting the spelling of /shən/. The major goal of these exercises is to help students realize that they do not need to memorize every word in the language. They may be able to spell a word if they can analyze it. As you are working through this lesson, note the patterns with which students are having difficulty. Provide reinforcement activities using other words that follow those patterns.

3 Words That End in *-tion*

In this exercise, students discover patterns by writing root words of words ending in *-tion* and then practice using those patterns. Keep reminding students of one important strategy for spelling /shən/: to look the words up in the dictionary.

Strategy 1: Using probabilities is a useful spelling strategy, but students should not rely on it as a substitute for using a dictionary when one is available.

Strategy 2: By writing the root words of words that end in *-tion* students will discover a pattern. It has been our experience that very few students think of a related word to give them the clue to the spelling of a word they don't know. By focusing on root words, they can begin to develop and practice this important strategy. Make sure students restore the silent *e* in numbers 3 and 4.

Strategy 3: The extra letters (usually *a* or *i*) added before the

-tion in these words normally do not present spelling problems because they are easy to hear. If students write *definite* for number 4, point out that the root for both words is *define*.

When students are adding *-ion* to the 10 words at the end of Exercise 3, make sure that they pronounce the whole words before writing them. Numbers 2, 4, 6, and 8–10 all require extra letters, and the silent *e* should be dropped in numbers 3 and 8.

Additional activity:

For advanced students, point out that the root words are verbs and the words with *-ion* added are nouns. Have them use pairs of words in sentences. Using different forms of the same word in context helps students to understand how affixes change the meaning and function of words and to develop the concept of related words.

4 Words That End in *-sion*

As in Exercise 3, students discover patterns by writing the root words of words with *-sion* added, and then practice using those patterns.

Knowing the roots of words is important for predicting when a word ends in *-sion*. You may have to help students derive the root words. Several of the roots and their variant forms to which *-ion* is added will be studied later in the book. Spelling /shən/ will be reviewed and practiced again as appropriate.

Strategy 1: The title of the strategy will help students to write the correct roots. Make sure that they include the silent *e* as part of the root. Point out that the pronunciation changes when *-ion* is added to *televise* and *revise*.

Strategy 2: The title of the strategy will help students to write the correct roots. Make sure that they include the silent *e* as part of the root in numbers 1–3. Point out that the pronunciation changes when *-ion* is added to *decide*.

Strategy 3: The root *vert* is presented in Lesson 18. There,

students will see that *-ion* is actually added to the variant form of the root, *verse*, after the silent *e* is dropped. The simplified strategy presented here is easier for students at this point.

When students are adding *-ion* to the 10 words at the end of Exercise 4, make sure that they pronounce the new words before writing them. Note whether students drop the silent *e* in numbers 1, 7, and 9, and change the *de* to *s* in numbers 4, 6, and 10.

---

4 Words That End in *-sion*

The second most common spelling of /shən/ is *-sion*. Here are some strategies for predicting when to use *-sion*.

Strategy 1: Root words that end in *se*. Write the root words for these words.

1. tension ___tense___
2. television ___televise___
3. revision ___revise___
4. confusion ___confuse___

Pattern: When a root word ends in *se*, the silent *e* is dropped and *-ion* is added.

Strategy 2: Root words that end in *d* or *de*. Write the root words for these words.

1. invasion ___invade___
2. explosion ___explode___
3. decision ___decide___
4. extension ___extend___

Pattern: When a root word ends in *d* or *de*, those letters are often changed to *s*, and *-ion* is added.

Strategy 3: The root *vert*. Write the root words for the following words.

1. conversion ___convert___
2. introversion ___introvert___

Pattern: When *-ion* is added to words with the Latin root *vert*, the *t* is changed to *s*.

Add *-ion* to the words below following these strategies.

1. verse ___version___
2. divert ___diversion___
3. revert ___reversion___
4. include ___inclusion___
5. expand ___expansion___
6. collide ___collision___
7. precise ___precision___
8. subvert ___subversion___
9. transfuse ___transfusion___
10. conclude ___conclusion___

32   Lesson 7

Additional strategy: The syllable *-sion* is often pronounced /zhən/, as in *version* and *conclusion.* For students who can easily hear the distinction, this can become another strategy for predicting the *-sion* spelling.

Additional activity:

For advanced students, point out that most of these root words are verbs and that the *-ion* forms are nouns. Have them use pairs of words in sentences.

5 **Words That End in** *ssion*

The suffix *-ion* is added directly to words ending in *ss.* This is the easiest pattern for students to learn. There are no common exceptions.

Miss and *cess* are variant forms of the roots *mit* and *ceed/cede,* which students will study in Lessons 31 and 29 respectively. There they will learn that *-ion* is added to the variant forms ending in *ss.*

Part C: Make sure that students change the roots when adding *-ion* to numbers 1, 3, 4, and 6.

6 **The Suffix** *-ian*

In this exercise, students learn that when /shən/ is spelled *-cian,* it usually refers to a person. Point out that words ending in *-cian* usually have related words ending in *-ic* or *-ics.* Remind students that there are many words in which *-ian* does not follow *c,* but these are usually not difficult to spell.

When students are adding *-ian* to the given roots, make sure that they pronounce each new word before writing it. Note whether students drop the *s* in numbers 4–6.

Note these four exceptions to the more common spellings for /shən/: In *fashion* and *cushion,* /shən/ is spelled *shion.* In *suspicion* and *coercion,* it is spelled *cion.*

Quizzes

Give a graded spelling quiz on the words in this lesson. For advanced students, you may want to include other words that contain these suffixes.

Sentences

Sentences for dictation are available at the back of this book if you wish to use them.

Lesson 8

The Suffixes *-ant,* *-ance,* *-ent,* and *-ence*

Objectives

- **Suffixes:** Learn to recognize and spell words with *-ant,* *-ance,* *-ent,* and *-ence.*
- **Word Building:** Join morphemes to build whole words.
- **Strategies:** Learn and practice strategies for spelling /ənt/, /əns/, and /ənsē/ at the end of words.
- **Patterns:** Review patterns for spelling hard and soft *c* and *g.* Discover that roots ending in *qu* are usually followed by *-ent/-ence/-ency.*
- **Homophones:** Practice using context to determine the correct spelling of homophones.

The suffixes included in this lesson present spelling problems because they usually form an unstressed syllable of the words in which they are used. Thus, *-ant* and *-ent* are both pronounced /ənt/, *-ance* and *-ence* are often pronounced /əns/, and *-ancy* and *-ency* are pronounced /ənsē/.

Predicting the spelling of /ənt/, /əns/, and /ənsē/, therefore, is another of the more difficult spelling problems addressed in this book. These suffixes are introduced here in order to provide practice in spelling words that contain them throughout the rest of the book.

General strategies for predicting the spelling of the schwa are presented in this lesson. Strategies related to specific roots are included later in the book.

-ant, -ance, -ent, and *-ence*

1 Recognizing Suffixes

In each group of words below, underline the suffixes listed on the left.

-ant	inclined to; being in a state of;			someone who
	redundant	pleasant	hesitant	occupant
	significant	dominant	expectant	assistant

-ance, -ancy	state or quality of; action			
	assistance	fragrance	hesitancy	vacancy
	significance	dominance	expectancy	occupancy

-ent	inclined to; being in a state of;			someone who
	innocent	recent	urgent	agent
	convenient	delinquent	frequent	patient

-ence, -ency	state or quality of; action			
	innocence	sequence	urgency	agency
	convenience	patience	frequency	emergency

2 Word Building

Join the morphemes that follow to build whole words. Write the words on the lines provided. Remember to change letters if necessary.

1. defy + ant   defiant
2. reluct + ant   reluctant
3. exist + ence   existence
4. persist + ent   persistent
5. appear + ance   appearance
6. insist + ence   insistence
7. intellig + ent   intelligent
8. adolesc + ent   adolescent
9. attend + ance   attendance
10. consist + ency   consistency

Tell your students that this lesson contains a great deal of information, so they should not feel discouraged if they don't remember it all at once. They will be practicing and reinforcing these strategies in later lessons. They can refer to this lesson whenever necessary.

1 Recognizing Suffixes

Read aloud the representative words listed for each suffix. Read the words in a normal speaking voice without stressing the suffixes. Instruct students to underline the suffix as you read each word.

Remind students that usually a suffix is spelled the same way in every word. Then draw attention to the fact that *-ant* and *-ent* sound alike by pronouncing a few word pairs such as *pleasant* and *recent.* Do the same for *-ance* and *-ence.* Point out that all of these suffixes contain a schwa. Explain that this lesson will present strate-

3 **Strategies for Spelling /ənt/, /əns/, and /ənsē/**

The suffixes *-ant* and *-ent* are pronounced the same way. This is usually true of *-ance* and *-ence* as well. Saying the word will not help you spell the suffix because these suffixes nearly always have a schwa sound. The exercises in this lesson will give you some strategies for predicting the spelling of /ənt/, /əns/, and /ənsē/.

Strategy 1: Using the dictionary. Looking a word up in a dictionary is the most basic strategy for dealing with these sounds, and even the best spellers use it.

Strategy 2: Related words. Words ending in *-ant* often have related forms ending in *-ance* or *-ancy*. Words ending in *-ent* often have related forms ending in *-ence* or *-ency*.

Fill in the blanks in this chart following Strategy 2. The first one is done for you.

-ant	-ance/-ancy	-ent	-ence/-ency
extravagant	extravagance	indulgent	indulgence
truant	truancy	coherent	coherence
ignorant	ignorance	existent	existence
relevant	relevancy	inconsistent	inconsistency

4 **Reviewing Patterns: Hard and Soft *c* and *g***

The letters *c* and *g* each spell two sounds. When *c* spells /k/ and *g* spells /g/, we say they are hard. When *c* spells /s/ and *g* spells /j/, we say they are soft. The letters that follow the *c* or *g* usually signal whether they will be hard or soft. An *a* usually signals a hard *c* or *g*, while an *e* signals a soft *c* or *g*.

Add *-ant/-ance/-ancy* or *-ent/-ence/-ency* to each of the roots below and write the words under the appropriate headings. Say each word before you write it, so you know if the *c* or *g* is hard or soft.

arrog   dec   dilig   extravag   innoc   signific   urg   vac

-ant	-ance/-ancy	-ent	-ence/-ency
arrogant	arrogance	decent	decency
extravagant	extravagance	diligent	diligence
significant	significance	innocent	innocence
vacant	vacancy	urgent	urgency

gies for choosing the correct suffix.

Students may understand the definitions better when they see how words with these suffixes function in sentences.

2 **Word Building**

Remind students to pronounce the new words before writing them and to proofread their work.

Make sure that students change the *y* to *i* in *defiant*.

Note: The next five exercises focus on strategies for predicting the spelling of /ənt/, /əns/, and /ənsē/. The major goal of these exercises is to help students realize that they do not need to memorize every word in the language. They may be able to spell a word if they can analyze it. As you work through this lesson, note the strategies with which students are having difficulty. Provide reinforcement activities using other words that follow those strategies.

3 **Strategies for Spelling /ənt/, /əns/, and /ənsē/**

Strategy 1: Stress to students that most people must use the dictionary sometimes to check the spellings of words with these sounds.

Strategy 2: Students learn to relate words ending in *-ant* or *-ent* to words ending in *-ance/-ancy* or *-ence/-ency*. You may want to work one or two of the items with students. Once they start filling in the blanks, the relationships among the words will become obvious. Encourage them to use a dictionary even with this strategy to check their spelling.

4 **Reviewing Patterns: Hard and Soft *c* and *g***

In this exercise, students use the pronunciation of *c* and *g* to predict the spelling of the suffixes. Soft *c* and *g* are followed by suffixes beginning with *e*, while hard *c* and *g* are followed by suffixes beginning with *a*.

We assume that students studying in this book know that *e* and *i* following *c* and *g* generally signal a soft *c* and *g* and that *a*, *o*, and *u* signal hard *c* and *g*. If your students are unfamiliar with this pattern, you may need to preteach it. If you do preteach this pattern, remember that it is more reliable for *c* than for *g*. There are many common words, such as *get* and *begin*, in which hard *g* is followed by *e* or *i*.

Before you begin this exercise, you may want to have students underline roots in Exercise 1 that end in *c* or *g* and then pronounce those words.

Students are required to categorize roots according to the suffixes they take. It is important that students pronounce a whole word before they write it in order to determine whether the *c* or *g* is soft or hard. You may want to read through the information at the beginning of the exercise with students and do one word with them. Be sure that students write whole words, not just roots, on the lines. Encourage them to use a dictionary if they are unsure of related forms (e.g., *diligent* and *diligence*).

5 Another Related-Word Strategy: Words That End in *-ant*

In this exercise, the relationships among related forms of the same roots are emphasized. By filling in the blanks, students learn that if words ending in *-ation* have a form ending in /∂nt/, it will usually be spelled *-ant*. Point out to them that verbs ending in *-ate* are likely to have related forms ending in *-ation* and *-ant*.

Make sure that students drop the silent *e* from the verbs ending in *-ate* before adding suffixes.

Additional activity:

Have students write the corresponding *-ance/-ancy* form of the words ending in *-ant* if there is one (numbers 2–6, and 8).

---

5 Another Related-Word Strategy: Words That End in *-ant*

In Lesson 7 you added *-ion* to verbs to form nouns. Many nouns formed this way end in *-ation*. When there is a related word ending in /∂nt/, the suffix will usually be spelled *-ant*. Fill in the chart below. The first one is done for you.

Verbs	Nouns ending in *-ation*	Words ending in *-ant*
1. irritate	irritation	irritant
2. expect	expectation	expectant
3. consult	consultation	consultant
4. occupy	occupation	occupant
5. hesitate	hesitation	hesitant
6. tolerate	toleration	tolerant
7. immigrate	immigration	immigrant
8. dominate	domination	dominant
9. intoxicate	intoxication	intoxicant
10. participate	participation	participant

6 Discovering a Pattern: Words That End in *-ent/-ence/-ency*

Fill in the blanks in the chart below. Then answer the questions that follow.

Words ending in *-ent*	Related words ending in *-ence/-ency*
1. frequent	frequency
2. delinquent	delinquency
3. eloquent	eloquence
4. consequent	consequence

1. What two letters come before the suffix in all of these words? __qu__

2. When a root ends in *qu*, what suffixes are usually used? __-ent/-ence/-ency__

36   Lesson 8

---

6 Discovering a Pattern: Words That End in *-ent/-ence/-ency*

Through the discovery approach, students deduce that roots ending in *qu* are followed by the suffixes *-ent/-ence/-ency*. (Exceptions to this rule are the words *piquant* and *piquancy*.)

7 Words in Context: A Strategy for Homophones

The endings *-ance* and *-ants* or *-ence* and *-ents* sound alike. Students must learn to use context clues to predict accurately which spelling to use.

In this exercise, students are required to select one of two words below the blank in each sentence and to write the word on the blank to complete the sentence.

Tell students to read a whole sentence first to decide which word to select. After they've written words in the blanks, they should reread the sentence to be sure that it makes sense.

Remind students before they begin that the noun ending *s* usually signifies more than one person or thing.

Note the pronunciation of *patient.* Point out that the *ti* sound is the same as in the ending *-tion.* The endings *-tient* and *-cient* (as found in words such as *impatient, efficient,* and *sufficient*) are not dealt with in this book. It is hoped that most students will be able to make the transfer to *-tient* and *-cient* from *-tion/-sion, -tious/-cious, -tial/-cial,* and *-cian,* all of which are included in this book. You may want to provide reinforcement activities for students who have particular difficulty with these sounds.

Additional Exercises

1. On a separate piece of paper, have students write the same column headings as in Exercise 4. Dictate the following words, asking students to place them in the correct column. Give students ample time to think about adding the correct suffix.

1. dominance   7. hesitancy
2. evident   8. informant
3. different   9. resident
4. assistant   10. excellent
5. defiant   11. elegance
6. magnificence   12. intelligent

If students are unsure of any spellings, have them check the dictionary.

2. Generally we do not recommend error-based instruction that can reinforce an incorrect spelling, but we recognize that proofreading for these minimal differences in spelling is something that students must do. You may want to give your students a proofreading exercise for these suffixes. One possible format is to write words spelled both ways (i.e. *dominant/dominent, emergancy/emergency,* etc.). Ask students to underline the correct one, verify their choice with the dictionary, and finally write the whole word correctly.

Quizzes

Give a graded spelling quiz on the words in this lesson or other words that contain these suffixes.

Sentences

Sentences for dictation are available at the back of this book.

Unit 2

Review of Lessons 4-8

Objectives

- **Suffixes:** Review suffixes studied in Unit 2.
- **Changing Meanings:** Add suffixes to roots to change the meaning of words.
- **Composing Sentences:** Write original sentences using selected words.
- **Word Building:** Reorder and combine morphemes to build words.
- **Completing Words in Sentences:** Build words to fit in context by adding suffixes to given roots.
- **Strategies:** Review and practice strategies for spelling words ending in /ər/, /shən/, and /ənt/, /əns/, and /ənsē/.

You may need to review some of the patterns for adding and spelling suffixes before beginning this review, depending on how well students have managed with individual lessons. Remind them that they can refer to the lessons whenever necessary. One of the most important things they may learn from this unit is that it is often necessary to verify the spellings of some of these suffixes in the dictionary.

For detailed information about strategies and patterns, refer to lesson notes for individual lessons.

Suffixes Presented in This Unit

-ance	-ency	-hood	-ness
-ancy	-ent	-ian	-or
-ant	-er	-ion	-ory
-ary	-ery	-less	-ry
-en	-est	-ly	-ship
-ence	-ful	-ment	-ward

1 Adding Suffixes to Change the Meaning of Words

Add one or more of the suffixes above to each word below to make a new form of the word. Remember to add, drop, or change letters if necessary. Write the new words on the lines provided.

1. act — actor
2. like — likely
3. help — helpfulness
4. fresh — freshen
5. direct — direction
6. refine — refinement
7. expect — expectation
8. discuss — discussion
9. civil — civilian
10. advise — advisory
11. ignore — ignorance
12. indulge — indulgent
13. inspect — inspection
14. intrude — intruder
15. consist — consistency
16. occupy — occupant

Use two of the new words in original sentences.

_____

_____

---

1 Adding Suffixes to Change the Meaning of Words

In this exercise, students change the meaning and function of given words by selecting and adding suffixes from the list of those presented in the unit.

Remind students to pay special attention if they are forming words ending in /əry/, /shən/, /ənt/, /əns/, or /ənsē/. Make sure they proofread the words they write.

Answers given on the replica of the student page are examples. Accept all correctly spelled words.

Students are asked to write original sentences using two of the new words. The exercise instructions are deliberately flexible about how many sentences should be written. If students need more room to write, encourage them to use their notebooks.

Help them to correct misspellings by using what they already know. Errors in words not yet studied should not be treated negatively.

2 Jumbled Word Building

Build words by putting the morphemes below in the correct order. Write the words on the lines provided. Remember to add, drop, or change letters if necessary. The first one is done for you.

1. spect re ful __respectful__
2. less ly self __selflessly__
3. ful stress ly __stressfully__
4. ug ness ly __ugliness__
5. er lead ship __leadership__
6. ly like hood __likelihood__
7. ate spect or __spectator__
8. en deep ed __deepened__
9. y wealth est __wealthiest__
10. pent ry car __carpentry__
11. fresh re ment __refreshment__
12. for straight ward __straightforward__

3 Predicting the Spelling of /ər/

Part A. Complete the sentences below.

1. The most common way to spell /ər/ at the end of a word is _er_.

2. The most common spelling after words ending in -*ate*, *t*, or *ess* is _or_.

3. When /ər/ means *more*, it is spelled _er_.

Part B. Add -*er* or -*or* to the words below and write them in the correct column.

angry	carry	catch	collect	custom
fast	listen	legislate	messy	operate
perform	investigate	radiate	true	young

-er	-er	-or
angrier	catcher	investigator
faster	messier	legislator
performer	truer	radiator
carrier	customer	collector
listener	younger	operator

Additional activities:

Ask students to write sentences using pairs of words (given words and the same words with suffixes added). This will help them to see how suffixes change the function of words.

Ask students to make as many other words as they can by adding suffixes to the given words.

2 Jumbled Word Building

In this exercise, students build words from morphemes that are not in the correct order. Students must be able to identify prefixes, roots, and suffixes before they can start to build the words.

Note whether students make the *y* to *i* conversion in numbers 4, 6, and 9, and whether they drop the silent *e* in number 7.

Remind students to pronounce the words before they write them and to proofread them afterward.

Additional activity:

Have students generate exercises of this sort for each other using words from Exercise 2 of previous lessons.

3 Predicting the Spelling of /ər/

Part A: Students complete sentences stating the strategies and patterns from Lesson 6.

Part B: Students use the information from Part A to categorize words according to which form of /ər/ can be added to make new words. The fact that many more words end in -*er* than in -*or* is reinforced through the format of this exercise.

Make sure that students change the *y* to *i* in *angrier, carrier,* and *messier,* and that they drop the silent *e* from *true* and words ending in -*ate.*

4 Completing Words in Sentences

In this exercise, students add the suffix *-ery* or one of its variant forms to roots to form words that are appropriate in the context of the sentences. Remind them that the best strategy for correctly spelling words with these suffixes is to check them in the dictionary.

Make sure that students read a whole sentence first to decide which form of the suffix to use and that they proofread completed sentences.

Additional activity:

Have students use any of the words they complete here in other sentences.

5 Reviewing and Practicing Strategies for Spelling /shən/

In this exercise, students review strategies and patterns for predict-ing the spelling of /shən/ at the end of words. Review any part of Lesson 7 before students begin this exercise if necessary.

Part A: Students complete sentences stating strategies and patterns presented in Lesson 7.

Part B: Students use the information from Part A to predict whether the spelling of /shən/ at the end of given roots is *-tion, -sion, ssion,* or *-cian*. Make sure they add, drop, or change letters according to the patterns they've studied. Remind them to check a dictionary if they are unsure of any spellings.

Note if students are having trouble with particular patterns and review them.

Additional activity:

Ask students to write sentences using pairs of words (given words and the same words with suffixes added).

---

4 Completing Words in Sentences

Add one of the following forms of the suffix *-ery* to the root given under each blank below and write the completed word in the blank. The word you build must make sense in the sentence.

-ery   *-ary*   *-ory*   *-ry*

1. Paying taxes isn't __voluntary__, it's __obligatory__.
   (volunt)   (obligat)

2. That __machinery__ is __necessary__ to build car bodies.
   (machin)   (necess)

3. Using a __dictionary__ is one way to build __vocabulary__.
   (diction)   (vocabul)

4. There was a __burglary__ at the __factory__ last night.
   (burgl)   (fact)

5. The __scenery__ from the window is quite __ordinary__.
   (scen)   (ordin)

6. The __laundry__ room in our building is __satisfactory__.
   (laund)   (satisfact)

5 Reviewing and Practicing Strategies for Spelling /shən/

Part A. Complete the sentences below.

1. The most common spelling of /shən/ is __tion__.

2. When a root word ends in *t* or *te,* or when other letters are added to the root before *-ion,* /shən/ is probably spelled __tion__.

3. When a root word ends in *se, d,* or *de,* /shən/ is probably spelled __sion__.

4. In words with the Latin root *vert,* /shən/ is spelled __sion__, and in words with the roots *mit* or *cede,* or when a root ends in *ss,* /shən/ is spelled __ssion__.

5. When a word ending in /shən/ means a person who does something, /shən/ is probably spelled __cian__.

40   Unit 2 Review

48   Unit 2 Review

Part B. Add *-ion* or *-ian* to each root word below. Write the new words on the lines provided. Remember to add, drop, or change letters if necessary.

1. erode __erosion__
2. ignite __ignition__
3. music __musician__
4. inform __information__
5. educate __education__
6. product __production__
7. confuse __confusion__
8. transmit __transmission__
9. relax __relaxation__
10. politics __politician__
11. correct __correction__
12. confess __confession__
13. electric __electrician__
14. pervert __perversion__
15. concede __concession__
16. appreciate __appreciation__

6 Reviewing and Practicing Strategies for Spelling /ənt/, /əns/, and /ənsē/
Part A. Complete the sentences below.

1. Words ending in *-ent* often have related forms ending in __-ence__ or __-ency__ .

2. Words ending in *-ance* or *-ancy* often have related forms ending in __-ant__ .

3. If you hear a soft *c* or *g* at the end of a root word, use the suffixes __-ent__ , __-ence__ , or __-ency__ .

4. A hard *c* or *g* will be followed by the suffixes __-ant__ , __-ance__ , or __-ancy__ .

5. After *qu*, /ənt/ is spelled __-ent__ and /əns/ is spelled __-ence__ .

Part B. Add *-ant* or *-ent* to the roots below. Write the new words on the lines provided.

1. urg __urgent__
2. dilig __diligent__
3. frequ __frequent__
4. domin __dominant__
5. immigr __immigrant__
6. occup __occupant__
7. arrog __arrogant__
8. expect __expectant__
9. subsequ __subsequent__
10. magnific __magnificent__

6 Reviewing and Practicing Strategies for Spelling /ənt/, /əns/, and /ənsē/

In this exercise, students review patterns for predicting the spelling of /ənt/, /əns/, and /ənsē/ at the end of words. Review any part of Lesson 8 before students begin this exercise if necessary.

Part A: Students complete sentences stating strategies and patterns presented in Lesson 8.

Part B: Students use the information from Part A to predict whether the spelling of the suffixes at the end of given roots is *-ant/-ance/-ancy* or *-ent/-ence/-ency*. Remind them to check a dictionary if they are unsure of any spellings.

Students should write whole words and not just the suffixes on the lines provided.

Note if students are having trouble with particular patterns and review them if necessary.

Sentences

Sentences for dictation are available at the back of this book if you wish to use them.

Unit 2 Test

We recommend that you test your students on the words from Unit 2 before going on. The following is a suggested list of words from Unit 2. You may want to substitute other words to meet the needs of your students.

Dictate each word and use it in a simple sentence. Students should be able to spell 90 percent of these words correctly.

thankfully	factory
afterward	carpentry
useful	bigger
carelessly	inspection
cheerfulness	discussion
relationship	politician
neighborhood	pleasant
arrangement	assistance
machinery	patient
spectator	frequency

Lesson 9

The Prefixes *a-*, *ad-*, *in-*, and *un-*

Objectives

- **Prefixes:** Learn to recognize and spell words with *a-*, *ad-*, *in-*, and *un-*.
- **Word Building:** Join morphemes to build whole words.
- **Assimilative Prefixes:** Learn and practice spelling the assimilative forms of *ad-* and *in-*.
- **Taking Words Apart:** Divide words into morphemes.
- **Changing Meanings:** Add prefixes to roots to change the meaning of words.
- **Composing Sentences:** Write original sentences using selected words.
- **Recognizing Morphemes in Context:** Identify prefixes in context.

For general information on prefixes, refer to page 8 in the introduction.

Lesson 9 — Prefixes
a–, *ad–*, *in–*, and *un–*

1 Recognizing Prefixes
In each group of words below, underline the prefixes listed on the left.

a-	without;		on, in; in a state of	
	atypical	amoral	afield	apart
	asymmetrical	asexual	ashore	aboard

ad-, ac-, ap-, as-	toward, to, near, or in			
	adapt	admit	accept	appear
	addition	adoption	accessory	assistance
	adhesive	adjustment	approaches	assignment

in-, im-	in			
	involved	insert	imminent	impact
	including	installation	important	impressive

in-, im-, il-, ir-	not			
	inhuman	impatient	illegal	irrational
	incomplete	immature	illogical	irrelevant
	inexcusable	impossible	illegible	irresistible

un-	not, opposite of;		reverse an action	
	unkind	unhappy	undo	unfold
	unusual	unemployed	unload	unlock
	unnatural	unnecessary	undress	uncover

42   Lesson 9

1 Recognizing Prefixes

Read aloud the representative words listed for each prefix. Read the words in a normal speaking voice without stressing the prefixes. Instruct students to underline the prefix as you read each word. Do this exercise orally so that students can both see and hear the prefixes.

Remind students that the definitions of the prefixes are listed above the representative words. Point out the prefixes that have more than one meaning.

Emphasize that usually a prefix is spelled the same way in every word. Point out the prefixes that are spelled the same way in each word. Tell students that a few prefixes, such as *ad-*, do change in predictable ways. Later in this lesson they will learn how to predict these changes.

The pronunciation of *a-* changes according to the meaning of the prefix. It is pronounced /ā/ when it means *without* (*atypical*) and /ə/ when it means *on, in* or *in a state of* (*afield*).

Point out that the prefix *a-* in *afield, ashore, apart,* and *aboard* changes the part of speech when added to the root word, but that this is unusual.

When you come to *ad-*, ask students to identify the different forms of *ad-* in the representative words.

2 Word Building

Join the morphemes that follow to build whole words. Write the words on the lines provided. Remember to drop the silent *e* if necessary.

1. il + lus + ion ___illusion___
2. im + mobile ___immobile___
3. un + fast + en ___unfasten___
4. ap + prove + al ___approval___
5. ad + vent + ure ___adventure___

6. im + per + fect ___imperfect___
7. in + cred + ible ___incredible___
8. un + pre + pare + ed ___unprepared___
9. un + ac + cept + able ___unacceptable___
10. ac + commod + ation ___accommodation___

3 Recognizing Patterns: Prefixes That Change

When prefixes are added to roots, the spelling of the prefix usually does not change. A few prefixes, however, do change when added to roots that start with certain letters. These changes often account for double consonants near the beginning of words. Study the following charts.

Part A. The Prefix *ad-*

Prefix	Changes to	Before	Examples
ad-	ac-	c	ad + cuse = accuse
ad-	ap-	p	ad + pear = appear
ad-	as-	s	ad + sume = assume

In a few words, *ad-* changes to *af-, al-,* and *at-* before roots that begin with *f, l,* and *t* respectively. Example words are *afflict, allocate,* and *attend.*

Join the morphemes below, changing *ad-* if necessary.

1. ad + fect ___affect___
2. ad + point ___appoint___
3. ad + semble ___assemble___
4. ad + tempt ___attempt___

5. ad + here ___adhere___
6. ad + cident ___accident___
7. ad + lowance ___allowance___
8. ad + proximate ___approximate___

Lesson 9   43

Additional activities:

Have students work in small groups to generate as many words as they can that start with these prefixes. You may want to have them use a dictionary to find additional words.

Have students identify suffixes that they recognize in the representative words.

2 Word Building

In this exercise, students combine morphemes to build words. Emphasize that students should add one morpheme at a time to minimize the chance of making errors. Remind them to pronounce the new words before writing them and to proofread their work.

Make sure that students drop the silent *e* in numbers 4 and 8.

The suffix *-ate* will be introduced in Lesson 23, at which point students will learn that although *-ation* is listed as a suffix in some dictionaries, it is usually a combination of *-ate* and *-ion.*

3 Recognizing Patterns: Prefixes That Change

In this exercise, students are introduced to prefixes that undergo assimilative changes. An assimilative prefix is one in which the final consonant changes before roots that begin with certain consonants. Learning which prefixes change, and before which consonants, can help students to remember when to double a consonant near the beginning of a word.

Make sure that students understand that the prefixes that change are exceptions and that it is not an overwhelming task to learn them.

Point out that the changes are regular and that they occur each time *ad-* and *in-* come before certain letters.

Part A: Students should study the charts carefully before attempting to join the morphemes that follow them. You may want students to underline double consonants once they have built the words.

Only assimilative forms occurring frequently in familiar words are included here. *Ad-* also changes to *ag-, an-,* and *ar-* in a few words.

There are actually more common words starting with *ap-* than *ad-,* even though *ad-* is the original form of the prefix.

Lesson 9   **51**

Part B: Point out to students that the prefix will not change in every case (numbers 2 and 9).

Additional activities:

Have students use some of the words they build in original sentences.

Have students try to find words in their dictionaries beginning with *ad-* and roots that start with *c, f, l, p, s,* or *t* (*adc-, adf-, adl-,* etc.). Then have them try to find words that begin with *in-* and roots that start with *b, m, p, l,* or *r* (*inb-, inm-, imp-,* etc.). They will find few exceptions to the patterns presented in this lesson.

For advanced students, you may want to point out that *en-,* a variant form of *in-,* changes to *em-,* following the same pattern as *in-* to *im-,* before certain consonants (*en + bark = embark, en + ploy = employ, en + balm = embalm*). The prefix *en-* is not included in the lesson as it is less common. Have students use the dictionary to make a list of five words beginning with *em-* as a variant form of *en-.*

4 Taking Words Apart

In this exercise, students divide words into their component morphemes. All of these words follow regular patterns. Encourage students to refer to the glossary or a dictionary if necessary.

Students who have difficulty should first identify the prefixes presented in this lesson.

Part B. The Prefix *in-*

Prefix	Changes to	Before	Examples
in-	im-	b, m, or p	in + balance = imbalance
			in + moral = immoral
			in + practical = impractical
in-	il-	l	in + legible = illegible
in-	ir-	r	in + regular = irregular

Join the morphemes below, changing *in-* if necessary.

1. in + port ___import___
2. in + ability ___inability___
3. in + mortal ___immortal___
4. in + rational ___irrational___
5. in + personal ___impersonal___
6. in + limitable ___illimitable___
7. in + resistible ___irresistible___
8. in + legitimate ___illegitimate___
9. in + vulnerable ___invulnerable___
10. in + replaceable ___irreplaceable___

4 Taking Words Apart

Divide the following words into morphemes and write each one under the correct heading. You may write either the original form of the prefix or the variation used in the word. Check prefixes and suffixes in the glossary if necessary.

	Prefixes		Roots	Suffixes
1. assorted	as/ad		sort	ed
2. immortal	im/in		mort	al
3. addiction	ad		dict	ion
4. imported	im/in		port	ed
5. unadjusted	un	ad	just	ed
6. appearance	ap/ad		pear	ance
7. unimportant	un	im/in	port	ant
8. acceptance	ac/ad		cept	ance

44   Lesson 9

If a word contains a variant form of a prefix, students may write either the original form of the prefix or the form that is used in the word. For example, *assorted* could be either *ad + sort + ed* or *as + sort + ed. Addiction* and *unadjusted* are the only words in this exercise that do not contain variant forms of assimilative prefixes.

Note whether students divide the two prefixes in *unadjusted* and *unimportant.* Review those prefixes if necessary. Point out that

un- is often added to words that already have a prefix.

Additional activity:

Encourage your students to make a habit of looking at the words they encounter in their daily lives to see if those words can be divided into morphemes. Students can practice taking apart the words they find in any printed material, such as newspapers, magazines, or ads.

Students may write two sentences using a pair of words each, four sentences using one word each, or any other combination. If they need more room, encourage them to use their notebooks.

Remind students to proofread their words and sentences.

6 **Recognizing Prefixes in Context**

This exercise will help students to see how individual morphemes are used in context.

Tell students to underline in the sentences all of the prefixes from the given list. Tell them also to read the sentences before they start underlining.

Additional activities:

Have students circle any suffixes that they recognize in these sentences.

Recognizing morphemes in context can be done using printed material such as newspapers, magazines, or ads.

Quizzes

Give a graded spelling quiz on the words in this lesson or other words that include these prefixes.

Sentences

Sentences for dictation are available at the back of this book.

5 **Changing the Meaning of Words**

This exercise has students generate antonyms since all of the prefixes convey an opposite or negative meaning. By selecting and adding these prefixes, students change the meanings of the given words. They are then asked to use two pairs of words in original sentences.

Point out that adding prefixes is easier than adding suffixes because the spelling of the root doesn't change.

Make sure students understand that they are to use pairs of words—the positive and the negative form—in their sentences. Using different forms of the same word in context helps students to understand how prefixes change the meaning of words. It also helps them to develop the concept of related words. The exercise instructions are deliberately flexible about how many sentences should be written.

The Prefixes *con-*, *de-*, *dis-*, *di-*, *ex-*, and *per-*

Objectives

- **Prefixes:** Learn to recognize and spell words with *con-*, *de-*, *dis-*, *di-*, *ex-*, and *per-*.
- **Word Building:** Join morphemes to build whole words. Select and combine morphemes to build 10 or more words.
- **Assimilative Prefixes:** Learn and practice spelling the assimilative forms of *con-*, *dis-*, and *ex-*.
- **Completing Words in Sentences:** Build words to fit in context by adding prefixes to given roots.

1 Recognizing Prefixes

Read aloud the representative words listed for each prefix. Read the words in a normal speaking voice without stressing the prefixes. Instruct students to underline the prefix as you read each word.

Point out that the prefixes *con-*, *dis-*, and *ex-* change and that in this lesson students will learn how to predict these changes.

When you come to *decongestant* and *discontinue*, ask students to identify both prefixes. When you come to the prefixes with assimilative forms, ask students to identify the different forms in the

representative words. Have students circle double consonants near the beginnings of words and see if they can identify a pattern based on what they learned in Lesson 9.

Point out the following:

The prefixes *de-* and *di-* sound alike in many words, so students must learn which prefix goes with which roots.

The prefix *per-* sounds like *pur-*, but *per-* is the more common spelling of /pur/.

The pronunciation of *sequence* changes when the prefix *con-* is added.

Additional activities:

Have students work in small groups to generate as many words as they can that start with these prefixes. You may want to have them use a dictionary to find additional words.

Have students identify suffixes that they have studied or recognize in the representative words.

---

1 Recognizing Prefixes

In each group of words below, underline the prefixes listed on the left.

con-, col-, com-, cor-	*with, together*			
	congress	conversation	companion	collide
	connecting	consequence	communicate	correction

de-	*reverse, remove, reduce*			
	deflate	decay	depreciate	desegregate
	decrease	deficit	descending	decongestant

dis-, dif-	*absence; opposite; reverse, remove*			
	distribute	discount	dislike	difficult
	discontinue	disagreement	dishonest	different

di-	*separation, twoness*			
	divorce	diverse	divest	dioxide
	division	diluted	direction	dilemma

ex-, ef-, e-	*out of, from*			
	export	exterior	effort	eject
	exception	exclusive	effective	emerge
	expedition	expanding	emigrate	eruption

per-	*through; thoroughly*			
	perspire	percolator	perfect	perturbed
	perforate	permeable	permanent	perseverance

2 Word Building

Join the morphemes that follow to build whole words. Remember to drop the silent *e* if necessary. Write the words on the lines provided.

1. dis + sect dissect	6. e + limin + ate eliminate
2. con + stant constant	7. dif + fuse + ion diffusion
3. ef + fici + ent efficient	8. per + spect + ive perspective
4. di + gress + ion digression	9. com + pare + ed compared
5. ex + pect + ant expectant	10. de + con + gest + ant decongestant

3 Recognizing Patterns: More Prefixes That Change

When prefixes are added to roots, their spelling usually does not change. The prefixes *con-*, *dis-*, and *ex-*, however, do change when added to roots that begin with certain letters. Study the chart below. Remember that these changes often account for double consonants near the beginning of words.

The Prefixes *con-*, *dis-*, and *ex-*

Prefix	Changes to	Before	Examples
con-	com-	b, m, or p	con + bine = combine con + merce = commerce con + pete = compete
con-	col-	l	con + laborate = collaborate
con-	cor-	r	con + respond = correspond
dis-	dif-	f	dis + ficult = difficult
ex-	ef-	f	ex + fort = effort

Join the morphemes below, changing *con-*, *dis-*, and *ex-* if necessary.

1. con + pos + ed composed	5. con + lect + or collector
2. con + rupt + ion corruption	6. con + bust + ion combustion
3. con + mand + er commander	7. con + vent + ion convention
4. dis + fer + ent different	8. in + ex + fect + ive ineffective

Lesson 10 47

2 Word Building

Students should drop the silent *e* in numbers 7 and 9.

If students have trouble with the /shənt/ sound in *efficient*, point out that the *ci* sound is the same as in the ending *-cian*. It is hoped that most students will be able to make the transfer. You may want to provide reinforcement activities for students who have particular difficulty with these sounds.

3 Recognizing Patterns: More Prefixes That Change

In this exercise, students continue their study of prefixes that undergo assimilative changes. Remind students that the changes are regular and that they occur each time *con-*, *dis-*, or *ex-* comes before certain letters. Only the more common assimilative forms are presented here.

Students should study the chart carefully before attempting to join the morphemes that follow it. You may want students to underline double consonants once they have built the words.

Students will not need to change the prefix in number 7.

Notes: The prefix *ex* changes to *e* in front of many consonants. It is not presented here as an assimilative prefix since it usually does not cause spelling problems. The *e* can be heard clearly in most words.

Technically, *con-* is a variant form of *com-*. Since *com-* is commonly used only before roots that begin with *b, m,* and *p,* however, we think that it will be less confusing to students to present these variant forms following the pattern set in Lesson 9.

Additional activities:

Have students use some of the words they build in sentences.

Have students try to find in a dictionary words starting with *dif-* or *ef-* with a single *f*. They will find few or none, depending on the dictionary they use.

4 Completing Words in Sentences

Add one of the following prefixes to the root given under each blank below, and write the completed word in the blank. The word you build must make sense in the sentence.

con-   com-   de-   dis-   di-   ex-   e-   ef-   per-

1. The loud music from the next apartment is really __disturbing__.
   <small>turbing</small>

2. Are you __committed__ to __excelling__ in this course?
   <small>mitted   celling</small>

3. Please make an __effort__ to __complete__ the job today.
   <small>fort   plete</small>

4. My __concentration__ was __divided__ between two projects.
   <small>centration   vided</small>

5. I __persuaded__ him to __examine__ the __evidence__.
   <small>suaded   amine   vidence</small>

5 Challenge Word Building

On a separate piece of paper, combine the morphemes below to build at least 10 words. Use as few or as many morphemes as you need for each word. Remember that the prefixes *de-* and *di-* often sound the same, so use a dictionary if you are unsure of a word.

Prefixes	Roots	Suffixes
de-	bate	-er
di-	cept	-ery
dis-	cov	-ive
	rect	-ion
	script	-or
	sign	

48   Lesson 10

---

words begin with *de-* or *di-*. Make sure they drop the silent *e* when necessary.

Possible responses are listed here. There may be others. Accept all correctly spelled words.

bate	designer
cover	direct
debate	direction
debater	directive
deception	director
deceptive	discover
description	discoverer
descriptive	discovery
descriptor	script
design	sign

Additional Exercises: Using the Dictionary

1. Tell students to find one word in the dictionary that starts with each of the following prefixes. Encourage them to find words that haven't been included in this lesson. Then have them use some of the words in sentences.

1. con-	4. e-
2. de-	5. ex-
3. dis-	6. per-

2. Have students find six words that start with *de-* and six that start with *di-*. Then have them use one word beginning with each prefix in a sentence.

Quizzes

Give a graded spelling quiz on the words in this lesson or other words that include these morphemes.

Sentences

Sentences for dictation are available at the back of this book.

---

4 Completing Words in Sentences

Remind students to read a whole sentence first to decide which prefixes to use. After they've written words in the blanks, they should reread the sentence. Make sure that they use assimilated forms of prefixes and double consonants when necessary.

5 Challenge Word Building

Emphasize that students can use as few or as many morphemes as needed for a particular word. For instance, the roots *bate, script,* and *sign* function as whole words.

Tell students to apply what they have already learned about adding suffixes such as *-ion* to roots.

Encourage students to use a dictionary if necessary. For instance, they may need to check whether

Lesson —11—

The Prefixes *pre-*, *post-*, *re-*, *pro-*, and *mis-*

Objectives

- **Prefixes:** Learn to recognize and spell words with *pre-*, *post-*, *re-*, *pro-*, and *mis-*.
- **Word Building:** Join morphemes to build whole words.
- **Using Meanings:** Select prefixes based on the definitions of words to be formed.
- **Taking Words Apart:** Divide words into morphemes.
- **Building and Using Words:** Select, reorder, and combine morphemes to build words. Use selected words in context.
- **Recognizing Morphemes in Context:** Identify prefixes in context.
- **Word Game:** Play a game to build words.

1 Recognizing Prefixes

Read aloud the representative words listed for each prefix. Read the words in a normal speaking voice without stressing the prefixes. Instruct students to underline the prefix as you read each word. Do this exercise orally so that students can both see and hear the prefixes.

Remind students that the definitions of the prefixes are listed above the representative words.

Emphasize that usually a prefix is spelled the same way in every

---

Lesson —11— Prefixes
pre-, post-, re-, pro-, and *mis-*

1 Recognizing Prefixes
In each group of words below, underline the prefixes listed on the left.

pre-	**before**		
	preview	prejudice	prefix
	prepared	premature	pretax
	precaution	preoccupied	prevention

post-	**after, later; behind**			
	postdate	posterity	postscript	postgraduate
	postpone	posterior	postmortem	posthumously

re-	**back, again, anew**			
	return	release	renew	review
	retreat	reversal	remember	rediscovered
	rejection	replacing	reproduction	reappointment

pro-	**forth, forward**		
	proceed	project	prominent
	progressive	produce	promotion

mis-	**wrongly, badly**		
	mistaken	misdeeds	mislaid
	mistimed	misbehave	misfortune
	mistrust	misunderstood	misleading

Lesson 11   49

---

word. If the spelling changes, it changes in predictable ways.

When you come to *reproduction, rediscovered,* and *reappointment,* ask students to identify both prefixes.

Point out the following:

The prefixes *pre-* and *post-* have opposite meanings.

There are two words spelled *pro,* one meaning *professional (pro football)* and the other meaning *in favor of (pros and cons).*

Several of the prefixes in this lesson have more than one pronunciation. *Pre-* and *pro-* are both sometimes pronounced /prə/, so knowing the meaning is important for predicting the correct spelling. The prefix *re-* is also sometimes pronounced /rə/. The prefix *post-* is pronounced /pōst/ if the other part of the word can stand alone, as in *postdate,* but /post/ if the prefix is an indispensable part of the word as in *posterior.*

Additional activities:

Have students work in small groups to generate as many words as they can that start with these prefixes. You may want to have them use a dictionary to find additional words.

Have students identify suffixes that they have studied or recognize in the representative words.

2 Word Building

Emphasize that students should add one morpheme at a time to minimize the chance of making errors. Remind them to pronounce the new words before writing them and to proofread their work.

Students should drop the silent *e* in numbers 4 and 9. For number 7, both *programmer* and *programer* are acceptable spellings.

3 Looking at Meanings: *pre-*, *pro-*, and *per-*

Using meaning to determine spelling is an important strategy. This exercise encourages students to pay close attention to the meanings of individual morphemes and then of whole words.

Before students begin, review the definitions of *pre-*, *pro-*, and *per-*.

It is easy to confuse the prefixes *pre-*, *pro-*, and *per-* because of the schwa sound. Mistaking *per-* for

pre- is an especially common error. Point out that the prefix *pre-* is sometimes mispronounced as *per-*. Stress that when students are learning any new word with either prefix, they should pay particular attention to the correct pronunciation of the prefix. Learning to relate the meanings of these prefixes to the words in which they are used should help students to spell the prefixes correctly.

If students make errors, discuss the meaning of the incorrect prefix and the definition of the word to show how they are mismatched.

Additional activities:

Once they have written the word suggested by the definition and partial word given, have students underline the portion of the definition that led them to choose a certain prefix.

Have students use the words in sentences.

---

2 Word Building
Join the morphemes below to build whole words. Write the words on the lines provided.

1. post + nasal _____postnasal_____
2. re + miss + ion _____remission_____
3. pro + vis + ion _____provision_____
4. pre + cede + ing _____preceding_____
5. mis + con + duct _____misconduct_____
6. re + ject + ion _____rejection_____
7. pro + gram +er _____programmer_____
8. pre + vent + ion _____prevention_____
9. post + operate + ive _____postoperative_____
10. mis + con + cept + ion _____misconception_____

3 Looking at Meanings: *pre-*, *pro-*, and *per-*
Below is a list of roots. Next to each root is the definition of a word that has that root. Add either *pre-*, *pro-*, or *per-* to the root to make a word that fits the definition. Write the whole word on the line provided. The first one is done for you.

Roots	Meaning of words	Whole words
1. dawn	before dawn	predawn
2. turb	disturb thoroughly	perturb
3. scribe	write beforehand	prescribe
4. vade	go through thoroughly	pervade
5. gress	step forward	progress
6. pare	make ready in advance	prepare
7. mote	move forward or up	promote
8. mit	give leave, let through	permit
9. ceed	go forward	proceed
10. caution	care taken in advance	precaution

4 Taking Words Apart

Divide the following words into morphemes and write each one under the correct heading. Remember to add the silent *e* to the root if necessary.

	Prefixes		Roots	Suffixes
1. pretext	pre		text	
2. provider	pro		vide	er
3. mistrusted	mis		trust	ed
4. proportion	pro		port	ion
5. improvising	im/in	pro	vise	ing
6. posthumous	post		hum	ous
7. postponement	post		pone	ment
8. reappointment	re	ap/ad	point	ment

5 Jumbled Morphemes

Use the morphemes in each group below to create three different words. Choose two words from each group and use them in phrases or short sentences. The first one is started for you.

Phrases or sentences

1. pro   un   tect   ed

   protect   Lee is a protected child.

   protected   unprotected from the rain

   unprotected

2. pre   able   dict   un

   predict   The weather is unpredictable.

   predictable   Do you predict success?

   unpredictable

4 Taking Words Apart

In this exercise, students divide words into their component morphemes. All of these words follow regular patterns. Encourage students to refer to the glossary or a dictionary to check any individual morphemes if necessary.

Remind students that they should write the original form of a root. They should restore the silent *e* in *pro vide er* and *im pro vise ing*.

Students who have difficulty should first identify the prefixes presented in this lesson.

Note whether students divide the two prefixes in *improvising* and *reappointment*. Review those morphemes if necessary.

Additional activity:

Encourage your students to make a habit of looking at the words they encounter in their daily lives to see if those words can be divided into morphemes. Students can practice taking apart the words they find in any printed material, such as newspapers, magazines, or ads.

5 Jumbled Morphemes

In this exercise, students are required to build three words from a group of morphemes that are not in correct order. Not every morpheme will be used in each word. Students are then asked to use some of their words in phrases or sentences. By using the words in context, students will show how well they understand the functions of various morphemes.

Encourage students to use a dictionary to check their spelling and to determine if the words they form are actual words. Remind them to proofread their work.

The answers on the replica of the student page are examples. Accept all correctly spelled words.

3. pro ion duct re

<u>product</u>   <u>That's a poor reproduction of</u>

<u>production</u>   <u>the original product.</u>

<u>reproduction</u>

6 Recognizing Prefixes in Context

Underline the following prefixes in the sentences below.

pre-   *post-*   *re-*   *pro-*   *mis-*

1. It's redundant to keep on restating the same idea.
2. They requested that the proceeds be shared equally.
3. Juan is a sales representative for a refrigerator company.
4. The rebels were mistaken in persisting in violent behavior.
5. That was a good proposal, and I think you'll be promoted for it.
6. She's not prepared to provide for him or to promise him anything.
7. My father misunderstood how to get reimbursed for medical expenses.
8. We can't prevent this misfortune, but we can postpone telling anyone about it.

7 Word Pyramid

Use the letters found in *pre-* to complete the words below. Each word contains the letters *p, r,* and *e* at least once in any order. The first one is done for you.

P RE

P u <u>R</u> <u>E</u>

P <u>R</u> o v <u>E</u>

<u>E</u> x <u>P</u> <u>R</u> <u>E</u> s s

c a <u>R</u> <u>P</u> <u>E</u> n t e <u>R</u>

a <u>P</u> <u>P</u> <u>E</u> a <u>R</u> a n c <u>E</u> s

words. With the exception of the first two words, the answer words contain morphemes that students have studied.

Remember that word games are intended to be fun. Students may want to work in pairs or small groups. If they find this game confusing or frustrating, let them skip it.

Quizzes

Give a graded spelling quiz on the words in this lesson or other words that include these prefixes.

Sentences

Sentences for dictation are available at the back of this book if you wish to use them.

6 Recognizing Prefixes in Context

Instruct students to underline in the sentences only the prefixes from the given list and to read each sentence before they start underlining.

In *representative,* have students draw a vertical line between the two prefixes.

Additional activities:

Have students circle any suffixes that they recognize in these sentences.

Have them develop exercises of this sort for one another to do.

This kind of activity can be done using any printed material, such as newspapers, magazines, or ads.

7 Word Pyramid

In this word game, students build complete words by filling in the letters *p, r,* and *e.* These letters can be in any order, and some will be used more than once in some

Unit 3

Review of Lessons 9–11

Objectives

- **Prefixes:** Review prefixes studied in Unit 3.
- **Changing Meanings:** Add prefixes to change the meaning of words.
- **Composing Sentences:** Write original sentences using selected words.
- **Assimilative Prefixes:** Review the assimilative forms studied in Unit 3.
- **Taking Words Apart:** Divide words into morphemes.
- **Creating and Using Words:** Create words and use them in context.
- **Related Words:** List words related to given words.
- **Completing Words in Sentences:** Build words to fit in context by adding prefixes to given roots.
- **Word Game:** Play a game to build words.

You may need to review some of the patterns for adding and spelling prefixes before beginning this review, depending on how well students have managed with individual lessons. Remind them that they can refer to the lessons whenever necessary.

For detailed information about patterns and strategies, refer to the lesson notes for individual lessons.

Prefixes Presented in This Unit

a-	con-	ef-	per-
ac-	cor-	ex-	post-
ad-	de-	il-	pre-
ap-	di-	im-	pro-
as-	dif-	in-	re-
col-	dis-	ir-	un-
com-	e-	mis-	

1 **Adding Prefixes to Change the Meaning of Words**
Add one or more of the prefixes above to each word below to make a new form of the word. Write the new words on the lines provided.

1. fort _____comfort_____
2. port _____report_____
3. press _____depress_____
4. cover _____uncover_____
5. treated _____mistreated_____

6. play _____display_____
7. view _____preview_____
8. count _____discount_____
9. quest _____conquest_____
10. formation _____information_____

Use three of the new words in original sentences.

_____

_____

_____

Unit 3 Review　　53

---

1 Adding Prefixes to Change the Meaning of Words

In this exercise, students are required to choose among the prefixes listed at the beginning of the review to build new words. The exercise helps to illustrate that each root can take different prefixes and that each prefix can be used with more than one root.

Make sure that students proofread the words they write and that they form real words.

You may want to discuss how adding these prefixes affects the meaning of the words.

The answers given on the replica of the student page are examples. More than one answer is possible for all of these items. Accept all correctly spelled words.

Students are also asked to use three of the new words in original sentences. The exercise instructions are deliberately flexible about how many sentences should be written in order to accommodate different student styles and abilities. Advanced students may enjoy trying to use three of their words in a single sentence. Allow students to use any form of the words they create in their sentences. If students need more room, encourage them to use their notebooks. Make sure that they proofread their work.

Help them to correct misspellings by using what they already know. Errors in words not yet studied should not be treated negatively.

2 Reviewing Prefixes That Change

In this exercise, students review prefixes that undergo assimilative changes. Remind them that these changes often account for double consonants near the beginning of words.

Remind them also that the changes are regular and that they occur each time these prefixes come before roots that start with certain letters.

Students should study the chart carefully before attempting to fill in the blanks. Remind them to refer to Lessons 9 and 10 if necessary. You may want students to underline double consonants once they have written their example words.

Additional activity:

Have students use some of their example words in original sentences. Using words in context is an important additional activity that should be included at any appropriate opportunity.

3 Taking Words Apart

In this exercise, students divide words into their component morphemes. All of these words follow regular patterns. Encourage students to refer to the glossary or a dictionary to check any individual morphemes if necessary.

Note whether students restore the silent *e* and separate the two prefixes in *unexciting*. Students may write either the original form of the prefix or the form that is used in the word.

Additional activity:

Students can practice taking apart the words they find in any printed material, such as newspapers, magazines, or ads.

4 Creating and Using Words

Add two of the following prefixes to each root listed below to create two different words. Then use each word in an original phrase or short sentence.

com-　　con-　　de-　　ex-　　di-　　dis-　　re-

	Whole words	Phrases or sentences
1. pel	dispel	_____
	compel	_____
2. press	depress	_____
	express	_____
3. serve	reserve	_____
	deserve	_____
4. vert	divert	_____
	convert	_____
5. duce	reduce	_____
	deduce	_____

5 Using the Dictionary

For each word below, list all the related words you can think of. When you run out of ideas, check in a dictionary for other related words. The first one is done for you.

	Related words
1. progress	progression, progressive, progressively
2. prepare	preparation, unprepared, preparedness, preparatory
3. mistake	mistaken, unmistakably, mistook, mistakenly
4. reproduce	reproduction, reproductive, produce, reproducible
5. consider	considerate, inconsiderate, considerable, consideration

Unit 3 Review　　55

4 Creating and Using Words

In this exercise, students select and add prefixes to the given roots. Then they use the words they build in phrases or short sentences. Allow students to use any form of the words they build in their phrases and sentences.

Creating two words for each root emphasizes the consistency of the spelling of the root as well as the way that prefixes change the meaning.

If students make errors trying to spell words that are unfamiliar, discuss how to find those words in the dictionary. Help them to correct misspellings by using what they already know.

The answers on the replica of the student page are examples. Accept all correctly spelled words.

5 Using the Dictionary

This exercise emphasizes the relationships among words. It will help students to realize that they may be able to spell a word if they can analyze it. Predicting the spelling of a word by associating it with a related word is an important strategy.

Students may come up with only one or two related words. Encourage them to use a dictionary both to check spellings and to look for additional related words. Remind students that related words are sometimes listed at the end of the main entry. For example, *progressively* may be listed at the end of the entry for *progressive*.

You may want to set a target number of words to be written on the lines provided. Three or four would be reasonable.

The answers on the replica of the student page are examples. Accept all correctly spelled words.

Additional activity:

Have students compare the words they listed and develop a master list.

6 Completing Words in Sentences

Add one of the following prefixes to the root given under each blank below and write the completed word in the blank. The word you build must make sense in the sentence.

al-　　at-　　com-　　con-　　ef-　　ex-　　in-　　post-　　pre-　　un-

1. The __previous__ owner __allowed__ tenants to keep animals.
　　　　vious　　　　　　　　　lowed

2. A warm front is __expected__ to __precede__ the storm.
　　　　　　pected　　　　　　　cede

3. The clean-up was a __community__ __effort__.
　　　　　　　　munity　　　　fort

4. My girlfriend and I __attended__ an __excellent__ party last Saturday.
　　　　　　　tended　　　　　　cellent

5. I __postponed__ doing the shopping because I was __unwell__.
　　poned　　　　　　　　　　　　　　　well

6. My friend is __interested__ in going to the __concert__.
　　　　terested　　　　　　　　　　cert

7 Missing Morphemes

One of the prefixes from this unit can be added to every root in each group below. Fill in the missing prefixes to make whole words. Use a different prefix for each group.

1. __re__view　　__re__duce　　__re__ceive　　__re__cess　　__re__act

2. __pro__duce　　__pro__cess　　__pro__duct　　__pro__vide　　__pro__voke

3. __de__mand　　__de__tract　　__de__duct　　__de__fine　　__de__ceive

4. __con__ceive　　__con__sist　　__con__vert　　__con__duct　　__con__fine

5. __ex__tract　　__ex__ist　　__ex__haust　　__ex__act　　__ex__cess

6. __per__ceive　　__per__tain　　__per__mit　　__per__sist　　__per__jury

56　　Unit 3 Review

6 Completing Words in Sentences

In this exercise, students add prefixes to roots to form words that are appropriate in the context of the sentences. All of the necessary forms of assimilative prefixes have been listed.

Remind students to read a whole sentence first to decide which prefix to use. After they've written words in the blanks, they should reread the sentence.

7 Missing Morphemes

In this word game, one of the prefixes studied in Unit 3 is missing from each group of roots. A different prefix is missing from each group. Only one prefix can be used with all of the roots in each group. If students have trouble getting started, you may want to provide them with a list of the prefixes they will use: con-, de-, ex-, per-, pro-, and re-.

Remember that word games are intended to be fun. Students may want to work in pairs or small groups. If they find this game confusing or frustrating, let them skip it.

Sentences

Sentences for dictation are available at the back of this book if you wish to use them.

Unit 3 Test

We recommend that you test your students on the words from Unit 3 before going on. The following is a suggested list of words from Unit 3. You may want to substitute other words to meet the needs of your students.

Dictate each word and use it in a simple sentence. Students should be able to spell 90 percent of these words correctly.

apart	distribution
adaptation	different
acceptance	division
including	exception
impatient	permanent
irrational	preparation
unhappiness	postponement
connection	rediscovery
companion	prominent
descending	mistakenly

64　　Unit 3 Review

Lesson 12

The Roots *act, cent, cord, cure,* and *fact*

Objectives

- **Roots:** Learn to recognize and spell words with *act, cent, cord, cure,* and *fact*.
- **Word Building:** Join morphemes to build whole words.
- **Taking Words Apart:** Divide words into morphemes.
- **Building and Using Words:** Select, reorder, and combine morphemes to build whole words. Use the words in context.
- **Completing Words in Context:** Build words to fit in context by adding roots to partial words.

For general information on roots, refer to page 8 in the introduction.

1 Recognizing Roots

Read aloud the representative words listed for each root. Read the words in a normal speaking voice without stressing the roots. Instruct students to underline the root as you read each word. Do this exercise orally so that students can both see and hear the roots.

Remind students that the definitions of the roots are listed above the representative words. The definitions of all roots are given when the root is first introduced and in the glossary.

---

1 Recognizing Roots

In each group of words below, underline the roots listed on the left.

act	do			
	actor	active	transact	inactivity
	exactly	actually	enactment	interaction

cent	one hundred;		center	
	cent	centimeter	center	concentric
	century	percentage	centralize	concentration

cord	heart			
	cordial	accord	recording	
	discordant	accordingly	concordance	

cure	care			
	curator	security	accurate	incurable

fact, fect, fit, fic(t)	make, do			
	factory	affects	fitness	fiction
	manufacture	effective	benefit	artificial
	dissatisfaction	infection	profitable	sufficient

2 Word Building

Join the morphemes that follow to build whole words. Write the words on the lines provided. Remember to drop the silent *e* or to double letters if necessary.

1. re + cord + er   recorder
2. pro + fit + ing   profiting
3. ef + fici + ency   efficiency
4. counter + act + ing   counteracting

Note that sometimes the sound of a root changes even if the spelling does not change. Tell students that some roots have variant forms that are related in meaning but are pronounced and spelled differently. The most common variant forms are listed with the original root. When you come to *fact*, point out the variant forms and ask students to underline the form that appears in each representative word as you read it. Remind them that if they are learning new words with these roots, they should pay particular attention to how the root sounds in each word.

Emphasize that roots provide the core or central meaning of a word. Note that the spelling of a root may change when certain suffixes are added, according to the patterns reviewed in Lesson 3.

Point out the following:

The roots *act* and *fact* take the suffix *-or (actor, factor)* rather than *-er.*

The root *cord* takes the suffixes *-ant* and *-ance*, as in *discordant* and *concordance*, and *fic(i)* takes *-ent*, as in *sufficient*. Generally, Latin roots take either *-ant/-ance/-ancy* or *-ent/-ence/-ency* but not both.

The *ci* spelling of /sh/ in *artificial* and *sufficient* is the same spelling as in the syllable *-cian*.

Additional activities:

Have students work in small groups to generate as many words as they can that include these roots.

Have students identify prefixes or suffixes that they have studied or recognize in the representative words.

2 Word Building

Remind students to pronounce the new words before writing them and to proofread their work.

Note whether students drop the silent *e* in number 9.

Make sure they don't double the *t* in number 2.

3 Taking Words Apart

All of these words follow regular patterns. Encourage students to refer to the glossary or a dictionary to check any individual morphemes if necessary.

Remind students that they should write the original form of a root. They should restore the silent *e* to the root *cure*.

Note whether students divide the two prefixes in *prerecorded* and the two suffixes in *factional*. Review those morphemes if necessary.

The suffix of *concentrate* is *-ate*. Since students have not yet studied this, accept either *con centr ate* or *con cent rate*.

Students who have difficulty should first identify the roots presented in this lesson.

Additional activity:

Students can practice taking apart the words they find in any printed material, such as newspapers, magazines, or ads.

4 Jumbled Morphemes

Students are asked to build words from a group of morphemes that are not in correct order. Not every

2. suf ency fici ent in

sufficient _____   _____

insufficient _____   _____

sufficiency _____

3. cure se in able ity

insecure _____   _____

security _____   _____

curable _____

5 Adding Roots to Make Complete Words

Write one of the following roots in each blank below to make a whole word that
makes sense in the phrase or sentence. Then write the whole word on the right. The
first one is done for you.

act   cent   cord   cure   fect/fit/fic

Whole words

1. ex__act__ly right   exactly _____

2. a difficult sacri__fic__e   sacrifice _____

3. an imper__fect__ match   imperfect _____

4. That was a bold __act__ion.   action _____

5. It's a de__fect__ive product.   defective _____

6. Uranium is radio__act__ive.   radioactive _____

7. ac__cord__ing to the newspaper   according _____

8. the bi__cent__ennial celebrations   bicentennial _____

9. Without locks, a house is inse__cure__.   insecure _____

10. A pro__fit__able business makes money.   profitable _____

morpheme will be used in each
word. Students are then asked to
use some of their words in
phrases or sentences.

Remind students to use a dictionary if necessary and to proofread
their work.

Help students with number 2 if
they have difficulty with the *ci* in
sufficient. Make sure that they
drop the silent *e* from the root
cure when necessary in number 3.

As students become more comfortable with the exercise formats

and the morpheme approach, you
might encourage them to become
more adventurous in the phrases
and sentences they write. If they
are using notebooks, they can
write extra sentences or longer
ones than space in the book
allows for.

The answers on the replica of the
student page are examples.
Accept all correctly spelled words.

5 Adding Roots to Make Complete Words

In this exercise, students must
form complete words by filling in
missing roots. Affixes and contexts are supplied, so that only
one root should make sense in
each blank. Students then write
the whole word to ensure that
they can spell it correctly.

Seeing words with roots missing
helps students to understand that
it is the root that gives a word its
essential meaning.

Have students read a whole
phrase or sentence before they fill
in the blank, and again afterward
to be sure it makes sense.

Students having trouble doing this
exercise should ignore the contexts at first and just focus on a
root that would fit in the blank to
form a word.

Additional activities:

Have students write another
phrase or sentence for each word.

Ask students to underline prefixes
from Unit 3.

Quizzes

Give a graded spelling quiz on the
words in this lesson or other
words that include these roots.

Sentences

Sentences for dictation are available at the back of this book.

Lesson 13

The Roots *file, fine, found,* and *fuse*

Objectives

- **Roots:** Learn to recognize and spell words with *file, fine, found,* and *fuse.*
- **Word Building:** Join morphemes to build whole words. Reorder and combine morphemes to build whole words.
- **Creating and Using Words:** Create words and use them in context.
- **Recognizing Morphemes in Context:** Identify roots in context.
- **Word Game:** Play a game to build words.

1 Recognizing Roots

Read aloud the representative words listed for each root. Read the words in a normal speaking voice without stressing the roots. Instruct students to underline the root as you read each word.

Emphasize that roots provide the core or central meaning of a word while affixes qualify that meaning and provide an indication of the part of speech. Note that the spelling of a root may change when certain suffixes are added. These changes generally follow the patterns reviewed in Lesson 3.

When you come to the root *found,* be sure students can identify its variant form *fund* in the representative words.

---

file, fine, found, and *fuse*

1 Recognizing Roots

In each group of words below, underline the roots listed on the left.

file	line, thread; draw a line		
	filing	fillet	profile
	filament	filigree	defilement

fine	end		
	final	infinity	confine
	finish	indefinitely	refinement

found, fund	bottom; pour		
	foundation	funding	confound
	profoundly	refunded	fundamentalist

fuse	pour; melt		
	fuse	profusely	refusal
	diffuse	confusion	infusion

2 Word Building

Join the morphemes that follow to build whole words. Write the words on the lines provided. Remember to drop the silent *e* if necessary.

1. con + found   confound
2. af + fine + ity   affinity
3. mis + file + ed   misfiled
4. re + fuse + ing   refusing
5. fin + ance + ial   financial
6. pro + fuse + ion   profusion
7. pro + found + ly   profoundly
8. con + fine + ment   confinement
9. un + de + file + ed   undefiled
10. fund + a + ment + al   fundamental

Ask students to identify words in which the silent *e* of a root has been dropped.

Point out the following:

The pronunciation of *file* sometimes changes in words in which the silent *e* has been dropped. The pronunciation of *fine* and *fuse* changes in some of the representative words.

Not all words have prefixes. Have students identify words that start with roots.

When the suffix *-ion* is added to the root *fuse,* the ending syllable is pronounced /zhən/. For students who can hear the distinction between /shən/ and /zhən/, listening for this can be another strategy for predicting the *-sion* spelling.

Additional activities:

Have students work in small groups to generate as many words as they can that include these roots.

3 Jumbled Word Building

Build words by putting the morphemes below in the correct order. Write the words on the lines provided. Remember to drop the silent *e* if necessary.

1. al fine ist __finalist__
2. ed fuse de __defused__
3. file pro ed __profiled__
4. ery fine re __refinery__
5. ite fine de __definite__
6. ate ion found __foundation__
7. found dumb ed __dumbfounded__
8. in ion fuse __infusion__
9. ion fuse con __confusion__
10. fuse trans ion __transfusion__

Say the last three words aloud. Notice how they are pronounced. When you hear the ending /zhən/, it is probably spelled *-sion*.

4 Creating and Using Words

Add one or more of the following prefixes or suffixes to each root listed below to create two different words. Remember to add or drop letters if necessary. Then use each word in an original phrase or short sentence.

con-   de-   pro-   re-   -al   -ance   -er   -ion

	New words	Phrases or sentences
1. file	defile	
	profile	
2. fine	finance	
	refiner	
3. found	profound	
	founder	
4. fuse	confusion	
	refusal	

Have students identify prefixes and suffixes that they recognize in the representative words.

2 Word Building

Emphasize that students should add one morpheme at a time to minimize the chance of making errors. Remind them to pronounce the new words before writing them and to proofread their work.

3 Jumbled Word Building

In this exercise, students build words from morphemes that are not in the correct order.

Remind students to pronounce the words before they write them and to proofread them afterward.

Students should drop the silent *e* from the root in numbers 2–6 and 9.

Note whether students drop the silent *e* in all words except *dumbfounded*. Review the pattern if necessary.

Additional activity:

Have students develop exercises of this sort for one another to do using words from Exercise 2 of previous lessons.

4 Creating and Using Words

In this exercise, students select and add affixes to the given roots. Then they use the words they build in phrases or short sentences.

Encourage them to use more than one affix for some of the words. Remind them that they will need to drop the silent *e* from the roots *file, fine,* and *fuse* before adding the suffixes.

Creating two words for each root emphasizes the consistency of the spelling of the root as well as the function of morphemes.

Spelling words in context is an important additional activity that should be included whenever appropriate. If students make errors in words not yet studied, point out any parts of the word that are spelled correctly and praise their effort.

The answers on the replica of the student page are examples. Accept all correctly spelled words.

5 Recognizing Roots in Context

Underline the following roots in the sentences below.

file   *fine*   *found/fund*   *fuse*

1. This is definitely your fin al chance to refuse
2. Refile those files when you've fin ished with them.
3. He was profoundly sorry and apologized profuse ly.
4. She had a blood transfus ion and is confin ed to bed.
5. If it's not too confus ing, let's fin alize the plans now.
6. He fin ally realized how infin ite the possibilities were.
7. In all the confus ion, the thief managed to confound the clerk.
8. The found ers of the company appealed for an infus ion of fund s.

6 Word Pyramids

Use the letters found in *fin* and *fil* to complete the words in each pyramid. Each word contains the letters at the top of the pyramid at least once in any order. Most of the words are from this lesson.

F I N		F I L
N I F T Y		F I N A L
F I N A N C E		M I S F I L E
P R O F U S I O N		D I F F I C U L T
C O N F I N E M E N T		E F F E C T I V E L Y

62   Lesson 13

---

5 Recognizing Roots in Context

Instruct students to underline in the sentences only the roots from the given list. Remind them that the silent *e* has been dropped from some of the roots.

Remind students that not all words have prefixes. Ask them to identify some that start with roots.

Remind students to read the sentences before they start underlining.

Additional activities:

Have students circle any prefixes or suffixes that they recognize in these sentences.

Have them develop exercises of this sort for one another to do.

This kind of activity can be done using any printed material, such as newspapers, magazines, or ads.

6 Word Pyramids

In this word game, students build complete words by filling in the letters *f, i, n* and *f, i, l.* The letters can be in any order, and some will be used more than once in some words. With the exception of the first word, the answer words are from Lessons 10, 12, or 13.

Remember that word games are intended to be fun. Students may want to work in pairs or small groups. If they find this game confusing or frustrating, let them skip it.

Quizzes

Give a graded spelling quiz on the words in this lesson or other words that include these roots.

Sentences

Sentences for dictation are available at the back of this book.

70   Lesson 13

Lesson 14

The Roots *mand, merge, muse, pass,* and *ply*

Objectives

- **Roots:** Learn to recognize and spell words with *mand, merge, muse, pass,* and *ply.*
- **Word Building:** Join morphemes to build whole words.
- **Related Words:** List words related to given words.
- **Using Meanings:** Select roots based on the definitions of words to be formed.
- **Building and Using Words:** Build words by adding roots to partial words. Use the whole words in context.
- **Recognizing Morphemes in Context:** Identify roots in context.

1 Recognizing Roots

Read aloud the representative words listed for each root. Read the words in a normal speaking voice without stressing the roots. Instruct students to underline the root as you read each word.

Point out that *mend, merse,* and *pat* are variant forms of the roots *mand, merge,* and *pass.* Variant forms of a root share the meaning of the original form. Be sure students can identify the variant forms of these roots in the representative words. If students are learning new words with these roots, they should pay particular

attention to how the root sounds in a word.

Point out the following:

The pronunciation of *pass* changes when *-ion* is added.

The root *ply* follows the *y* to *i* conversion pattern and is also pronounced in two distinct ways. Have your students listen to the difference between the pronunciation of *apply* and *application.*

The root *ply* takes the suffixes *-ant/-ance/-ancy.* The roots

merge and *pat* take the suffixes *-ent/-ence/-ency.*

The sound /sh/ is spelled *ti* in *patient* and *impatiently.*

Additional activities:

Have students work in small groups to generate as many words as they can that include these roots.

Have students identify prefixes and suffixes that they have studied or recognize in the representative words.

Lesson 14 — Roots
mand, merge, muse, pass, and *ply*

1 Recognizing Roots
In each group of words below, underline the roots listed on the left.

mand, mend	*entrust; order*		
	de**mand**ing	**mand**atory	com**mend**able
	com**mand**ed	com**mand**ment	recom**mend**ation

merge, merse	*plunge, immerse, dip*		
	e**merge**	**merg**er	sub**merg**ible	im**merse**
	sub**merge**	e**merg**ency	ree**merg**ence	sub**mers**ion

muse	*gaze, ponder; source of artistic inspiration*		
	music	**mus**ician	**mus**ings
	museum	a**mus**ement	be**mus**ed

pass, pat	*endure, suffer*		
	passion	**pass**ivity	**pat**ient
	com**pass**ionate	incom**pat**ible	im**pat**iently

ply	*fold together; fill*		
	sup**ply**	ap**ply**	re**ply**
	sup**pli**er	ap**pli**cation	com**pli**ment

2 Word Building
Join the morphemes that follow to build whole words. Write the words on the lines provided. Remember to drop or change letters if necessary.

1. re + ply + ing   replying
2. pass + ion + ate   passionate
3. ap + ply + ance   appliance
4. com + pat + ible + ly   compatibly

Lesson 14   63

5. e + merge + ent ___emergent___   8. muse + ic + ian + ship ___musicianship___

6. de + mand + ed ___demanded___   9. com + ply + cate + ed ___complicated___

7. a + mend + ment ___amendment___   10. im + merse + ion ___immersion___

Say the last word aloud. Notice how it is pronounced. When you hear the ending /zhən/, it is probably spelled -sion.

3 Related-Word Strategy

The *y* to *i* pattern is followed when writing words with the root *ply*. Beside each word below, write as many related words using the spelling *pli* as you can. When you run out of ideas, check a dictionary for other forms.

Related *pli* words

1. supply ___supplier, supplies, supplied___

2. apply ___application, reapplied, applies, appliance, applicable___

3. comply ___complied, noncompliance, compliant, complies, complier___

4. imply ___implication, implies, implied, implicit, implicitly___

4 Looking at Meanings

Add one of the following roots to each partial word below. The word you create must fit the definition on the left. Remember to drop the silent *e* if necessary. Use a dictionary if you are unsure of a word. The first one is done for you.

mand/mend	merge	muse	ply

Definitions	Partial words	Words with roots added
1. plunge under	sub	submerge
2. exercise authority	com	command
3. entertain	a	amuse
4. indicate, suggest	im	imply
5. mention favorably	recom	recommend

64   Lesson 14

2 Word Building

Note whether students change the *y* to *i* in numbers 3 and 9 and whether they drop the silent *e* in numbers 5 and 8–10. By now students should be making these changes almost automatically.

Number 4 presents a special difficulty, as students must drop the *le* from *compatible* before adding *-ly*. Be sure that students do not write *compatiblly*. The suffixes *-able* and *-ible* are presented in Lesson 23.

Note that when the suffix *-ion* is added to the root *merse,* the ending syllable is pronounced /zhən/. For students who can hear the distinction between /shən/ and /zhən/, listening for this can be another strategy for predicting the *-sion* spelling.

3 Related-Word Strategy

This exercise emphasizes the relationships among words. It will help students realize that they may be able to spell a word if they can analyze it. Predicting the spelling of a word by associating it with a related word is an important strategy.

Review the *y* to *i* conversion pattern before students begin if necessary.

Students may come up with only one or two related words. Encourage them to use a dictionary both to check spellings and to look for additional related words.

Remind them that they can also add prefixes to form related words.

You may want to set a target number of words to be written. Three or four would be reasonable.

The answers on the replica of the student page are examples. Accept all correctly spelled words.

Additional activity:

Have students compare their words and develop a master list.

4 Looking at Meanings

Learning to relate the meanings of roots to the words in which they are used should help students to recognize and spell those roots correctly whenever they occur in a word.

Make sure that students proofread the words they write and that their words make sense according to the definitions given. If students have difficulty, they might work in pairs or small groups.

5 Adding Roots to Make Complete Words

Write one of the following roots in each blank below to make a whole word.
Remember to change or drop letters if necessary. Then use the word in an original
phrase or short sentence.

mand   merge   muse   pass/pat   ply

Phrases or sentences

1. e_merg_ed   _____

2. _mus_ical   _____

3. a_mus_ing   _____

4. _pass_ively   _____

5. sim_pli_fy   _____

6. com_mand_er   _____

7. repri_mand_ed   _____

8. im_pat_ience   _____

6 Recognizing Roots in Context

Underline the following roots in the paragraph below.

mand/mend   pass/pat   ply

The framers of the Constitution of the United States had a com_pli_cated task. They did a
com_mend_able job. Ten a_mend_ments were then added to encom_pass_ rights that were not
originally stated in the Constitution. These a_mend_ments ap_ply_ to all citizens and _mand_ate
basic rights. They include freedom of speech (and the im_pli_ed freedom of expression),
freedom of assembly, and the right to a fair trial. The remaining a_mend_ments were made
later and encom_pass_ other rights, but the first 10 a_mend_ments alone are known as the Bill
of Rights.

Lesson 14   65

Additional activities:

Have students use the words in sentences.

Have advanced students make up similar exercises of their own to try out on other students.

5 Adding Roots to Make Complete Words

In this exercise, students must form complete words by filling in missing roots. Affixes are supplied, so that only one root should make sense in each blank.

Have students pronounce the whole word before they fill in the blank, and then reread it afterward. Be sure they drop the silent *e* from *merge* and *muse* in numbers 1–3 and change the *y* to *i* in number 5.

Additional activity:

Ask students to write another phrase or sentence for each word.

6 Recognizing Roots in Context

This exercise will help students to see how individual morphemes are used in a sustained context. When students see morphemes used in a variety of ways, it will help to improve their spelling and writing.

Remind students to underline in the paragraph only the roots listed above it, and to read the whole paragraph before they start underlining.

Note whether students recognize the root *ply* in *implied*.

Additional activities:

Have students circle any prefixes or suffixes that they recognize in the paragraph.

Students may want to discuss the contents of the paragraph. Although it will not help their spelling, it may generate extra interest in the exercise.

This kind of activity can be done using any printed material, such as newspapers, magazines, or ads.

Quizzes

Give a graded spelling quiz on the words in this lesson or other words that include these roots.

Sentences

Sentences for dictation are available at the back of this book.

Lesson 15

The Roots *pone, port,* and *prove*

Objectives

- **Roots:** Learn to recognize and spell words with *pone, port,* and *prove*.
- **Word Building:** Join morphemes to build whole words. Select and combine morphemes to build 20 or more words.
- **Completing Words in Context:** Build words to fit in context by adding roots to partial words.
- **Building and Using Words:** Build new words by removing and replacing affixes. Use the new words in context.
- **Studying Contexts:** Use context to determine the correct form of *suppose*.

1 Recognizing Roots

Read aloud the representative words listed for each root. Read the words in a normal speaking voice without stressing the roots. Instruct students to underline the root as you read each word.

Point out that *pose, post,* and *pound* are variant forms of the root *pone*. Be sure students can identify these variant forms in the representative words. The variant forms share the meaning of the original form *pone*. Students should pay particular attention to how this root and its variant forms sound.

Point out that the pronunciation of *post* changes in *posture* and *imposter*.

Additional activities:

Have students work in small groups to generate as many words as they can that include these roots.

Have students identify prefixes and suffixes that they recognize or have studied in the representative words.

2 Word Building

Note whether students drop the silent *e* in numbers 4–7 and 10. Be sure that they don't drop the silent *e* in number 9.

Additional activity:

Challenge students to identify the prefixes that have undergone assimilative changes in this exercise (*compost, composer,* and *unimportant*).

Lesson 15 — Roots
pone, port, and *prove*

1 Recognizing Roots

In each group of words below, underline the roots listed on the left.

pone, pose, post, pound	*put, place*			
	op ponent	position	poster	im pound
	ex ponent	ex posure	posture	ex pounded
	com ponent	com position	im postor	com pounding

port	*carry*		
	portable	sup porter	re ported
	trans portation	im portance	op portunity

prove	*test*		
	prove	ap prove	re proved
	im provement	disap proving	un provable

2 Word Building

Join the morphemes that follow to build whole words. Write the words on the lines provided. Remember to drop the silent *e* if necessary.

1. com + post ___compost___
2. op + pose ___oppose___
3. ex + port + er ___exporter___
4. pro + pose + al ___proposal___
5. com + pose + er ___composer___
6. un + prove + en ___unproven___
7. dis + pose + able ___disposable___
8. un + im + port + ant ___unimportant___
9. post + pone + ment ___postponement___
10. dis + ap + prove + al ___disapproval___

66   Lesson 15

---

3 Adding Roots to Make Complete Words

In this exercise, students must form complete words by filling in missing roots. Affixes and contexts are supplied, so one root should make the most sense in each blank.

Have students read a whole phrase or sentence before they fill in the blank and then reread it afterward.

Students having trouble doing this exercise should ignore the contexts at first and just focus on a root that will fit in the blank to form a word.

Additional activities:

Have students write another phrase or sentence for each word.

Encourage interested students to test mathematically the statement in number 8. For example: Transposing 38 gives you 83. The difference between 38 and 83 is 45, which is a number divisible by

9. Have students try this with other two-digit numbers.

4 Changing Morphemes

By removing one affix and replacing it with another, students are using morphemes as practical building blocks of words. This exercise reinforces the essential role of roots in meaning. Point out that the affixes to be replaced are in italics.

If students have difficulty with this exercise, go over with them the one that has been done. Encourage them to use a dictionary if they are uncertain of a word. They can also use the glossary to find alternative affixes.

Encourage advanced students to replace both affixes in some words.

Answers given on the replica of the student page are examples. Accept any answer that forms a correctly spelled word.

Additional activities:

Have students use the original word in a phrase or sentence.

For advanced students: See how many different words students can build from any of the given words by removing and replacing one affix at a time.

5 Telling the Difference: *Suppose* and *Supposed*

This exercise is included to help students overcome a common error that arises from the elision of the *d* at the end of *supposed* and the *t* at the beginning of *to* when

5 Telling the Difference: *Suppose* and *Supposed*

Writing *suppose* instead of *supposed* is a common spelling error. Write the correct form, *suppose* or *supposed*, in each blank below to make sense in the sentence.

1. I am ___supposed___ to pass an exam tomorrow. ___Suppose___ I don't?

2. What do you ___suppose___ happened? She was ___supposed___ to arrive at 3.

3. I was ___supposed___ to work tomorrow. ___Suppose___ I work today instead?

4. He was ___supposed___ to be at home. His mother ___supposed___ that he was out playing football.

6 Challenge Word Building

On a separate piece of paper, combine the morphemes below to build at least 20 words. Use as few or as many morphemes as you need for each word. Remember to drop the silent *e* if necessary. Use a dictionary if you are unsure of a word.

Prefixes	Roots	Suffixes
com-	port	-able
dis-	pose	-al
ex-	prove	-ation
im-		-ition
re-		-ment
sup-		-ure
trans-		

The suffixes listed include *-ation* and *-ition*. Strictly speaking, these are combinations of the suffixes *-ate* + *-ion* and *-ite* + *-ion*. The suffixes *-ate* and *-ite* are presented in Lesson 23.

Some responses are listed here. There are others. Accept all correctly spelled words.

comport	port
comportment	portable
compose	portal
composition	pose
composure	position
disposable	provable
disposal	prove
dispose	report
disposition	reportable
disprove	repose
export	reprove
exportable	supportable
exportation	supposable
expose	suppose
exposure	supposition
import	transport
importable	transportable
importation	transportation
impose	transposable
imposition	transpose
improve	transposition
improvement	

Additional activities:

Have students compare their words and develop a master list.

Have students use some of the words they build in sentences.

Quizzes

Give a graded spelling quiz on the words in this lesson or other words that include these roots.

Sentences

Sentences for dictation are available at the back of this book.

people say "supposed to." For advanced students, you may want to explain the grammatical reason for the spellings. For other students, simply tell them that the word is always spelled *supposed* when followed by *to*.

Additional activities:

Have students make up some sentences of their own to try out on one another.

Although not related to roots in this lesson, the phrase "used to" presents exactly the same spelling problem as "supposed to." You may want to include some work on this phrase as well.

6 Challenge Word Building

Emphasize that students can use as few or as many morphemes as needed for a particular word. For instance, the roots *port, pose,* and *prove* function as whole words.

Encourage students to use a dictionary if necessary.

Lesson 16 —

The Roots *tend, quest, sane, sect, serve,* and *side*

Objectives

- **Roots:** Learn to recognize and spell words with *tend, quest, sane, sect, serve,* and *side.*
- **Word Building:** Join morphemes to build whole words.
- **Creating and Using Words:** Create words and use them in context.
- **Strategy:** Learn two ways to spell /tenshən/ at the end of words.
- **Recognizing Morphemes in Context:** Identify roots in context.

1 Recognizing Roots

Read aloud the representative words listed for each root. Read the words in a normal speaking voice without stressing the roots. Instruct students to underline the root as you read each word.

Emphasize that roots provide the core or central meaning of a word. Note that the spelling of a root may change when certain suffixes are added.

Point out the following:

Tent and *tense* are variant forms of the root *tend. Quer* and *quire* are variant forms of *quest.* When you come to these roots, be sure students can identify the variant forms in the representative words.

Lesson 16 —

Roots

tend, quest, sane, sect, serve, and *side*

1 Recognizing Roots

In each group of words below, underline the roots listed on the left.

tend, tent, tense	*stretch*		
	ex**tend**	ex**tent**	pre**tense**
	pre**tend**	in**tent**ion	ex**tens**ion
	at**tend**ance	at**tent**ive	os**tens**ibly
quest, quer, quire	*seek, ask*		
	question	con**quest**	**quer**y	in**quir**y
	un**quest**ioning	re**quest**ed	con**quer**or	re**quir**e
sane	*healthy*		
	sane	**san**itarium	**san**itize
	in**san**ity	un**san**itary	**san**itation
sect	*cut*		
	section	**sect**or	bi**sect**
	inter**sect**ion	dis**sect**	in**sect**s
serve	*keep, save; guard*		
	re**serve**	de**serve**	ob**serv**ant
	pre**serv**ation	con**serv**ative	con**serv**ationist
side	*sit, settle*		
	re**side**	pre**sid**ent	re**sid**ue
	re**sid**ential	sub**sid**iary	dis**sid**ent

Lesson 16   69

The pronunciation of *quer, quire, sane,* and *side* changes in certain words. Remind students that morphemes are units of meaning whose spelling rarely changes even if the pronunciation does.

Tend can take both the suffixes *-ant* and *-ent* (e.g., *attendance, tendency, superintendent*).

The root *sect* takes the suffix *-or* rather than *-er.*

Most of these roots can have the suffix *-ion* added. Practice in the two ways of spelling the ending /tenshən/ is given in Exercise 4.

Additional activities:

Have students work in small groups to generate as many words as they can that include these roots.

Have students identify prefixes and suffixes that they have studied or recognize in the representative words.

2 Word Building

Join the morphemes that follow to build whole words. Write the words on the lines provided. Remember to change or drop letters if necessary.

1. tend + ency ___tendency___
2. quer + y + ed ___queried___
3. sane + it + ary ___sanitary___
4. sub + side + ize ___subsidize___
5. dis + sect + ion ___dissection___
6. quest + ion + able ___questionable___
7. re + quire + ment ___requirement___
8. in + sect + i + cide ___insecticide___
9. in + tent + ion + al ___intentional___
10. un + re + serve + ed ___unreserved___

3 Creating and Using Words

From each root listed below, create two new words by adding one or more of the following prefixes or suffixes. Remember to add, drop, or change letters if necessary. Then use the new words in phrases or short sentences.

con-   de-   in-   re-   -ent   -ion   -er

	New words	Phrases or sentences
1. quest	conquest	
	questioner	
2. serve	reserve	
	deserve	
3. side	resident	
	insider	
4. tense	tension	
	intense	
5. tent	detention	
	content	

2 Word Building

Emphasize that students should add one morpheme at a time to minimize the chance of making errors. Remind them to pronounce the new words before writing them and to proofread their work.

Students should change the *y* to *i* in number 2 and drop the silent *e* in numbers 3, 4, and 10. Be sure that students keep the double *s* in *dissection* and that they do not drop the silent *e* in *requirement.*

3 Creating and Using Words

In this exercise, students select and add affixes to the given roots. Then they use the words they build in short phrases or sentences.

Encourage them to use more than one affix for some of the words. Make sure they drop the silent *e* before adding suffixes when appropriate.

Creating two words for each root emphasizes the consistency of the spelling of the root as well as the function of morphemes.

Having students write phrases or sentences allows you to see if they are transferring their skills from doing exercises to writing words in context. If students make errors in words not yet studied, point out any parts of the word that are spelled correctly and praise their effort.

The answers on the replica of the student page are examples. Accept all correctly spelled words.

The common word *consider* comes from a root different from *side* meaning *sit* or *settle.* It presents similar spelling problems, however. Accept it in this exercise as long as it is spelled and used correctly.

4 **Spelling /tensh∂n/**

When *-ion* is added to words with the root *tend*, the root plus the suffix is usually pronounced /tensh∂n/. The /sh∂n/ ending may be spelled either *-tion* or *-sion*, however. Sometimes there is a related word that will help you remember how to spell the ending. If you are unsure of whether to use *-tion* or *-sion*, the best strategy is to look the word up in the dictionary. Add *-tion* or *-sion* to the partial words below and write the whole word under the correct heading. Use a dictionary if necessary.

| inten | atten | exten | deten | preten | ten |

-tion

intention

attention

detention

-sion

extension

pretension

tension

5 **Recognizing Roots in Context**

Underline the following roots in the paragraph below.

| tend/tent | quest/quire | sane | sect | serve | side |

If you pay attention to the way you spell, you may make some useful observations. When a word gives you particular difficulty, question yourself about how you write it. You might observe that you have a tendency to see if the word "looks right." Notice whether it is built from familiar word parts. If so, dissect the word by breaking it into sections. With other words, the answer to your inquiry might reside in the way the word sounds. In that case, phonetics may deserve a try. Some words simply require memorization. Don't forget, you can preserve your sanity by looking the word up in a dictionary.

Lesson 16   71

Remind students of the difference between morphemes and syllables: morphemes are units of meaning, while syllables are units of sound.

Additional activity:

Have students think of at least one other word with the same prefix and root as each of those listed.

5 **Recognizing Roots in Context**

This exercise will help students to see how individual morphemes are used in a sustained context. When students see morphemes used in a variety of ways, it will help to improve their spelling and writing.

Remind students to underline only the roots listed above the paragraph and to read the whole paragraph before they start underlining.

Additional activities:

Have students circle any prefixes or suffixes that they recognize in the paragraph.

Students may want to discuss the spelling strategies mentioned in the paragraph.

This kind of activity can be done using any printed material, such as newspapers, magazines, or ads.

Quizzes

Give a graded spelling quiz on the words in this lesson or other words that include these roots.

Sentences

Sentences for dictation are available at the back of this book.

4 **Spelling /tensh∂n/**

Words with the root *tend* can present spelling problems when the suffix *-ion* is added, since the syllable /sh∂n/ can be spelled either *-sion* or *-tion*. Latin roots usually take one spelling or the other.

In this exercise, students select either *-sion* or *-tion* and add the syllable to the roots listed. They must categorize these words by writing them under the correct heading.

Strategies taught in Lesson 7, particularly the related-word strategies, are not reliable for words formed from *tend*. This is because there is often more than one related word from which to choose (*intend, intent, intense*). Students should check each word in the dictionary, since that is the most reliable strategy for spelling these words correctly.

Lesson 17

The Roots *ten, sign, sort, stance, test,* and *tail*

Objectives

- **Roots:** Learn to recognize and spell words with *ten, sign, sort, stance, test,* and *tail.*
- **Word Building:** Join morphemes to build whole words. Select and combine morphemes to build as many words as possible.
- **Strategy:** Learn a related-word strategy for remembering the silent *g* in *sign.*
- **Composing Sentences:** Write an original sentence using selected words.
- **Completing Words in Context:** Build words to fit in context by adding roots to partial words.
- **Building and Using Words:** Build new words by removing and replacing prefixes. Use the new words in context.
- **Word Game:** Play a game to build words.

1 Recognizing Roots

Read aloud the representative words listed for each root. Read the words in a normal speaking voice without stressing the roots. Instruct students to underline the root as you read each word. Do this exercise orally so that students can both see and hear the roots.

Lesson 17 — Roots

ten, sign, sort, stance, test, and *tail*

1 Recognizing Roots

In each group of words below, underline the roots listed on the left.

ten, tain	**hold**			
	tenant	tenure	maintain	obtain
	tenacious	contented	maintenance	contain
sign	**mark, sign**			
	sign	designer	resignation	
	signature	significance	consignment	
sort	**chance, lot; go out**			
	sort	resort	presort	
	sorted	assortment	consort	
stance, stant	**stand**			
	substance	distance	instance	
	substantial	distantly	constantly	
test	**witness**			
	testify	detest	attested	
	testimony	protester	contestant	
tail	**cut**			
	tailor	detail	retail	

Emphasize that roots provide the core or central meaning of a word. Note that the spelling of a root may change when certain suffixes are added.

Point out that *tain* and *stant* are variant forms of the roots *ten* and *stance.* When you come to these roots, be sure students can identify the variant forms in the representative words.

Point out that the pronunciation of *sign* changes in the words *signature, significance,* and *resignation.* Remembering the silent *g* in words like *sign* is addressed in Exercise 3.

The word *curtail* is not included in this exercise as it comes from a root different from *tail* meaning *cut.* The spelling problems are the same, however, so you may wish to include it in an appropriate activity.

Additional activities:

Have students work in small groups to generate as many words as they can with these roots.

2 Word Building

Join the morphemes that follow to build whole words. Write the words on the lines provided. Remember to change letters if necessary.

1. re + tain _____ retain _____
2. en + tail + ing _____ entailing _____
3. as + sort + ed _____ assorted _____
4. in + stant + ly _____ instantly _____
5. de + sign + ate _____ designate _____
6. ten + ure + ed _____ tenured _____
7. de + test + able _____ detestable _____
8. Pro + test + ant _____ Protestant _____
9. circum + stance _____ circumstance _____
10. out + di + stance _____ outdistance _____

3 Related-Word Strategy: The Silent *g*

Some words that contain a silent consonant have related words in which that consonant is pronounced. Learning these related words can help you to remember the silent consonant in the root or other related words.

The root *sign* means *mark* or *sign*. This root always conveys that idea, regardless of the pronunciation.

Look up the word *signal* in the dictionary. Write the pronunciation and meaning below.

signal _(sĭg'nəl): an indicator, a message, something that incites action_

Remembering the word *signal* can help you remember the silent *g* in the word *sign*.

For each word below, write one related word in which the silent *g* is pronounced. Use a dictionary if necessary. The first one is done for you.

1. resign _____ resignation _____
2. assign _____ assignation _____
3. design _____ designate _____

Now use one of the pairs of words above in an original sentence.

I'll resign if you hand in your resignation, too.

_____

Lesson 17   73

Have students identify prefixes or suffixes that they have studied or recognize in the representative words.

2 Word Building

Students should drop the silent *e* in number 6.

Be sure that students do not confuse the root *stance* or *stant* with the suffixes *-ant* or *-ance* in words like *Protestant.*

3 Related-Word Strategy: The Silent *g*

In this exercise, a strategy is introduced for helping students to remember the silent *g* in words like *sign, resign,* or *design.* The answers given on the replica of the student page are examples.

Encourage students to put the dictionary definition into their own words. They should not copy everything. Selecting the key information is another useful dictionary skill.

Accept all correctly spelled words. Encourage students to use a dictionary if necessary.

Students are asked to use in a sentence one word with the silent *g* and one related word in which the *g* is pronounced. Once students can spell words, they need practice in using them correctly. If students ask how to spell a word they have not studied, encourage them to look it up in the dictionary.

We feel that it is acceptable for students to make phonetically correct misspellings of words they have not yet studied. If you choose to correct students, be supportive of their attempts.

4 Adding Roots to Make Complete Words

In this exercise, students must form complete words by filling in missing roots. Affixes and contexts are supplied, so that one root should make the most sense in each blank.

Seeing words with roots missing helps students to understand that it is the root that gives a word its essential meaning.

Have students read a whole phrase or sentence before they fill in the blank and then reread it afterward to be sure that it makes sense.

If students have trouble doing this exercise, have them ignore the contexts at first and just focus on a root that would fit in the blank to form a word.

Students may need help with number 5, *circumstantial.* Encourage them to use a dictionary to check the spelling.

Additional activity:

Ask students to write another phrase or sentence for each word.

5 Challenge Word Building

This exercise reinforces the fact that there are many ways to combine morphemes.

Emphasize that students can use as few or as many morphemes as needed for a particular word. More than one prefix can be added to build some of the words. The roots *sign, sort,* and *tail* function as whole words.

---

4 Adding Roots to Make Complete Words
Write one of the following roots in each blank below to make a whole word that makes sense in the phrase or sentence. Then write the whole word on the right.

tain   ten   sign   sort   stance/stant

Whole words

1. a _sign_ ificant event   significant
2. a table of con_ten_ts   contents
3. an enter_tain_ing show   entertaining
4. I re_sign_ed from my job.   resigned
5. circum_stant_ial evidence   circumstantial
6. an as_sort_ment of colors   assortment
7. She's a fashion de_sign_er.   designer
8. They traveled a great di_stance_.   distance
9. The suspects were de_tain_ed.   detained
10. a dangerous chemical sub_stance_   substance

5 Challenge Word Building
On a separate piece of paper, combine the morphemes below to build as many words as you can. Use as few or as many morphemes as you need for each word. Use a dictionary if you are unsure of a word.

Prefixes	Roots	Suffixes
con-	sign	-er
de-	sort	-ment
re-	tail	
	tain	

Remind students that using a dictionary is a necessary and ongoing strategy for good spelling and for checking words of which they are uncertain.

Possible responses are listed here. There may be others. Accept all correctly spelled words. (Check to be sure that students do not write *tailer.*)

consign	container
consigner	containment
consignment	design
consort	designer
contain	detail

detain	retain
detainer	retainer
detainment	retainment
redesign	sign
resigner	signer
resort	sort
retail	sorter
retailer	tail

Additional activities:

Have students compare their lists and develop a master list of all the words they form.

Have students use some of the words they build in sentences.

6 Changing Prefixes

Remove the prefix from each of the words below and replace it with one of the following prefixes. Then use the new word in a phrase or short sentence.

as-   con-   de-   in-   re-   sub-

	New words	Phrases or sentences
1. *re*tain	contain	_____
2. *en*sign	design	_____
3. *con*sort	resort	_____
4. *in*stance	substance	_____
5. *di*stantly	instantly	_____
6. *en*tailing	retailing	_____
7. *de*signation	assignation	_____

7 Missing Links

Add a root from this lesson that will link each pair below to form compound words or phrases. The missing link will form the end of the first word or phrase and the beginning of the second. You can use a root more than once. The number of blanks indicates how many letters are in each missing link. Study the example before you begin.

Example: count to t e n -spot

1. stop s i g n off
2. screen t e s t tube
3. five-and- t e n fold
4. turn t a i l light
5. high s i g n language
6. road t e s t pilot

Lesson 17   75

6 Changing Prefixes

By removing one prefix and replacing it with another, students are using morphemes as practical building blocks of words. Remind students to use a dictionary if they are uncertain of a word.

When students are writing phrases and sentences, allow them to use any form of the new words.

The answers on the replica of the student page are examples. Accept any answer that forms a correctly spelled word.

Additional activities:

Have students use the original word in a phrase or sentence.

For advanced students: See how many different words students can build from any of the given words by removing and replacing one prefix at a time.

7 Missing Links

In this word game, students form two unrelated compound words or phrases by writing a missing word in the blanks. The word that is filled in will form the end of the first word or phrase and the beginning of the second: *count to ten* and *ten-spot*. All of the missing words are roots from this lesson. The number of blanks indicates the number of letters in the missing word.

Remember that word games are intended to be fun. Students may want to work in pairs or small groups. If they find this game confusing or frustrating, let them skip it.

Quizzes

Give a graded spelling quiz on the words in this lesson or other words that include these roots.

Sentences

Sentences for dictation are available at the back of this book.

The Roots *vert, text, tour, vent,* and *verb*

Objectives

- **Roots:** Learn to recognize and spell words with *vert, text, tour, vent,* and *verb.*
- **Word Building:** Join morphemes to build whole words. Select, reorder, and combine morphemes to build whole words.
- **Taking Words Apart:** Divide words into morphemes.
- **Variant Forms:** Practice spelling words with variant forms of the root *vert.*
- **Building and Using Words:** Build words by adding roots to partial words. Use the whole words in context.
- **Recognizing Morphemes in Context:** Identify roots in context.

1 Recognizing Roots

Read aloud the representative words listed for each root. Read the words in a normal speaking voice without stressing the roots. Instruct students to underline the root as you read each word.

Point out that *verge* and *verse* are variant forms of the root *vert.* Be sure students can identify the variant forms in the representative words.

Point out that the pronunciation of *text* and *vent* changes when the suffix *-ure* is added. The *t* is

pronounced /ch/. When *-ion* is added to the root *verse,* the *s* is pronounced /zh/.

Additional activities:

Have students work in small groups to generate as many words as they can that include these roots.

Have students identify prefixes and suffixes that they have studied or recognize in the representative words.

2 Word Building

Emphasize that students should add one morpheme at a time to minimize the chance of making errors. Remind them to pronounce the new words before writing them and to proofread their work.

Students should drop the silent *e* in numbers 2–4, 8, and 9. Be sure they retain it in *venturesome.*

Lesson 18

Roots
vert, text, tour, vent, and *verb*

1 Recognizing Roots

In each group of words below, underline the roots listed on the left.

vert, verge, verse	*turn, bend, incline*		
	convert	converge	perverse
	diverted	divergent	inversion
	subverting	convergence	conversation

text	*weave, construct*			
	textile	texture	context	pretext

tour	*turn, around*		
	tourist	contoured	tournament

vent	*come, arrive*		
	events	intervention	inventor
	venture	adventurous	preventative

verb	*word*			
	verb	verbatim	verbose	adverb

2 Word Building

Join the morphemes that follow to build whole words. Write the words on the lines provided. Remember to drop the silent *e* if necessary.

1. verb + al + ize ___verbalize___   4. per + verse + ion ___perversion___
2. text + ure + al ___textural___   5. pre + vent + ion ___prevention___
3. re + verse + al ___reversal___   6. con + vent + ion ___convention___

7. en + tour + age ___entourage___   9. con + verge + ent ___convergent___

8. di + verse + ify ___diversify___   10. vent + ure + some ___venturesome___

3 Jumbled Morphemes

Use the morphemes in each group below to create four different words. Remember to change or drop letters if necessary. Write the words on the lines provided.

1. verge ly con ent di

   ___divergent___   ___divergently___

   ___converge___   ___convergent___

2. pre un able vent ly

   ___prevent___   ___unpreventable___

   ___preventable___   ___unpreventably___

3. verse ir ible ly re

   ___reversible___   ___reversibly___

   ___irreversible___   ___reverse___

4. vent ion al con un

   ___convention___   ___unconventional___

   ___conventional___   ___convent___

5. contro ial verse y con ly

   ___controversy___   ___conversely___

   ___controversial___   ___controversially___

3 Jumbled Morphemes

In this exercise, students are required to build four words from a group of morphemes that are not in correct order. Not every morpheme will be used in each word.

Note whether students drop the silent *e* when appropriate in numbers 1–3 and 5.

Encourage students to use a dictionary if they are uncertain of a word.

The answers on the replica of the student page are examples. Accept all correctly spelled words.

Additional activities:

Have students compare their answers and develop a master list of all the words they form from each group of morphemes.

Have students write original sentences using some of the words they form.

4 Taking Words Apart

Taking Words Apart

Divide the following words into morphemes and write each one under the correct heading. Remember to add the silent *e* to the root if necessary.

	Prefixes	Roots	Suffixes	
1. tourism		tour	ism	
2. university	uni	verse	ity	
3. invention	in	vent	ion	
4. contextual	con	text	ual	
5. conversion	con	verse	ion	
6. divergence	di	verge	ence	
7. proverbial	pro	verb	ial	
8. eventually	e/ex	vent	ual	ly

5 Variant Forms

Variant Forms

Verbs with the root *vert* often have related words ending in *verse* and *version*. Knowing the *verse* form will help you decide how to spell the /zhən/ at the end of related *version* words. Add the prefixes listed on the left to the roots *vert*, *verse*, and *version* and write the whole words under the correct headings.

	vert	verse	version
1. in-	invert	inverse	inversion
2. re-	revert	reverse	reversion
3. di-	divert	diverse	diversion
4. per-	pervert	perverse	perversion
5. con-	convert	converse	conversion

Say the words in the last column aloud. Notice how they're pronounced. When you hear the ending /zhən/, it is probably spelled -*sion*.

78   Lesson 18

---

4 Taking Words Apart

All of these words follow regular patterns. Encourage students to refer to the glossary or a dictionary to check any individual morphemes if necessary.

Remind students that they should write the original form of a root. They should restore the final *e* to the root in numbers 2, 5, and 6.

Students who have difficulty should first identify the roots presented in this lesson.

Note whether students divide the two suffixes in number 8.

Additional activity:

Students can practice taking apart the words they find in any printed material, such as newspapers, magazines, or ads.

5 Variant Forms

This exercise emphasizes the relationships among related forms of the same root. It also illustrates that a root may have different forms depending on how it is used in a sentence. Predicting the spelling of a word by associating it with a related word is an important strategy. If students are learning new words with these roots, they should pay particular attention to the sound the root makes in a word.

Stress to students that the variant form of the root, *verse,* is used when adding -*ion.* Point out how the pronunciation of *verse* changes when -*ion* is added. This is a reliable strategy for spelling the final syllable, /zhən/, in these words.

Some students may not be able to hear the difference between /shən/ and /zhən/. For those who can, remind them that /zhən/ is spelled *sion.*

Additional activity:

Have students use all three forms of one of the words in original sentences. Advanced students may enjoy trying to use all three forms in one sentence.

6 Adding Roots to Make Complete Words

Write one of the following roots in each blank below to make a whole word.
Remember to drop the silent *e* from the root if necessary. Then use the word in an
original phrase or sentence.

vert/verge/verse   text   tour   vent

Phrases or sentences

1. con_text_s _____

2. ad_vers_ity _____

3. uni_vers_al _____

4. in_vent_ory _____

5. in_vent_ion _____

6. une_vent_ful _____

7. di_verg_ence _____

8. intro_vert_ed _____

7 Recognizing Roots in Context

Underline the following roots in the sentences below.

vert/verse   text   tour   vent   verb

1. I like the new version of the story better.

2. Please don't take my words out of context

3. The tour of the city was quite an adventure.

4. Isn't there a proverb about too many cooks?

5. The advent of television changed people's lives.

6. Nonverbal communication takes place without words.

7. There are many controversial theories about the universe

8. A new fabric with the texture of cotton has been invented.

6 Adding Roots to Make Complete Words

In this exercise, students must form complete words by filling in missing roots. Affixes are supplied. In most of the blanks, only one root should make sense. Note that number 1, however, could be *converts, converges, converses, contexts, contours,* or *convents.* Number 5 could be *inversion* or *invention.*

Seeing words with roots missing helps students to understand that it is the root that gives a word its essential meaning, while affixes qualify that meaning and often indicate the part of speech.

Students are also asked to use the words they form in phrases or short sentences. Using words in context is an important additional activity that should be included at any appropriate opportunity.

Make sure that students proofread their work carefully.

7 Recognizing Roots in Context

Instruct students to underline in the sentences all of the roots from the given list. Remind students to read the sentences before they start underlining.

Additional activities:

Have students circle any prefixes and suffixes that they recognize.

Have them generate exercises of this sort for one another to do.

This kind of activity can be done using any printed material, such as newspapers, magazines, or ads.

Quizzes

Give a graded spelling quiz on the words in this lesson or other words that include these roots.

Sentences

Sentences for dictation are available at the back of this book.

Unit 4

Review of Lessons 12–18

Objectives

- **Roots:** Review roots studied in Unit 4.
- **Recognizing Morphemes in Context:** Identify roots in context.
- **Building and Using Words:** Build words by adding roots to partial words. Use the new words in context.
- **Strategies:** Practice spelling /shən/ and /ənt/, /əns/, and /ənsē/ at the end of words.
- **Composing Sentences:** Write an original sentence using selected words.
- **Word Building:** Select and combine morphemes to build as many words as possible.
- **Variant Forms:** Use context to determine the correct form of a root.
- **Word Game:** Play a game to build words.

You may need to review some of the patterns for adding endings before beginning this review, depending on how well students have managed with individual lessons. Remind them that they can refer to the lessons whenever necessary.

For detailed information about patterns and strategies, refer to the lesson notes for individual lessons.

Unit 4

Review
Lessons 12 through 18

Roots Presented in This Unit

act	mand	prove	tain
cent	mend	quer	ten
cord	merge	quest	tend
cure	merse	quire	tense
fact	muse	sane	tent
fect	pass	sect	test
fic(t)	pat	serve	text
file	ply	side	tour
fine	pone	sign	vent
fit	port	sort	verb
found	pose	stance	verge
fund	post	stant	verse
fuse	pound	tail	vert

1 Recognizing Roots in Context
Underline the roots from the list above in the following sentences.

1. I question how sanitary that canning factory is.
2. The detour diverted us through a residential area.
3. She's learning to conquer her dislike of intense cold.
4. It's our intention to start composting some of our garbage.
5. I'd recommend you wear that new outfit for the interview.
6. In this instance, it's beneficial to have a wide assortment of supplies.
7. The fundamental problem is compounded by the many details involved.
8. His health shows occasional signs of improvement, but the disease is actually incurable.

---

1 Recognizing Roots in Context

Instruct students to underline in the sentences all of the roots from the given list. Be sure that students read the sentences carefully before they begin. Suggest that they start by identifying roots and then check to see if the roots are included in the list.

Additional activities:

Have students circle any prefixes and suffixes that they recognize in the sentences.

Have them develop exercises of this sort for one another to do.

This kind of activity can be done using any printed material, such as newspapers, magazines, or ads.

2 Adding Roots to Make Complete Words

Write one of the following roots in each blank below to make a whole word. Remember to change or drop letters if necessary. Then use each word in a phrase or short sentence.

act   fect   pose   side   stant   tend   verge

Phrases or sentences

1. in_stant_ _____
2. sup_pose_ _____
3. _act_ive _____
4. re_side_ _____
5. con_verge_ _____
6. _tend_ency _____
7. ef_fect_ _____
8. com_pose_ _____

3 Practicing Strategies: Words Ending in /shən/

For each word listed below, write a related word that ends in *-ion*. Use the dictionary if necessary.

1. extend _extension_   6. divert _diversion_
2. intent _intention_   7. confuse _confusion_
3. revert _reversion_   8. attend _attention_
4. immerse _immersion_   9. convert _conversion_
5. contend _contention_   10. pretend _pretension_

Use one pair of words in an original sentence.

_____

_____

2 Adding Roots to Make Complete Words

In this exercise, students must form complete words by filling in missing roots and then use the words they form in phrases or short sentences. They choose the roots from the list at the beginning of the exercise.

When students are writing phrases and sentences, allow them to use any form of the word they have created.

Make sure that students proofread their work carefully. You may want to ask advanced students to explain why numbers 7 and 8 could each take only one of the listed roots. (*Ef-* is always followed by another *f* and *com-* is always followed by *b, m,* or *p.*)

Answers given on the replica of the student page are examples. Accept all correctly spelled words.

3 Practicing Strategies: Words Ending in /shən/

In this exercise, students practice spelling the syllable /shən/ after certain roots. Review the roots individually if necessary. Start by having students identify the roots (*tend, vert, merse,* and *fuse*) and see if they remember any patterns or strategies that apply. Refer students back to particular lessons if necessary. Encourage students to check their spelling in a dictionary.

Students are then asked to use one pair of words in an original sentence. Using different forms of the same word in context helps students to develop the concept of related words.

4 Practicing Strategies: /ənt/, /əns/, and /ənsē/

In this exercise, roots that take the suffixes *-ant/-ance/-ancy* or *-ent/-ence/-ency* are reviewed. Once students have completed the chart, they can use it for reference when necessary.

Encourage students to use a dictionary to help determine which suffixes can be added to which words if they are not sure. Remind them that the pronunciation will not help them to spell these suffixes. Point out that learning which roots take which pairs of suffixes will provide them with a strategy for spelling the schwa sound in these words.

Remind students that *tend* takes both *-ant/-ance/-ancy* and *-ent/-ence/-ency*.

Be sure that students drop the silent *e* in numbers 1, 4, 6, 8, and 10, and that they change the *y* to *i* in number 5.

Additional activity:

Have students use some of their example words in sentences.

5 Challenge Word Building

Emphasize that students can use as few or as many morphemes as needed for a particular word. For instance, the roots *act, side, tend,* and *tent* are also whole words.

Encourage students to use a dictionary if necessary. Have them check to be sure that they have dropped the silent *e* when necessary.

---

4 Practicing Strategies: /ənt/, /əns/, and /ənsē/

Several roots in this unit can have the suffixes *-ant/-ance/-ancy* or *-ent/-ence/-ency* added to them. For each root on the left, check the correct column to show which suffixes can be added. Then write an example of the root with one of the suffixes added on the right. Use a dictionary and remember to add, drop, or change letters if necessary. The first one is done for you.

	-ant/-ance/-ancy	-ent/-ence/-ency	Example words
1. fine	✓		finance
2. accord	√		accordance
3. disinfect	√		disinfectant
4. emerge		√	emergency
5. comply	√		compliance
6. compone		√	component
7. import	√		important
8. preside		√	presidency
9. attend	√		attendance
10. diverge		√	divergence

5 Challenge Word Building

On a separate piece of paper, combine the morphemes below to build as many words as you can. Use as few or as many morphemes as you need for each word. Remember to drop or change letters if necessary. Use a dictionary if you are unsure of a word.

Prefixes	Roots	Suffixes
at-	act	-ant/-ance/-ancy
pre-	side	-ent/-ence/-ency
re-	tend	-ion
	tent	

82   Unit 4 Review

Some morphemes that present special problems when combined are included here. Be sure that students spell *attendant/attendance* and *tendency* correctly, and that they do not try to write *pretention*.

Possible responses are listed here. There may be others. Accept all correctly spelled words.

act	attention
attend	preside
attendance	presidency
attendant	president
pretend	resident
react	retention
reactant	side
reaction	tend
reside	tendency
residence	tent
residency	

Additional activities:

Have students compare their lists and develop a master list.

Have students use some of the words they build in sentences.

6 Choosing the Correct Form of a Root

To complete the partial words in the following sentences, choose the correct form of the root from those under each blank and write it in the blank. Remember to drop the silent *e* if necessary.

1. That company sup__pli__es ex__tens__ion cords.
   ply/pli   tent/tense

2. His con__stant__ complaints are a re__vers__ion to his old habits.
   stance/stant   vert/verse

3. Are you im__ply__ing that I'm too lazy to walk that di__stance__?
   ply/pli   stance/stant

4. If your ap__pli__cation is late, you are in__stant__ly disqualified.
   ply/pli   stance/stant

5. I have every in__tent__ion of com__ply__ing with the regulations.
   tent/tense   ply/pli

7 Missing Letters

A pair of letters has been omitted twice from each word below. Fill in the missing letters to make whole words. Each word contains a root from this unit.

1. __r__ e qui __r__ e
2. m __a__ i nt __a__ i n
3. __i__ n f __i__ n ity
4. __e__ n actm __e__ n t
5. pr __e__ s erv __e__ s
6. rev __e__ r b __e__ r ate
7. __i__ n vert __i__ n g
8. d __e__ s erv __e__ s
9. __i__ n def __i__ n ite
10. m __e__ r g __e__ r
11. t __e__ n d __e__ n cy
12. p __e__ r v __e__ r se

6 Choosing the Correct Form of a Root

Some variant forms sound and look somewhat alike. Students must learn to use context and sound clues to predict accurately which form to use.

In this exercise, students select the correct form from two forms of a root below the blank and write it in the blank to complete the sentence. Students must choose a word that is appropriate in the sentence and correctly spelled.

Make sure that students read the whole sentence before they fill in the blanks. Then they should proofread it carefully afterward.

Note whether they have problems with any of the forms and review patterns if necessary.

7 Missing Letters

In this word game, students fill in pairs of letters in the same order to build complete words. In each word, the pair of letters is missing twice. Each complete word contains a root from Unit 4. More than one word may be formed for some of the items. Accept any correctly spelled word, even if it does not contain a root from Unit 4.

Sentences

Sentences for dictation are available at the back of this book.

Unit 4 Test

We recommend that you test your students on the words from Unit 4 before going on. The following is a suggested list of words from Unit 4. You may want to substitute other words to meet the needs of your students.

Dictate each word and use it in a simple sentence. Students should be able to spell 90 percent of these words correctly.

inexact	disapproval
accordance	intention
sufficient	unquestioning
concentration	observance
inaccurate	presidential
satisfactory	dissection
amusing	contentment
refinement	maintenance
confusion	significant
impatiently	designer
emergency	assortment
detailed	instantly
appliance	substance
composure	protester
importantly	recommendation

The Greek Roots *graph, gram, photo, phono, tele,* and *thermo*

Objectives

- **Greek Morphemes:** Learn to recognize and spell words with *graph, gram, photo, phono, tele,* and *thermo.*
- **Word Building:** Join morphemes to build whole words.
- **Combining Forms:** Understand the concept of combining forms.
- **Pattern:** Learn the *ph* spelling of /f/ in words of Greek origin.
- **Completing Words in Context:** Build words to fit in context by adding Greek morphemes to partial words.

Many Greek morphemes take on more than one role in English words. For example, *therm* is a root in a word like *thermal.* In a word like *thermonuclear,* it functions more as a prefix. For this reason, such morphemes are often known as combining forms. These combining forms are used in a way similar to words that form compound words. Also, there is often one form ending in *o* and one without the *o.*

Representative Greek morphemes are included in this unit. There is no attempt made to include them all. You may wish to point out to students that they are likely to encounter other Greek morphemes in their reading and writing.

---

1 Recognizing Roots

In each group of words below, underline the roots listed on the left.

graph	**write, draw**		
	graphics	telegraph	geography
	autograph	autobiography	photographic
gram	**write, draw**		
	grammar	program	diagram
	gramophone	telegram	anagram
photo	**light**		
	photocopy	photostat	telephoto
	photograph	photosynthesis	unphotogenic
phono, phone, phon	**sound**		
	phonetics	telephone	symphony
	phonology	microphone	gramophone
tele	**distant**		
	telegram	telegraph	telephoto
	television	telephone	telecommunications
thermo, therm	**heat**		
	thermal	thermostat	isotherm
	thermometer	thermonuclear	thermodynamics

84   Lesson 19

Many words from Greek are scientific or technical words that students will never have heard and are unlikely ever to need. Tell them that they should not feel intimidated by any of the less common words they may find in the dictionary when working on Greek morphemes.

For further general information on Greek morphemes, refer to page 9 in the introduction.

1 Recognizing Roots

Read aloud the representative words listed for each root. Read the words in a normal speaking voice without stressing the roots. Instruct students to underline the root as you read each word. Do this exercise orally so that students can both see and hear the roots.

Remind students that the definitions of the roots are listed above the representative words.

2 Word Building

Join the morphemes that follow to build whole words. Write the words on the lines provided. Remember to drop the silent *e* if necessary.

1. tele + scope ___telescope___
2. tele + path + y ___telepathy___
3. photo + gen + ic ___photogenic___
4. re + pro + gram ___reprogram___
5. geo + therm + al ___geothermal___
6. photo + copy + er ___photocopier___
7. stereo + phon + ic ___stereophonic___
8. biblio + graph + er ___bibliographer___
9. gram + mat + ic + al ___grammatical___
10. demo + graph + ic + s ___demographics___

3 Greek Roots as Combining Forms

Morphemes from Greek can often be used in more than one way to build words. Some Greek morphemes may be used as a prefix in one word, as a root in another, and as a suffix in a third word. This is why they are sometimes called *combining forms*.

Part A. Write each of the following words under the morphemes they contain.

telephone   phonograph   telephoto   photograph   telegraph

tele	*graph*	*photo*	*phono*
telephone	phonograph	telephoto	telephone
telephoto	photograph	photograph	phonograph
telegraph	telegraph		

Part B. Many Greek morphemes end in *o*. Several of these have a variant form without the final *o*. The form that ends in *o* is usually used before a morpheme that starts with a consonant. Underline the form of *phono* used in each word below.

phono**graph**   phono**logy**   micro**phone**   gramo**phone**

Now say these words aloud. The *o* ending on combining forms is sometimes pronounced as a schwa when the ending is added. Knowing that Greek combining forms usually have an *o* can help you to spell the schwa sound in these words.

Lesson 19   85

Emphasize that although a root usually provides the core or central meaning of a word, when a root acts as a combining form, its function may change from word to word. Have students identify morphemes that form the beginning, middle, or end of words.

Point out the following:

Phono and *thermo* also have forms without the final *o*.

There is often a shift in stress in these morphemes, e.g., in *photograph* and *photography,* in *graphics* and *autograph,* and in *telephone* and *symphony.*

There are few prefixes and suffixes in these words that students will recognize from previous lessons. Greek roots are often combined with other Greek morphemes rather than with Latin morphemes.

2 Word Building

Emphasize that students should add one morpheme at a time to minimize the chance of making errors. Remind them to pronounce the new words before writing them and to proofread their work.

Students should change the *y* to *i* in number 6.

3 Greek Roots as Combining Forms

Part A: Students categorize words made up of two combining forms according to the morphemes they contain. Listing the words under the morphemes contained in them demonstrates the versatile function of some combining forms. Each word is listed under two headings.

Part B: Students see that the form of a word ending in *o* is generally used before morphemes that begin with consonants. Knowing this provides a strategy for spelling words from Greek that have a schwa sound in the middle, such as *phonological, holocaust,* or *thermostat.*

Lesson 19   93

4 **Discovering Patterns: /f/ Spelled _ph_**

Underline the words below in which _ph_ spells /f/. Then fill in the blank in the pattern.

uphill   **peephole**   apostrophe   photography

digraph   philosophy   blasphemy   **reupholstered**

headphone   **upheaval**   shepherd   autobiographical

Notice that the words you underlined include Greek roots.

Pattern: In words from Greek, the /f/ sound is usually spelled _ph_ .

5 **Adding Morphemes to Make Complete Words**

Write one of the following morphemes in each blank below to make a whole word. The word must make sense in the phrase or sentence. Use a dictionary if necessary. Then write the whole word on the right.

graph   gram   photo   phone/phon   tele   thermo/therm

Whole words

1. a mono_gram_ med shirt   _monogrammed_

2. That's a long para_graph_ .   _paragraph_

3. an interesting pro_gram_   _program_

4. a talented choreo_graph_ er   _choreographer_

5. The debate was _tele_ vised.   _televised_

6. _Photo_ synthesis involves light.   _Photosynthesis_

7. Astronomers need _tele_ scopes.   _telescopes_

8. She's an excellent saxo_phon_ ist.   _saxophonist_

9. Please turn the _thermo_ stat down.   _thermostat_

10. The cheerleader used a mega_phone_ .   _megaphone_

4 **Discovering Patterns: /f/ Spelled _ph_**

Words from Greek are phonetically regular, but the letters that typically spell some sounds are not the same as in words of Latin derivation.

This exercise is designed to increase students' awareness of the sound /f/ spelled _ph_. If they know whether or not a word is of Greek origin, they are likely to know how to spell the /f/ sound.

Additional activity:

Have students use a dictionary to find 10 words that start with _ph_. Have them notice the origin of the words as they look them up. Have them list the words on a separate piece of paper or in their notebooks and then compare their lists.

5 **Adding Morphemes to Make Complete Words**

In this exercise, students must form complete words by filling in missing morphemes. Affixes and contexts are supplied, so that only one morpheme should make sense in each blank.

Have students read a whole phrase or sentence before they fill in the blank and then reread it afterward.

Be sure that students use the appropriate form of the morpheme.

Students having trouble doing this exercise should ignore the contexts at first and just focus on a morpheme that would fit in the blank to form a word.

If students are unfamiliar with any of the words, encourage them to use a dictionary. In number 6, the word _light_ is a clue to the morpheme _photo_ if they do not know the word _photosynthesis_.

Additional activity:

Have students write another phrase or sentence for each word.

Quizzes

Give a graded spelling quiz on the words in this lesson or other words that include these morphemes.

Sentences

Sentences for dictation are available at the back of this book.

Lesson 20 ——

The Greek Roots *bio, crat, cyclo, log, gen, astro,* and *geo*

Objectives

- **Greek Morphemes:** Learn to recognize and spell words with *bio, crat, cyclo, log, gen, astro,* and *geo.*
- **Word Building:** Join morphemes to build whole words.
- **Building and Using Words:** Select, reorder, and combine morphemes to build whole words. Use selected words in context.
- **Completing Words in Context:** Build words to fit in context by adding Greek morphemes to partial words.
- **Using Meanings:** Select Greek morphemes based on the definitions of words to be formed.

1 Recognizing Roots

Read aloud the representative words listed for each root. Read the words in a normal speaking voice without stressing the roots. Instruct students to underline the root as you read each word.

Emphasize that although a root usually provides the core or central meaning of a word, when a root acts as a combining form, its function may change from word to word. Have students identify morphemes that form the beginning, middle, or end of words.

Lesson 20 — Greek Roots
bio, crat, cyclo, log, gen, astro, and *geo*

1 Recognizing Roots
In each group of words below, underline the roots listed on the left.

bio	*life*			
	bio**log**y	anti**bio**tic	**bio**psy	
	sym**bio**tic	auto**bio**graphy	**bio**medical	
crat, cracy	*representative or form of government, power*			
	demo**crat**	bureau**cracy**	aristo**cracy**	
	demo**cracy**	bureau**crat**ic	idiosyn**crat**ic	
cyclo, cycle	*circle, wheel*			
	cyclone	**cycle**	re**cycle**	
	bi**cycl**ing	**cycl**ical	motor**cycle**	
log(ue), logy	*word, speech; study of*			
	logo	dia**log**(ue)	bio**log**y	eu**log**y
	logical	cata**log**(ue)	theo**log**y	antho**log**y
gen	*something produced; producer*			
	genetic	**gen**erate	oxy**gen**	
	genesis	**gen**eration	carcino**gen**ic	
astro, ast	*star, constellation*			
	astronaut	**astro**logy	**astro**nomical	**ast**erisk
geo	*earth*			
	geology	**geo**graphy	**geo**metry	**geo**physics

Lesson 20   87

Both *log* and *logue* are acceptable spellings for many words that end in /log/, e.g., *catalog/catalogue, dialog/dialogue.* This text uses *log* because it is easier to spell, but both spellings are correct.

Some of the words containing the morpheme *gen* are identified in the dictionary as being of Latin origin. The Latin form *genus* meaning *birth* came from the Greek *genes* meaning *born,* but dictionaries do not always go back to the Greek. If students question this, explain to them that some Latin words originated in Greek.

Point out the following:

The morpheme *crat* refers to a person, while *cracy* refers to a form of government or power. *Bureau* (meaning *desk*) is of French origin. The Greek morphemes *crat* and *cracy* are added to it to build new words in English.

The *g* in *log* can be either hard or soft, depending on the letters that follow it.

Words formed with *astro*, such as *astronaut*, sometimes have a schwa sound in the middle of the word. Knowing that the word is of Greek origin will help students to predict the spelling of the schwa.

Cycle is a variant form of *cyclo*, *logy* is a variant form of *log(ue)*, and *ast* is a variant form of *astro*. When you come to these roots, be sure students can identify the variant forms in the representative words.

2 Word Building

Students should drop the silent *e* in numbers 2 and 10.

If some of these words are unfamiliar to students, point out that by studying morphemes, they have a better chance of predicting both spelling and meaning correctly.

3 Jumbled Morphemes

Students are asked to build words from a group of morphemes that are not in correct order. Not every morpheme will be used in each word. Students are then asked to use some of their words in phrases or sentences.

Remind students to use a dictionary if necessary and to proofread their work. Make sure that they do not try to form *biologically* in number 2. The suffix given is *-y*, not *-ly*.

As students become more comfortable with the exercise formats and the morpheme approach, you might encourage them to become more adventurous in the phrases and sentences they write. If they are using notebooks, they can write extra sentences or longer ones than space in the book allows for. Allow them to use any form of the words they build.

The answers on the replica of the student page are examples. Accept all correctly spelled words.

---

2 Word Building

Join the morphemes that follow to build whole words. Write the words on the lines provided. Remember to drop the silent *e* if necessary.

1. eco + logy ___ecology___
2. cycle + ist ___cyclist___
3. mono + log ___monolog___
4. auto + cracy ___autocracy___
5. cyclo + rama ___cyclorama___

6. geo + metr + ic ___geometric___
7. bio + graph + er ___biographer___
8. astro + phys + ics ___astrophysics___
9. techno + crat + ic ___technocratic___
10. gen + er + ate + or ___generator___

3 Jumbled Morphemes

Use the morphemes in each group below to create three different words. Choose two words from each group and use them in phrases or short sentences.

Phrases or sentences

1. cycle   ist   bi   motor

   ___cyclist___

   ___bicycle___

   ___motorcyclist___

2. log   bio   al   ic   ist   y

   ___biology___

   ___biological___

   ___biologist___

3. crat   demo   ic   ly   al   cracy

   ___democracy___

   ___democratic___

   ___democratically___

4 Adding Morphemes to Make Complete Words

Write one of the following morphemes in each blank below to make a whole word. The word must make sense in the phrase or sentence. Then write the whole word on the right.

bio   crat   cycle   log/logy   gen   astro   geo

		Whole words
1.	studying __geo__ metry	geometry
2.	a careful motor __cycl__ ist	motorcyclist
3.	What a bureau __crat__ ic mess!	bureaucratic
4.	Is that trash __bio__ degradable?	biodegradable
5.	Three __astro__ nauts will be trained.	astronauts
6.	The twins are very photo __gen__ ic.	photogenic
7.	a recently discovered carcino __gen__	carcinogen
8.	The treaty banned bio __log__ ical warfare.	biological

5 Looking at Meanings

Add one of the following roots to each partial word below. The word you create must fit the definition on the left. Use a dictionary if necessary.

bio   log/logy   gen   ast   geo

Definitions	Partial words	Whole words
1. allergy producer	aller	allergen
2. study of the earth	logy	geology
3. star-shaped symbol	erisk	asterisk
4. conversation in a play	dia	dialog
5. story of someone's life	graphy	biography
6. words expressing regret	apo	apology

4 Adding Morphemes to Make Complete Words

In this exercise, students must form complete words by filling in missing Greek morphemes. Contexts and some morphemes are supplied, so that only one morpheme should make sense in each blank.

Seeing how Greek morphemes can fill different positions in words helps students to understand the concept of combining forms and how they function.

Have students read a whole phrase or sentence before they fill in the blank and then reread it afterward.

Students having trouble doing this exercise should ignore the contexts at first and just focus on a morpheme that would fit in the blank to form a word.

Additional activity:

Ask students to write another phrase or sentence for each word.

5 Looking at Meanings

Learning to relate the meanings of Greek morphemes to words in which they are used should help students to spell these words correctly.

Make sure that the words the students form make sense according to the definitions on the left. Each definition gives a key word to help the students identify the correct morpheme to add.

Additional activities:

Once they have written the word suggested by the definition and partial word, have students underline the portion of the definition that led them to choose a certain morpheme. Doing this helps to promote an awareness of the importance of meaning to correct spelling.

Have students use the words in sentences.

Quizzes

Give a graded spelling quiz on the words in this lesson or other words that include these morphemes.

Sentences

Sentences for dictation are available at the back of this book.

Lesson 21

The Greek Roots
aero, techno, mechan, metro, psycho, and *chrono*

Objectives

- **Greek Morphemes:** Learn to recognize and spell words with *aero, techno, mechan, metro, psycho,* and *chrono.*
- **Word Building:** Join morphemes to build whole words.
- **Patterns:** Learn to use *ch* spelling /k/ and to recognize the silent *p* in words of Greek origin.
- **Taking Words Apart:** Divide words into morphemes.
- **Building and Using Words:** Build new words by removing and replacing morphemes. Use the new words in context.
- **Recognizing Morphemes in Context:** Identify Greek morphemes in context.
- **Word Game:** Play a game to build words.

1 Recognizing Roots

Read aloud the representative words listed for each root. Read the words in a normal speaking voice without stressing the roots. Instruct students to underline the root as you read each word. Do this exercise orally so that students can both see and hear the roots.

Emphasize that although a root

usually provides the core or central meaning of a word, when a root acts as a combining form, its function may change from word to word. Have students identify morphemes that form the beginning, middle, or end of words.

Point out the following:

All the morphemes in this lesson except *mechan* end in *o* and have a variant form without the *o*. *Metro* has two variant forms, *metr* and *meter*. Be sure students can identify the variant forms in the

representative words. Remind students that the form ending in *o* is generally used before a morpheme beginning with a consonant and that knowing if a word is of Greek origin can help to predict the spelling of a schwa sound in the middle of a word like *metropolitan*.

There is a shift in stress in *meter* in the word *centimeter*. Encourage students to listen for such changes, so they learn to identify Greek morphemes that

---

Lesson **21**	Greek Roots
	aero, techno, mechan, metro, psycho, and *chrono*

1 Recognizing Roots

In each group of words below, underline the roots listed on the left.

aero, aer	*air, of aircraft*		
	aerobics	aerosol	aerial
	aerodynamic	aeronautical	aerate
techno, techn	*art, skill, science*		
	technocrat	technical	technician
	technology	technique	polytechnic
mechan	*machine*		
	mechanical	mechanics	mechanic
	mechanization	mechanism	mechanistic
metro, metr, meter	*measure*		
	metrical	diameter	geometry
	metropolitan	kilometer	optometrist
	symmetrical	centimeter	thermometer
psycho, psych	*mind, soul*		
	psychology	psychopath	psychiatrist
	psychoanalytical	psychodrama	psychotherapy
chrono, chron	*time*		
	chronometry	chronic	synchronize
	chronological	chronicle	anachronistic

90   Lesson 21

2 Word Building

Join the morphemes that follow to build whole words. Write the words on the lines provided.

1. psych + ic ____psychic____
2. peri + meter ____perimeter____
3. aero + space ____aerospace____
4. techn + ique ____technique____
5. mechan + ize ____mechanize____
6. syn + chron + ism ____synchronism____
7. un + aer + ate + ed ____unaerated____
8. a + sym + metr + y ____asymmetry____
9. chrono + metr + ic ____chronometric____
10. psycho + ana + lyst ____psychoanalyst____

3 Discovering Patterns: *Ch* Spelling /k/ and the Silent *p*

Part A. Underline the words below in which *ch* spells /k/.

teacher	French	chronicle	chimney	cherry
technicality	psychology	chronology	mechanize	psychoanalysis

Notice that the words you underlined include Greek roots.

Pattern: In words from Greek, the /k/ sound is usually spelled _ch_.

Part B. Look up the pronunciations and origins of the following words, and write the origins on the lines provided.

1. psalm ____Greek____
2. pseudo ____Greek____
3. pneumatic ____Greek____
4. pneumonia ____Greek____

Pattern: Words from Greek sometimes begin with a silent _p_.

Part C. Knowing that a word is of Greek origin will usually help you to spell it correctly. Fill in the blanks below.

1. In words from Greek, /f/ is usually spelled _ph_, and /k/ is usually spelled _ch_.

2. Words from Greek sometimes begin with a silent _p_.

Lesson 21   91

---

are spelled the same way despite variations in pronunciation.

Technician is an example of a word ending in *-cian* meaning a person skilled at certain work.

Additional activity:

Ask students to identify any Greek morphemes that they studied in Lessons 19 and 20.

2 Word Building

Emphasize that students should add one morpheme at a time to minimize the chance of making errors. Remind them to pronounce the new words before writing them and to proofread their work.

Reassure students that many of the words with Greek morphemes are scientific or technical words, and that they should not expect to know them all.

Students should drop the silent *e* in number 7.

You may want to explain that the spelling of /ēk/ in *technique* is unusual, and that it comes from French.

See if students remember the meaning of the prefix *a-* (*without*) from Lesson 9. It should help them to guess the meaning of *asymmetry* if they don't know it.

3 Discovering Patterns: *Ch* Spelling /k/ and the Silent *p*

Words from Greek are phonetically regular, but the letters that typically spell some sounds are not the same as in words of Latin derivation.

This exercise will increase students' awareness of the sound /k/ spelled *ch* and the silent *p*.

Part B: Remind students that if their dictionary gives more than one language of derivation, it is the last language listed that is the original one.

Part C: You may want your students to memorize the patterns for spelling the /f/ and /k/ sounds and the silent *p* in Greek morphemes, as they are unusual for English.

Lesson 21   99

4 Taking Words Apart

Note that the columns in this exercise do not have the usual headings. Combining forms are versatile and do not necessarily fall into the categories of prefixes, roots, and suffixes. The format of this exercise is another way for students to realize this.

Students who have difficulty should first identify the morphemes presented in this lesson.

For number 9, accept *psycho log ist* or *psycho logue ist*. Note whether students separate the two suffixes in *mechan ic al*.

Additional activity:

Students can practice taking apart the words they find in any printed material, such as newspapers, magazines, or ads.

5 Changing Morphemes

By removing one morpheme and replacing it with another, students are using morphemes as practical building blocks of words. This exercise also gives students another chance to see how interchangeable combining forms can be.

Remind students to use a dictionary if they are uncertain of a word.

The answers on the replica of the student page are examples.

Accept any answer that forms a correctly spelled word.

Additional activities:

Have students use the original words in phrases or sentences.

For advanced students: See how many different words students can build from any of the given words by removing and replacing one morpheme at a time.

6 Recognizing Morphemes in Context

Underline the following morphemes in the sentences below.

aero/aer   *techno*   *mechan*   *metr/meter*   *psycho/psych*   *chrono/chron*

1. Psychedelic drugs affect the mind.
2. A psychopathic killer has a diseased mind.
3. Technophobes fear science and its applications.
4. It has been measured carefully so it's symmetrical.
5. An anachronism places something in the wrong time.
6. Aerating the room helped to bring in some outside air.
7. The aerobatic team did amazing stunts in their airplanes.
8. The new machines led to mechanization and the loss of jobs.

7 Double Pyramid

Use the letters found in *aero* to complete the words below. Each word contains the letters *a*, *e*, *r*, and *o* at least once in any order. Most of the words are from previous lessons.

```
            A E R O
        S O A R E D
        A P P R O V E D
      T E C H N O C R A T
    M E T R O P O L I T A N
  R E F R I G E R A T O R
      P E R S U A S I O N
      H O M E W A R D
        A S H O R E
```

6 Recognizing Morphemes in Context

Tell students to underline in the sentences all of the Greek morphemes in the given list and to read the sentences before they start underlining.

Additional activity:

Have students underline a word or words in each sentence related to the meaning of the morpheme they have underlined (e.g., *time* for *chron, machines* for *mechan*).

7 Double Pyramid

In this word game, students build complete words by filling in the letters *a*, *e*, *r*, and *o*. The letters can be in any order, and some will be used more than once in some words. With the exception of the first word, the answer words are from lessons in this book.

Remember that word games are intended to be fun. Students may want to work in pairs or small groups. If they find this game confusing or frustrating, let them skip it.

Quizzes

Give a graded spelling quiz on the words in this lesson or other words that include these morphemes.

Sentences

Sentences for dictation are available at the back of this book.

Unit 5

Review of Lessons 19–21

Objectives

- **Greek Morphemes:** Review Greek morphemes studied in Unit 5.
- **Creating Words:** Select Greek morphemes to complete partial words.
- **Using Meanings:** Select Greek morphemes given their definitions and write example words.
- **Strategy:** Practice a strategy for choosing the correct form of Greek morphemes.
- **Creating Words in Sentences:** Build words to fit in context by reordering and combining morphemes.
- **Puzzle:** Review words from this unit by completing a cross-word puzzle.

You may need to review some of the patterns for adding and spelling Greek morphemes before beginning this review, depending on how well students have managed with individual lessons. Remind them that they can refer to the lessons whenever necessary.

For detailed information about patterns and strategies, refer to the lesson notes for individual lessons.

Greek Morphemes Presented in This Unit

aer	crat	logy	photo
aero	cycle	mechan	psych
ast	cyclo	meter	psycho
astro	gen	metr	techn
bio	geo	metro	techno
chron	gram	phon	tele
chrono	graph	phone	therm
cracy	log(ue)	phono	thermo

1 Creating Words

Use one of the morphemes above with each of the partial words below to create whole words. Remember to use the form ending in *o*, if there is one, when the next morpheme starts with a consonant. Write the words on the lines provided.

1. bi _bicycle_
2. etic _genetic_
3. dia _diagram_
4. demo _democracy_
5. genic _photogenic_
6. ic _graphic_
7. ical _technical_
8. ically _logically_
9. logy _phonology_
10. logist _biologist_
11. logical _psychological_
12. meter _thermometer_
13. pathic _telepathic_
14. pro _program_
15. tele _telephoto_
16. graphy _geography_

---

1 Creating Words

In this exercise, students create words by selecting and adding a Greek morpheme to the partial words given. They should add the morpheme as appropriate before or after the partial word and write the whole word on the line provided.

Be sure that students use the variant form ending in *o* when necessary.

Answers given on the replica of the student page are examples. Accept all correctly spelled words.

Additional activity:

Have students choose, or choose for them, one of the given partial words and see how many words they can build by adding Greek morphemes from the list. You may want to choose one such as *logical* or *tele* for them to be sure that many words can, in fact, be built.

2 Looking at Meanings

In the middle column below, write the Greek morphemes that have the meanings listed on the left. Use the glossary if necessary. Then write an example word for each morpheme. The first one is done for you.

Meanings	Morphemes	Example words
1. air, of aircraft	aero	aerosol
2. art, skill, science	techno	technology
3. circle, wheel	cycle	tricycle
4. distant	tele	television
5. earth	geo	geologist
6. form of government	cracy	democracy
7. word, speech	log	dialog
8. heat	thermo	thermometer
9. life	bio	biographical
10. light	photo	photographer
11. machine	mechan	mechanization
12. measure	meter	kilometer
13. mind	psycho	psychoanalysis
14. something produced	gen	carcinogen
15. sound	phone	telephone
16. star	astro	astronaut
17. time	chrono	chronicle
18. study of	logy	theology

2 Looking at Meanings

This exercise helps to reinforce the fact that morphemes have meaning and that knowing the meaning can help with spelling. For most meanings given, at least two forms of the Greek morpheme exist. Accept any form that was presented in Lessons 19–21.

Encourage students to use the glossary to check individual morphemes.

If students have trouble thinking of example words, encourage them to look back at individual lessons or to use a dictionary.

Additional activities:

Have students use some of their example words in sentences.

Have students compare their example words with one another.

3 Greek Morphemes Ending in *o*

Add the correct form of the morphemes listed on the left to each partial word below. Remember that Greek morphemes ending in *o* are usually used before morphemes beginning with consonants. The forms without the *o* are usually used before morphemes beginning with vowels. Remember to drop the silent *e* if necessary. Write the whole words on the lines provided.

Roots	Partial words	Whole words
1. aero/aer	_aer_ ial	aerial
2. astro/ast	_astro_ naut	astronaut
3. cyclo/cycle	_cycl_ ist	cyclist
4. techno/techn	_techn_ icality	technicality
5. psycho/psych	_psycho_ pathic	psychopathic
6. chrono/chron	_chrono_ logical	chronological
7. thermo/therm	_therm_ al	thermal
8. phono/phone/phon	_phon_ etic	phonetic

4 Creating Words in Sentences

Combine the morphemes under each blank to create words that make sense in the following sentences.

1. Our last ___telephone___ bill was really high.
   phone tele

2. I like animals and often watch ___zoological___ programs.
   ic log al zoo

3. Cigarette smoke is ___carcinogenic___ according to that TV ___program___.
   gen carcino ic   pro gram

4. The ___technical___ crew and the ___photographers___ were excellent.
   ic al techn   er graph s photo

5. The ___Democratic___ and Republican parties had productive ___dialogs___.
   crat Demo ic   s log dia

3 Greek Morphemes Ending in *o*

In this exercise, students add Greek morphemes to partial words, showing that they know when to use the form of Greek morphemes ending in *o*. Review the pattern with them before they begin if necessary.

Additional activity:

Have students use some of the words in sentences.

4 Creating Words in Sentences

In this exercise, students combine the morphemes below each blank to create a word that makes sense in the sentence.

Remind students to read a whole sentence before starting to combine the morphemes. After they've written words in the blanks, they should reread the sentence to be sure that it makes sense.

5 Crossword Puzzle

Use the clues below to complete this crossword puzzle. Many of the answers are words with Greek Morphemes.

B	U	R	E	A	U	C	R	A	T		B	E
I			A			H			R			U
O		P	S			R		R	A	N		L
G		H	Y	D	R	O	G	E	N		T	O
R		O				N			S			G
A	U	T	O	B	I	O	G	R	A	P	H	Y
P		O		A		L			C			
H	O	G		C	L	O	S	E	T		P	A
Y		R		K		G	A	P		A	R	E
		A	L	L		I		I	N	T	E	R
R	A	P		A		C		L		T		I
I		H		S		A		O		I		A
P	S	Y	C	H	O	L	O	G	I	C	A	L

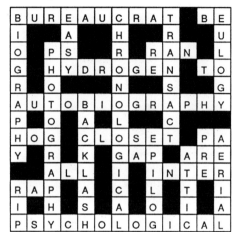

Across

1. Person who works in a government department
5. "To ____ or not to ____ . . ."
7. Abbreviation for postscript
8. Moved quickly on foot
9. Water is composed of oxygen and ____.
10. Homophone of two
11. One's own life story
13. Large pig
14. Place where clothes are kept
17. He goes with Ma.
19. An empty space
20. I am, you ____, he is
21. ____'s well that ends well.
22. Prefix meaning between or among
23. To knock on a door
24. Having to do with the mind

Down

1. Story of someone's life
2. Opposite of difficult
3. In the order that things happened in time
4. To carry out business
6. Speech given at a funeral
7. The process of taking and printing pictures
8. Prefix meaning back, again, or anew
12. A sudden backward whipping motion
15. Abbreviation for South America
16. A short section that follows the end of a book or play
17. Prefix meaning before
18. Antenna that brings a radio signal into your car
20. Room at the top of a house
23. Tear roughly

Unit 5 Review 97

5 Crossword Puzzle

Have students complete the crossword puzzle. Tell them that many of the answer words contain Greek morphemes. The clues are mostly definitions that rely on the students' general knowledge.

Encourage them to use a dictionary if they wish. You might want them to work in pairs or small groups. If necessary, give them the following list of answer words and have them check off words as they use them.

Answer words:

aerial	easy
all	epilog
are	eulogy
attic	gap
autobiography	hog
backlash	hydrogen
be	inter
biography	Pa
bureaucrat	photography
chronological	pre
closet	p.s.
psychological	rip
ran	S.A.
rap	to
re	transact

Sentences

Sentences for dictation are available at the back of this book.

Unit 5 Test

We recommend that you test your students on the words from Unit 5 before going on. The following is a suggested list of words from Unit 5. You may want to substitute other words to meet the needs of your students.

Dictate each word and use it in a simple sentence. Students should be able to spell 90 percent of these words correctly.

geographical	catalog(ue)
programming	generation
photographer	astronomical
telephone	geometrically
television	aerosol
thermometer	technician
biological	mechanization
democratic	centimeter
motorcyclist	psychological
chronic	autobiographical

Lesson 22

The Suffixes *-ic, -al, -ial, -ous,* and *-ious*

Objectives

- **Suffixes:** Learn to recognize and spell words with *-ic, -al, -ial, -ous,* and *-ious.*
- **Word Building:** Join morphemes to build whole words.
- **Combining Suffixes:** Practice combining *-ic, -al,* and *-ly.*
- **Patterns:** Learn that /chuəl/ is usually spelled *tual* at the end of words.
  Learn another pattern for spelling soft *g.*
- **Strategies:** Learn and practice strategies for spelling /shəl/ and /shəs/ at the end of words.

For general information on suffixes, refer to page 8 in the introduction.

The suffix *-ial* presents spelling problems when it follows *c* or *t* because the syllables *-cial* and *-tial* are both pronounced /shəl/. When *-ial* follows other letters, as in *material* or *trivial,* it does not present particular problems.

The suffix *-ious* also presents spelling problems when it follows *c* or *t.* The syllables *-tious* and *-cious* are both pronounced /shəs/.

Predicting the spelling of /shəl/ and /shəs/ is among the more difficult spelling problems addressed in this book. The problems parallel those in spelling the sound /shən/, addressed in Lesson 7. You may want to review that lesson before starting this one.

Lesson 22 — Suffixes

-ic, -al, -ial, -ous, and *-ious*

1 Recognizing Suffixes

In each group of words below, underline the suffixes listed on the left.

-ic — *relating to, characterized by*

med ic	log ic	athlet ic	Hispan ic
electr ic	dynam ic	magnet ic	individualist ic

-al — *relating to, characterized by*

typic al	logic al	glob al	usu al
medic al	nation al	form al	annu al
electric al	person al	comic al	gradu al

-ial — *relating to, characterized by*

triv ial	mart ial	rac ial	especi ally
mater ial	essent ial	offic ial	peren ially
memor ial	resident ial	benefic ial	confident ially

-ous — *full of, characterized by*

nerv ous	fam ous	outrage ous	gener ous
danger ous	mountain ous	advantage ous	simultane ous

-ious — *full of, characterized by*

cur ious	infect ious	prec ious	anxi ously
prev ious	nutrit ious	delic ious	feroci ously
myster ious	pretent ious	unconsc ious	conscient ious

98   Lesson 22

---

1 Recognizing Suffixes

Read aloud the representative words listed for each suffix. Read the words in a normal speaking voice without stressing the suffixes. Instruct students to underline the suffix as you read each word.

Remember that it is more important that students recognize the function of words that end with these suffixes than that they learn the complex conceptual meanings of the suffixes.

Some of these words contain more than one suffix. Ask students to identify each suffix in such words. There are three suffixes in *individualistic* and *confidentially.*

The suffixes *-al, -ic,* and *-ous* do not usually present spelling problems. All the suffixes presented in this lesson can be used to form adjectives. The suffix *-ic* sometimes denotes a noun, however. When

2 Word Building

Join the morphemes that follow to build whole words. Write the words on the lines provided. Remember to add, drop, or change letters if necessary.

1. glory + ous ___glorious___   6. bio + log + ic + al ___biological___
2. gen + er + ic ___generic___   7. hero + ic + al + ly ___heroically___
3. mystery + ous ___mysterious___   8. im + part + ial + ly ___impartially___
4. nature + al + ly ___naturally___   9. contro + verse + ial ___controversial___
5. ob + nox + ious ___obnoxious___   10. mono + tone + ous ___monotonous___

3 Combining Suffixes

Sometimes several suffixes are added to a root at once. The suffixes -ic, -al, and -ly are often combined. Add -ic, -al, and -ly to the partial words below. Write the new words on the lines provided. The first one is done for you.

1. democrat ___democratically___   5. techn ___technically___
2. pract ___practically___   6. crit ___critically___
3. mechan ___mechanically___   7. ident ___identically___
4. numer ___numerically___   8. polit ___politically___

4 Adding -al to Roots That End in tu

When the suffix -al is added to roots that end in tu, the sound of the t changes. Add -al to the following roots and write the whole words on the lines provided. Then answer the questions that follow.

1. actu ___actual___   4. mutu ___mutual___
2. factu ___factual___   5. punctu ___punctual___
3. eventu ___eventual___   6. perpetu ___perpetual___

Pronounce each word you formed. Notice how the endings sound.

When you hear /chuəl/ at the end of a word, how is it usually spelled? ___tual___

Lesson 22   99

---

such nouns are made into adjectives, the suffix -al is added (e.g., medic/medical).

Ask students to listen carefully to the representative -ial words and to listen for two different pronunciations of -ial. Point out -tial and -cial, the two different spellings of /shəl/. Explain that they will be learning strategies to help them predict the spelling of these syllables. Repeat this type of activity and explanation when you come to the words ending in -ious with

the two different spellings of the sound /shəs/.

Have students listen for the sound of du in individualistic and gradual. Exercise 4 deals with the sound change that occurs when -al is added to roots ending in tu. A similar change occurs when -al is added to roots ending in du.

Have students listen to the sound of the g in outrageous and advantageous. Exercise 6 will address retaining the silent e in words ending in -ous.

Additional activity:

Have students identify prefixes and roots that they have studied or recognize in the representative words.

2 Word Building

Students should change the y to i in numbers 1 and 3. They should drop the silent e in numbers 4, 9, and 10.

Ask students to pronounce the words in numbers 5, 8, and 9 and to notice the sounds /shəs/ and /shəl/.

3 Combining Suffixes

The suffixes -ic, -al, and -ly are often used together. This exercise gives students practice in combining these suffixes.

Knowing that -ally is a combination of -al and -ly should help students to remember the double l in these words.

Additional activity:

Have students write other forms of the root words using one or two of these suffixes, such as practical and mechanic.

4 Adding -al to Roots That End in tu

When the suffix -al is added to roots that end in tu, the sound of the t changes to /ch/. Be sure that students can hear the change in sound.

Lesson 22   107

Additional activity:

Have students add -ly to one of these words and then use both the original word and the adverb they have formed in a sentence.

5 Spelling /shəl/ and /shəs/

Several strategies are presented here to help students predict the different spellings of /shəl/ and /shəs/. All students will not retain all of the information, but they should remember that there are reasons for these spellings and that generally English is not arbitrary. Reinforce these concepts whenever appropriate.

We have found that very few of our students think of another related word to give them a clue to the spelling of a word of which they are unsure. Strategies presented for spelling /shəl/ and /shəs/ are mostly related-word strategies.

Point out that although the c or t before the suffixes -ial and -ious become an integral part of the syllable pronounced /shəl/ or /shəs/, the morphemes themselves are

---

5 Spelling /shəl/ and /shəs/

When -ial and -ious follow c or t, they create spelling problems because both -cial and -tial spell /shəl/. Likewise, both -cious and -tious spell /shəs/. The following exercises will give you some related-word strategies for deciding which spelling to use. Check your spellings in a dictionary when necessary.

Part A. If a word ends in ce and you are adding the suffixes -ial or -ious, you usually begin the final syllable with the letter c. Write a word ending in ce for each adjective below.

1. official ___office___
2. malicious ___malice___
3. vicious ___vice___
4. gracious ___grace___
5. financial ___finance___
6. commercial ___commerce___

Part B. There are exceptions to this pattern. When adding -ial or -ious to the following words, you change ce to t. Add -ial or -ious to the words below.

1. palace ___palatial___
2. essence ___essential___
3. conscience ___conscientious___
4. substance ___substantial___
5. preference ___preferential___
6. circumstance ___circumstantial___

Part C. If a word ends in t and you are adding the suffixes -ial or -ious, you usually begin the final syllable with the letter t. Add -ial or -ious to the words below. Remember to add, drop, or change letters if necessary.

1. infect ___infectious___
2. repeat ___repetitious___
3. resident ___residential___
4. confident ___confidential___
5. different ___differential___
6. consequent ___consequential___

Notice that the last four words end in -ent. Each of these words also has a form that ends in -ence. When there are related words that end in both -ent and -ence, /shəl/ is nearly always spelled -tial.

Benefit and suspect are exceptions to this strategy for words ending in t. Form the words below. Pronounce them first. Then check your spelling in a dictionary.

1. benefit + ial ___beneficial___   2. suspect + ious ___suspicious___

100   Lesson 22

-ial and -ious. This parallels the pattern with /shən/ presented in Lesson 7.

Part C: Students may need help in forming repetitious from repeat. Remind them that related words often sound different. Note also that the same pattern occurs in the word repetition.

Remind students that using a dictionary is one of the best strategies for correct spelling. They will probably need to use a dictionary to spell beneficial and

suspicious correctly. Make sure that they pronounce each word before they attempt to write it.

Additional strategy for advanced students:

Point out to students that if they can neither use a dictionary nor apply one of the strategies, there are more words ending in -tial than -cial, but almost twice as many words ending in -cious as in -tious. If they have to guess, they should guess the more common endings.

108   Lesson 22

6 Discovering Patterns: Keeping the Silent *e*

Join the morphemes below to build whole words. Write the words on the lines provided. Check your spelling in a dictionary.

1. gorge + ous ___gorgeous___   3. cour + age + ous ___courageous___

2. out + rage + ous ___outrageous___   4. ad + vant + age + ous ___advantageous___

Notice that the silent *e* is not dropped when *-ous* is added to these words. How does the silent *e* affect the way the *g* is pronounced in the words you built?

___It keeps the g soft.___

7 Another Related-Word Strategy

Some nouns ending in *-tion* can be made into adjectives by changing *-tion* to *-tious.* Change the nouns below to adjectives. Then complete the sentences by using the appropriate form of each word.

Nouns	Adjectives ending in *-ious*	Sentences
1. nutrition	nutritious	It is a ___nutritious___ cereal.
2. caution	cautious	Please proceed with ___caution___ .
3. ambition	ambitious	His ___ambition___ will take him a long way.
4. flirtation	flirtatious	She has a ___flirtatious___ manner.
5. infection	infectious	How long did the ___infection___ last?
6. superstition	superstitious	I am ___superstitious___ about black cats.

Strategy: If a noun that ends in *-tion* has a related word that ends in /shəs/, the ending will be spelled *-tious.*

Lesson 22   101

Discuss the answers students give to the question. Be sure that they understand how to use the hard and soft *c* and *g* sounds to help them to predict the spelling of words in which they occur.

7 Another Related-Word Strategy

This exercise presents a strategy for determining the spelling of /shəs/ in some words. When an adjective ending in /shəs/ has a related noun ending in *-tion,* then /shəs/ is spelled *-tious.*

Students are asked to form adjectives ending in *-tious* from nouns ending in *-tion.* They then have to show that they understand how to use nouns and adjectives in context by selecting the correct form to fit into a given sentence.

Have students pronounce the adjectives as they write them. Encourage them to check their spelling in a dictionary. Be sure that they read each sentence carefully before selecting the noun or adjective to write on the blank. They should then reread it.

Additional activity:

Have students write a sentence using the form of the word that was not used in the given sentence.

Quizzes

Give a graded spelling quiz on the words in this lesson or other words that include these suffixes.

Sentences

Sentences for dictation are available at the back of this book.

6 Discovering Patterns: Keeping the Silent *e*

This exercise draws students' attention to a few words that are exceptions to the silent *e* pattern. When *-ous* is added to words that end in *ge,* the silent *e* is retained in order to keep the soft *g* sound.

Before students begin, you may want to review these patterns: *a, o,* and *u* signal hard *c* and *g,* while *e* and *i* generally signal soft *c* and *g.* This pattern was previously reviewed in Lesson 8, Exercise 4.

As a preliminary exercise, you could have students circle the *c*'s and *g*'s in the representative words in Exercise 1 and to note whether they are soft or hard.

Make sure that students look each word up in a dictionary before writing it. Reinforce the fact that these words are exceptions to the silent *e* rule.

The Suffixes -*age*, -*ate*, -*ite*, -*able*, and -*ible*

Objectives

- **Suffixes:** Learn to recognize and spell words with -*age*, -*ate*, -*ite*, -*able*, and -*ible*.
- **Word Building:** Join morphemes to build whole words.
- **Combining Suffixes:** Practice combining -*ate* and -*ion*.
- **Strategies:** Learn and practice strategies for spelling /əbl/ at the end of words.
- **Dictionary Use:** Learn exceptions to the soft *c* and *g* strategy for spelling /əbl/.
- **Spelling the Schwa:** Practice spelling /ət/ at the end of words.
- **Recognizing Morphemes in Context:** Identify suffixes in context.

1 Recognizing Suffixes

Read aloud the representative words listed for each suffix. Read the words in a normal speaking voice without stressing the suffixes. Instruct students to underline the suffix as you read each word.

Point out the following:

Words with the suffix -*age* end with the sound /j/, but English words do not usually end with the letter *j*. That sound at the end of a word is usually spelled -*ge*. If a verb such as *block* or *use* has a related noun form ending in /j/, the final syllable is often spelled -*age*.

The pronunciation of -*ate* changes according to whether the word is a verb, an adjective, or a noun. The *a* is usually long in verbs and short in adjectives. It varies when the word is a noun that refers to a person. Have students think of sentences for the verbs and for the adjectives, noting the difference in the pronunciation of -*ate*.

Have students listen carefully to the words ending in -*ite* and see if they can identify the two pronunciations. The long or short *i* is not determined by the silent *e*. Generally, words that mean *follower or resident of* or *mineral product* are pronounced with the long *i*. *Granite* is an exception to this.

There is a schwa in the suffixes -*able* and -*ible*, which are often pronounced alike. Explain that strategies for predicting the spelling of the schwa will be presented in this lesson.

---

1 Recognizing Suffixes

In each group of words below, underline the suffixes listed on the left.

-age *action or result of an action; collection; state*

dam*age*	us*age*	post*age*	short*age*
block*age*	mess*age*	langu*age*	break*age*

-ate

cause, make;		*state, condition;*	*someone who*
evalu*ate*	activ*ate*	fortun*ate*	associ*ate*
stimul*ate*	decor*ate*	desper*ate*	candid*ate*

-ite *quality of; follower or resident of;*   *mineral product*

infin*ite*	favor*ite*	Israel*ite*	gran*ite*
defin*ite*	oppos*ite*	Mennon*ite*	graph*ite*

-able *able to, capable of, liable to*

ador*able*	toler*able*	profit*able*	flamm*able*
consider*able*	depend*able*	comfort*able*	remark*able*

-ible *able to, capable of, liable to*

terr*ible*	elig*ible*	incred*ible*	horr*ible*
poss*ible*	sens*ible*	comprehens*ible*	invis*ible*

2 Word Building

Join the morphemes that follow to build whole words. Write the words on the lines provided. Remember to change or drop letters if necessary.

1. rely + able ___reliable___
2. gradu + ate ___graduate___
3. dis + pose + able ___disposable___
4. ir + re + sist + ible ___irresistible___

When you come to *eligible,* have students point out what letter keeps the *g* soft. Point out that in general, a suffix beginning with an *i* keeps a *c* or a *g* soft at the end of a root.

Additional activities:

Have students work in small groups to generate as many words as they can that end with these suffixes.

Have students identify prefixes and roots that they recognize in the representative words.

2 Word Building

Students should change the *y* to *i* in number 1 and drop the silent *e* in numbers 3 and 9. Be sure that they drop both silent *e*'s in number 10.

Ask students why the *r* is doubled at the beginning of *irresistible.* (See Lesson 9, Exercise 3.)

3 Combining Suffixes

The suffixes *-ate* and *-ion* are often used together and are included in many dictionaries as one suffix (*-ation*). Knowing that *-ation* is usually a combination of *-ate* and *-ion* should help students to remember the *t.*

Be sure that students drop the silent *e* in numbers 2, 6, and 8 and change the *y* to *ic* in *qualification.*

Additional activity:

Review the strategy for determining the spelling of /ər/ presented in Lesson 6, Exercise 5: When a root ends in *-ate,* /ər/ is usually spelled *-or.* You may want to give students appropriate roots to which they can add *-ate* and *-or,* e.g., *decor, oper, radi.*

4 Related-Word Strategy: Words That End in /əbl/

This exercise presents a strategy for predicting the spelling of /əbl/. Review the sound of *-ation* in the words students formed in Exercise 3. Tell students to look first for words in Exercise 4 that end in *-ation.* In words related to these, /əbl/ will be spelled *-able.*

Caution students against assuming that the reverse of this strategy is reliable. It is not. Words ending in *-sion* or *-tion* may have related words that end in either *-able* or *-ible.* Remind students that they will often need to use the dictionary when spelling words that end in /əbl/.

5 Using Probabilities to Predict the Spelling of /əbl/

This exercise presents two other strategies for predicting the spelling of the schwa sound in /əbl/.

Strategy 1: Using probabilities is a useful spelling strategy, but students should not rely on it as a substitute for using a dictionary. Point out that -*able* is four times as common as -*ible*, but that many common words, such as those in Exercise 1, are spelled with -*ible*.

Strategy 2: Briefly review the sounds of hard and soft *c* and *g*. Have students tell you which vowels follow the soft sounds and which follow the hard sounds. Tell students to pronounce the whole words before writing them on the lines provided.

Be sure that students drop the silent *e* in numbers 6, 9, and 10. In many words, such as *like* and *move*, the silent *e* can be either dropped or retained. We recommend teaching the more common form, which is to drop the silent *e*. Students may find the other form in the dictionary. If so, explain to them that either spelling is acceptable, but that retaining the silent *e* is unusual unless it affects the pronunciation of a word.

---

5 Using Probabilities to Predict the Spelling of /əbl/

There are two other strategies to use in predicting the spelling of /əbl/.

Strategy 1: There are four words with the suffix -*able* for every word that has the suffix -*ible*. So if you have to guess how to spell a word that ends in /əbl/, you should probably guess -*able*.

Strategy 2: If the root ends in a soft *c* or *g*, the suffix -*ible* is probably added to keep the /s/ or /j/ sound of the root.

Add -*able* or -*ible* to the roots below using these two strategies. Remember to change or drop letters if necessary. Use a dictionary if you are unsure of a spelling.

1. like	likable	6. force	forcible
2. avail	available	7. neglig	negligible
3. move	movable	8. applic	applicable
4. break	breakable	9. invince	invincible
5. inelig	ineligible	10. reproduce	reproducible

6 Using the Dictionary

A few words don't follow Strategy 2 above. Look up the /əbl/ form of each word below and write it on the line provided. Then answer the question that follows.

1. notice	noticeable	7. trace	traceable
2. change	changeable	8. peace	peaceable
3. service	serviceable	9. charge	chargeable
4. enforce	enforceable	10. salvage	salvageable
5. replace	replaceable	11. marriage	marriageable
6. manage	manageable	12. knowledge	knowledgeable

Notice that the silent *e* is not dropped when -*able* is added to these words. What does the silent *e* do in these words?

It keeps the *c* or *g* soft.

104   Lesson 23

---

6 Using the Dictionary

Words in which the silent *e* is retained before -*able* is added are presented in this exercise. Have students look the words up one by one, write them on the lines provided, and then explain why the silent *e* is retained.

The most common words that end in -*eable* are included in this exercise.

Explain to students that after a soft *c* or *g*, /əbl/ is spelled -*ible* or -*eable*. Other words that take this spelling are *challengeable*, *unpronounceable*, and other negative forms of the given words, such as *unmanageable*. Students may need to memorize them.

Additional activity:

Have students use any of the words from Exercises 3–6 in sentences.

7 ## The Suffixes -ate and -ite

Unless the suffixes -ate and -ite are accented, they sound alike.

Remind students that even the best spellers sometimes need to check the spelling of a schwa in a dictionary.

You may want to review the suffixes they have studied so far that start with the schwa sound: /ər/ and /əry/ (Lesson 6); /ənt/, /əns/, and /ənsē/ (Lesson 8); and /əj/, /ət/, and /əbl/ (this lesson).

8 ## Recognizing Suffixes in Context

Tell students to underline in the sentences all of the suffixes in the given list and to read the sentences before they start underlining.

Additional activities:

Have students circle any prefixes and roots that they recognize in these sentences.

This kind of activity can be done using any printed material, such as newspapers, magazines, or ads.

Additional Exercises to Practice Spelling /əbl/

Dictation: Dictate the following words, which students should write under the column headings -able and -ible. Give students adequate time to think about how to spell the suffix. You may want to add other words.

1. answerable   5. adaptable
2. deductible   6. reducible
3. horrible   7. reversible
4. suitable   8. navigable

Proofreading: Consider designing a proofreading exercise using words that end in /əbl/. Write some of the words from this lesson spelled both ways, (horrable–horrible). Then ask students to underline the correct one. They should verify their choice in a dictionary and then write the word correctly.

Quizzes

Give a graded spelling quiz on the words in this lesson or other words that include these suffixes.

Sentences

Sentences for dictation are available at the back of this book.

Lesson 24

The Suffixes *-ist, -ism, -ive, -ize,* and *-ine*

Objectives

- **Suffixes:** Learn to recognize and spell words with *-ist, -ism, -ive, -ize,* and *-ine.*
- **Word Building:** Join morphemes to build whole words.
- **Combining Suffixes:** Practice combining *-ize, -ate,* and *-ion.*
- **Creating and Using Words:** Create words and use them in context.
- **Completing Words in Sentences:** Build words to fit in context by adding suffixes to given roots.
- **Word Game:** Play a game to build words.

1 Recognizing Suffixes

Read aloud the representative words listed for each suffix. Read the words in a normal speaking voice without stressing the suffixes. Instruct students to underline the suffix as you read each word.

Point out the following:

It is more important to recognize the function of words that end with these suffixes than to learn the complex conceptual meanings of the suffixes.

When you come to *cooperative* and *finalize,* ask students to identify both suffixes.

Lesson 24

Suffixes
-ist, -ism, -ive, -ize, and *-ine*

1 Recognizing Suffixes
In each group of words below, underline the suffixes listed on the left.

-ist   *someone who*

artist	racist	tourist	optimist
scientist	realist	motorist	idealistic

-ism   *act, condition, doctrine, or practice of*

racism	capitalism	hypnotism	Judaism
realism	patriotism	alcoholism	communism

-ive   *performing or tending toward an action*

addictive	expensive	festive	selective
distinctive	constructive	cooperative	progressive

-ize   *cause to be or become*

civilize	finalize	terrorize	equalize
criticize	organize	apologize	mechanize

-ine   *of, pertaining to;*   *chemical substance*

famine	routine	chlorine	
feminine	medicine	antihistamine	

2 Word Building
Join the morphemes that follow to build whole words. Write the words on the lines provided. Remember to drop the silent *e* if necessary.

1. div + ine ___divine___
2. genu + ine ___genuine___
3. pessim + ist ___pessimist___
4. familiar + ize ___familiarize___

106   Lesson 24

Suffixes beginning with *i* signal a soft *c* or *g* at the end of a root, as in *racist, racism, criticize, apologize,* and *medicine.* Contrast the hard *c* at the end of *critic* and *medic.*

In the suffix *-ism,* /z/ is spelled *s.* This can cause spelling problems, so be sure to draw students' attention to it. Contrast the suffix *-ize,* in which /z/ is spelled *z.*

In spite of the silent *e* at the end of the suffix, adjectives with the suffix *-ive* are pronounced with a short *i* or even with a schwa.

Words ending in *-ive* are usually adjectives and words ending in *-ize* are usually verbs. You may want to have students use some of each kind of word in sentences.

Words ending in *-ine* are pronounced with either a short *i* or a long *e.* Ask students to listen for the two pronunciations in the words as you read them. Words meaning *a chemical substance* are usually pronounced with a

5. art + ist + ic ___artistic___ 8. altern + ate + ive ___alternative___

6. penal + ize ___penalize___ 9. imagin + ate + ive ___imaginative___

7. social + ism ___socialism___ 10. in + con + clus + ive ___inconclusive___

3 Combining Suffixes

Sometimes several suffixes are added to a root at once. The suffixes *-ize, -ate,* and *-ion* are often combined. Add *-ize, -ate,* and *-ion* to the roots below. Write the new words on the lines provided. Remember to add, drop, or change letters if necessary.

1. civil ___civilization___ 6. central ___centralization___

2. final ___finalization___ 7. modern ___modernization___

3. organ ___organization___ 8. dramat ___dramatization___

4. brutal ___brutalization___ 9. hospital ___hospitalization___

5. fertile ___fertilization___ 10. alphabet ___alphabetization___

4 Creating and Using Words

For each root listed below, create two different words by adding two of the following suffixes. Then use each word you form in a phrase or short sentence.

-ist　　*-ism*　　*-ize*

New words	Phrases or sentences
1. ideal ___idealism___	_____
___idealize___	_____
2. critic ___criticize___	_____
___criticism___	_____
3. optim ___optimist___	_____
___optimism___	_____

long *e,* as in *chlorine.* It is harder to remember the silent *e* when *-ine* is pronounced with a short *i.*

Additional activities:

Have students work in small groups to generate as many words as they can that end with these suffixes.

Ask students to identify roots in Exercise 1 to which more than one of these suffixes can be added. If students learn to relate words to one another in this way, they will see that the spelling of every word does not have to be learned in isolation.

2 Word Building

Students should pay special attention to the sound of the *i* at the beginning of the suffixes in all the words. They should drop the silent *e* in numbers 8 and 9.

3 Combining Suffixes

In this exercise, the suffix *-ize* is added before the combination *-ation.* These suffixes are often used together and are included in some dictionaries as one suffix (*-ization*). This exercise gives practice in combining these suffixes. Practice in combining the suffixes *-ate* and *-ion* was given in Lesson 23, Exercise 3.

Knowing that the ending *-ization* is a combination of three suffixes they have studied should help students to spell it correctly.

Be sure that students drop the silent *e* from *fertile* and that they drop the silent *e* from *-ize* and *-ate* in each word.

Point out to students that this ending indicates a noun.

Additional activities:

Have students make each of the root words into a verb by adding the suffix *-ize.*

Have them use the verb and noun form of some of the words (e.g., *hospitalize* and *hospitalization*) in sentences.

4 Creating and Using Words

Encourage students to pronounce their words before writing them.

The roots *ideal* and *optim* can have any of the three suffixes added to build different words. The answers on the replica of the student page are examples. Accept all correctly spelled words.

5 Completing Words in Sentences

Add one of the following suffixes to the root listed under each blank below and write the completed word in the blank. The word must make sense in the sentence. Use a dictionary if necessary.

-ist   -ism   -ive   -ize   -ine

1. Her grandson is an __active__ and __aggressive__ child.
   act   aggress

2. I __recognize__ that the treatment will be __expensive__ .
     recogn   expens

3. The __scientist__ was angry about the __criticism__ of her work.
       scient   critic

4. The new __tourist__ attraction gave a boost to __tourism__ in the area.
        tour   tour

5. The doctor will __examine__ her and prescribe some __medicine__ for her.
       exam   medic

6 Missing Morphemes

One of the suffixes from this lesson can be added to every root in each group below. Fill in the missing suffixes to make whole words. Use a different suffix for each group.

1. national__ist__   solo__ist__   cycl__ist__   pessim__ist__   extrem__ist__

2. pessim__ism__   hero__ism__   national__ism__   extrem__ism__   vandal__ism__

3. furt__ive__   creat__ive__   attent__ive__   intens__ive__   effect__ive__

4. vandal__ize__   national__ize__   hospital__ize__   categor__ize__   glamor__ize__

5 Completing Words in Sentences

Remind students to read a whole sentence first to decide which suffix to use. After they've written words in the blanks, they should reread the sentence to be sure that it makes sense.

The suffixes can be added without any spelling changes at the end of the roots.

6 Missing Morphemes

In this word game, one of the suffixes from Lesson 24 is missing from each group of roots. A different suffix is missing from each group. Only one suffix can be used with all of the roots in each group.

Remember that word games are intended to be fun. Students may want to work in pairs or small groups. If they find this game confusing or frustrating, let them skip it.

Quizzes

Give a graded spelling quiz on the words in this lesson or other words that include these suffixes.

Sentences

Sentences for dictation are available at the back of this book.

Lesson 25

The Suffixes *-ure, -y, -ty,* and *-ice*

Objectives

- **Suffixes:** Learn to recognize and spell words with *-ure, -y, -ty,* and *-ice.*
- **Word Building:** Join morphemes to build whole words.
- **Changing Functions:** Add suffixes to roots to create verbs and nouns.
- **Composing Sentences:** Write original sentences using selected words.
- **Patterns:** Learn to spell /chər/ and /zhər/ at the end of words.
- **Recognizing Morphemes in Context:** Identify suffixes in context.
- **Taking Words Apart:** Divide words into morphemes.
- **Creating and Using Adjectives:** Create adjectives and use them in context.

1 Recognizing Suffixes

Read aloud the representative words listed for each suffix. Read the words in a normal speaking voice without stressing the suffixes. Instruct students to underline the suffix as you read each word.

When you come to *availability, festivity, maturity,* and *inactivity,* ask students to identify both suffixes. An extra *i* has been added in *availability.* Without it, the word would be very hard to pronounce.

Ask students to listen carefully to the pronunciation of the final syllable in words like *measure* and *nature.* An *s* preceding the suffix *-ure* is usually pronounced /zh/, and a *t* is usually pronounced /ch/. This is addressed in Exercise 4.

Point out the following:

Some nouns become adjectives when the suffix *-y* is added. The *-y* is pronounced /ē/.

The *i* in the suffix *-ice* is generally pronounced with a short *i.* When *-ice* is part of the root, however, there are other pronunciations. In *advice, suffice,* and *twice,* for example, the *i* is long. In *police* it is pronounced as a long *e.*

Malicious ends in the /shəs/ sound studied in Lesson 22.

Additional activities:

Have students work in small groups to generate as many words as they can that end with these suffixes.

Have students identify prefixes and roots that they have studied or recognize in the representative words.

Lesson 25 — Suffixes
-ure, -y, -ty, and *-ice*

1 Recognizing Suffixes
In each group of words below, underline the suffixes listed on the left.

-ure	*act, process; function or body performing a function*			
	measure	nature	adventure	failure
	exposure	picture	agriculture	legislature

-y	*characterized by*			
	shiny	dirty	funny	agony
	cloudy	rainy	healthy	remedy

-ty, -ity	*state or quality of*			
	loyalty	certainty	quality	maturity
	honesty	availability	festivity	inactivity

-ice	*state or quality of*			
	justice	notice	novice	malice
	service	prejudice	practice	malicious

2 Word Building
Join the morphemes that follow to build whole words. Write the words on the lines provided. Remember to add, drop, or change letters if necessary.

1. thirst + y ___thirsty___
2. fidel + ity ___fidelity___
3. cult + ure ___culture___
4. fract + ure ___fracture___
5. difficul + ty ___difficulty___
6. un + health + y ___unhealthy___
7. im + moral + ity ___immorality___
8. serv + ice + able ___serviceable___
9. mal + pract + ice ___malpractice___
10. dis + please + ure ___displeasure___

Lesson 25   109

Many suffixes change the way words are used. Adding -ize to words can change them to verbs. The suffixes -y or -ity can change words to nouns. For each root below, write a verb ending in -ize and a noun ending in -y or -ity. Remember to drop the silent e if necessary. The first one is done for you.

Roots	Verbs ending in -ize	Nouns ending in -y or -ity
1. agon	agonize	agony
2. fertile	fertilize	fertility
3. apolog	apologize	apology
4. mobile	mobilize	mobility
5. special	specialize	speciality
6. harmon	harmonize	harmony
7. national	nationalize	nationality
8. personal	personalize	personality

Use one pair of words that you formed in original sentences.

_____

_____

4 **Adding -ure to Roots That End in s or t**

When the suffix -ure follows s or t, the sounds of the s and t change. Add -ure to the following roots and write the whole words on the lines provided. Then pronounce each whole word and notice the sound of the ending.

1. nat	nature		5. treas	treasure
2. fut	future		6. depart	departure
3. leis	leisure		7. pleas	pleasure
4. meas	measure		8. struct	structure

110   Lesson 25

2 **Word Building**

Have students pay attention to the sound of the last syllable in numbers 3, 4, and 10. They should also proofread their work.

Be sure that students do not drop the silent e in *serviceable*. Ask them how the word would be pronounced if they did. Review Lesson 23, Exercise 6 if necessary.

Students should drop the silent e in number 10.

3 **Changing the Function of Words**

This exercise reinforces the concept that suffixes change the functions of root words.

First, students are asked to form verbs by adding the suffix *-ize* to the given roots. Then they form nouns by adding the suffixes *-y* or *-ity* to the same roots. Finally, they are required to use one pair of the words (i.e., the verb and the noun) in original sentences.

Accept either *speciality* or *specialty* for number 5.

Additional activity:

Have students use all of the words they formed here in sentences. Advanced students may enjoy trying to use a pair of words in a single sentence.

4 **Adding -ure to Roots That End in s or t**

When the suffix *-ure* is added to roots that end in s or t, the sound of the final consonant changes. This exercise focuses on syllables with the suffix *-ure* that are pronounced /chər/ and /zhər/. Be sure the students can hear these sounds.

Remind students that the pronunciation of the *t* in *tual* is similar. Review Lesson 22, Exercise 4 if appropriate.

5 Alternative Spellings for /chər/

Pronounce the words below and notice how the endings sound.

picture   pitcher

1. What suffix was added to the root *pict?*   <u>ure</u>

2. What suffix was added to the root *pitch?*   <u>er</u>

When *-ure* is added to a root that ends in *t,* it sounds the same as when *-er* is added to a word that ends in *ch.* Remove the suffixes from the words below and write the roots on the lines provided.

1. catcher   <u>catch</u>   5. feature   <u>feat</u>

2. teacher   <u>teach</u>   6. creature   <u>creat</u>

3. searcher   <u>search</u>   7. miniature   <u>miniat</u>

4. stretcher   <u>stretch</u>   8. manufacture   <u>manufact</u>

Look at the roots and fill in the blanks in the pattern below.

Pattern: For words that end in /chər/, if the root is a whole word that ends in *-ch,* the suffix will be spelled <u>er</u>.

When the root is not a whole word, the suffix will be spelled <u>ure</u>.

6 Recognizing Suffixes in Context

Underline the following suffixes in the sentences below.

-ure   -y   -ty   -ity   -ice

1. My daughter's room is dusty and messy.
2. He practiced those gestures until they looked natural.
3. She has the ability to solve a problem of this complexity.
4. That is a dangerous activity, and failure could result in their death.
5. Do you know the pledge that ends "with liberty and justice for all"?
6. The vice president's signature will grant the authority to order that service.

5 Alternative Spellings for /chər/

This exercise builds on Exercise 4. There is more than one group of letters that is pronounced /chər/ at the end of a word.

In this exercise, students practice identifying roots and using the root as a clue to the spelling of the ending. Be sure students understand that the key is recognizing whether or not the root is a word that ends in *ch.*

6 Recognizing Suffixes in Context

Instruct students to underline in the sentences all of the suffixes in the given list and to read the sentences before they start underlining.

Be sure that students identify the suffixes even when they are not at the end of a word, e.g., prac*tic*ed or nat*ur*al.

Additional activities:

Have students circle any prefixes or roots that they recognize in these sentences.

Have them develop exercises of this sort for one another to do.

This kind of activity can be done using any printed material, such as newspapers, magazines, or ads.

7 Taking Words Apart

Divide the following words into morphemes and write each one under the correct heading.

	Prefixes	Roots	Suffixes
1. gesture		gest	ure
2. maturity		mat	ure ity
3. humanity		human	ity
4. exposure	ex	pose	ure
5. unworthy	un	worth	y
6. apprentice	ap/ad	prent	ice

8 Creating and Using Adjectives

Adding the suffix -y can change a noun to an adjective. Choose five of the following nouns and change them to adjectives by adding -y. Note that the suffix -y is considered a vowel, so the silent e is dropped when the suffix -y is added. Then use each adjective in an original phrase or sentence. One is done for you.

dirt	fish	sleep	taste	storm
grass	greed	shade	hand	wealth

Adjectives	Phrases or sentences
1. dirty	a very dirty car
2. greedy	
3. shady	
4. wealthy	
5. grassy	
6. sleepy	

112   Lesson 25

7 Taking Words Apart

Remind students that they should write the original form of a root or suffix. They should restore the silent e in *mat ure ity* and *ex pose ure.*

Students may write either the original form of the prefix or the form that is used in the word. Ask them why there is a double p at the beginning of *apprentice.* (See Lesson 9, Exercise 3.)

Students who have difficulty should first identify the suffixes presented in this lesson.

Additional activity:

Students can practice taking apart the words they find in any printed material, such as newspapers, magazines, or ads.

8 Creating and Using Adjectives

In this exercise, students add the suffix -y to make adjectives from five nouns that they choose from the list given. Then they use the adjectives in phrases or short sentences.

Remember that errors in words not yet studied should not be treated negatively. Help students to correct misspellings by using what they already know.

The answers on the replica of the student page are examples. Accept all correctly spelled words. If students choose the nouns *shade* or *taste,* be sure that they drop the silent e before adding the suffix.

Additional activity:

Have students use pairs of words— nouns and adjectives—in sentences.

Additional Exercise

If your students need extra practice in spelling words ending with the sounds /chər/ and /zhər/, dictate the following words and have students write them under the column headings *ture, sure,* and *cher.*

1. fixture	7. exposure
2. preacher	8. structure
3. denture	9. gesture
4. pleasure	10. treasure
5. archer	11. butcher
6. manufacture	12. adventure

Quizzes

Give a graded spelling quiz on the words in this lesson or other words that include these suffixes.

Sentences

Sentences for dictation are available at the back of this book.

Unit 6

Review of Lessons 22–25

Objectives

- **Suffixes:** Review suffixes studied in Unit 6.
- **Taking Words Apart:** Divide words into morphemes.
- **Strategies:** Review and practice strategies for spelling words ending in /əbl/, /shəl/, and /shəs/.
- **Changing Meanings:** Add suffixes to roots to change the meaning of words.
- **Composing Sentences:** Write original sentences using selected words.
- **Word Building:** Select and combine morphemes to build at least 15 words.
- **Word Game:** Play a game to build words.

You may need to review some of the patterns for adding and spelling suffixes before beginning this review, depending on how well students have managed with individual lessons. Remind them that they can refer to the lessons whenever necessary.

For detailed information about patterns and strategies, refer to the lesson notes for individual lessons.

1 Taking Words Apart

Encourage students to refer to the glossary or a dictionary to check any individual morphemes if necessary. The number of blanks will also guide them in dividing the words.

Remind students that they should write the original form of a root or suffix. They should restore the silent *e*'s in numbers 4 (in *-ize* and *-ate*) and 8. If a word contains a variant form of a prefix, students may write either the original form of the prefix or the form that is used in the word.

Ask students why the silent *e* is not dropped in *damageable*.

Students who have difficulty should first identify the suffixes presented in this unit.

Note whether students divide the multiple suffixes in numbers 1, 4–6, and 8–10. Review those morphemes if necessary.

Additional activity:

Students can practice taking apart the words they find in any printed material, such as newspapers, magazines, or ads.

Suffixes Presented in This Unit

-able	-ible	-ism	-ize
-age	-ic	-ist	-ous
-al	-ice	-ite	-ty
-ate	-ine	-ity	-ure
-ial	-ious	-ive	-y

1 Taking Words Apart

Divide the following words into morphemes and write one on each blank.

1. logically — log — ic — al — ly
2. antisocial — anti — soc — ial
3. elaborate — e/ex — labor — ate
4. realization — real — ize — ate — ion
5. nationalism — nat — ion — al — ism
6. damageable — dam — age — able
7. constructive — con — struct — ive
8. accumulation — ac/ad — cumul — ate — ion
9. subconsciously — sub — consci — ous — ly
10. unmentionable — un — ment — ion — able

Unit 6 Review   113

2 **Reviewing and Practicing Strategies for Spelling /əbl/**

Review any part of Lesson 23 before students begin this exercise if necessary.

Part A: Students are required to complete sentences stating the strategies and patterns presented in Lesson 23.

Part B: Students add *-able* or *-ible* to 12 roots and write the words under the appropriate heading. The fact that many more words end in *-able* than in *-ible* is reinforced through the format of this exercise.

Note that the silent *e* should be dropped from *believe* and *excuse*.

Make sure that students pay special attention to the roots *elig, force,* and *knowledge,* all of which

have a soft *c* or *g* after the suffix is added.

Remind students that they should check any spelling of which they are unsure in a dictionary.

3 **Reviewing and Practicing Strategies for Spelling /shəl/ and /shəs/**

Review any part of Lesson 22 before students begin this exercise if necessary.

Part A: Students complete sentences stating the strategies and patterns presented in Lesson 22.

If students write *-ive* as the answer to question 4, point out that it is not incorrect (e.g., *cooperation/cooperative*), but that this exercise is dealing strictly with syllables pronounced /shəl/ and /shəs/.

Part B. Add *-ial* or *-ious* to each of the words below. Say the word aloud before you write it. Remember to add, drop, or change letters if necessary.

1. race _____racial_____
2. part _____partial_____
3. grace _____gracious_____
4. infect _____infectious_____
5. malice _____malicious_____
6. caution _____cautious_____
7. artifice _____artificial_____
8. residence _____residential_____
9. province _____provincial_____
10. confident _____confidential_____
11. suspicion _____suspicious_____
12. ambition _____ambitious_____

4 Changing the Meaning of Words

Add the suffixes *-ism*, *-ist,* and *-ize* to the roots below and write the words in the correct columns.

	-ism	-ist	-ize
1. real	realism	realist	realize
2. terror	terrorism	terrorist	terrorize
3. social	socialism	socialist	socialize
4. plagiar	plagiarism	plagiarist	plagiarize
5. national	nationalism	nationalist	nationalize

Notice how adding different suffixes changes the meaning of a word. Now use all three forms of two of the above roots in original sentences.

_____

_____

_____

_____

_____

_____

Unit 6 Review   115

Part B: Students use the information from Part A to add the suffixes *-ial* or *-ious* to the given words. Be sure that students pronounce the new words before writing them. Note that the silent *e* should be dropped in numbers 1, 3, 5, 7, and 9 and that the suffix *-ion* is changed to *-ious* in numbers 6, 11, and 12.

4 Changing the Meaning of Words

Review any part of Lesson 24 before students begin this exercise if necessary.

In this exercise, students change the meaning and function of given roots by adding the suffixes *-ism*, *-ist,* and *-ize.*

Make sure that students proofread the words they write.

You may want to discuss how adding these suffixes affects the function of the words and to review the appropriate grammatical terms. Students can find these terms defined on page 5 of the student text.

Students are also asked to use all three forms of two of the given word roots in original sentences. Advanced students may enjoy trying to use all three forms in a single sentence. Encourage your students to be increasingly ambitious in their own writing as their spelling skills develop. If they need more room, encourage them to use their notebooks. Make sure that they proofread their sentences.

Help students to correct misspellings by using what they already know. We feel that it is acceptable for students to make phonetically correct misspellings in words they have not yet studied. If you choose to correct them, be supportive of their attempts.

Using words in context is an important additional activity that should be included at any appropriate opportunity.

5 Challenge Word Building

Emphasize that students can use as few or as many morphemes as needed for a particular word. For instance, the roots *fine* and *pose* function as whole words. More than one prefix or suffix can be added to build some of the words.

Encourage students to use a dictionary if necessary. Have them check to be sure that they have added, dropped, or changed letters when necessary.

than one word may be formed for some of the items. Accept any correctly spelled word, even if it does not contain a suffix from Unit 6.

5 Challenge Word Building

On a separate piece of paper, combine the morphemes below to build at least 15 words. Use as few or as many parts as you need for each word. Use a dictionary if you are unsure of a word.

Prefixes	Roots	Suffixes
af-	fect	-able
de-	fine	-ate
dis-	pose	-ion
in-		-ite
re-		-ity
		-ive

6 Missing Letters

A pair of letters has been omitted twice from each word below. Fill in the missing letters to make whole words. All of the words contain suffixes from Unit 6.

1. m __o__ __u__ ntain __o__ __u__ s
2. supers __t__ __i__ t __i__ on
3. op __t__ __i__ mis __t__ __i__ c
4. __o__ __u__ trage __o__ __u__ s
5. to __l__ __e__ rab __l__ __e__
6. m __o__ __n__ ot __o__ __n__ ous

7. c __o__ __u__ rage __o__ __u__ s
8. __i__ __n__ v __i__ __n__ cible
9. p __e__ __a__ c __e__ __a__ ble
10. __p__ __a__ rtici __p__ __a__ tion
11. fem __i__ __n__ __i__ __n__ e
12. ava __i__ __l__ ab __i__ __l__ ity

Remember that word games are intended to be fun. Students may want to work in pairs or small groups. If they find this game confusing or frustrating, let them skip it.

Sentences

Sentences for dictation are available at the back of this book.

Unit 6 Test

We recommend that you test your students on the words from Unit 6 before going on. The following is a suggested list of words from Unit 6. You may want to substitute other words to meet the needs of your students.

Dictate each word and use it in a simple sentence. Students should be able to spell 90 percent of these words correctly.

electrician	remarkably
gradually	impossible
essential	optimistic
official	racism
material	disorganized
delicious	finalization
infectious	medicine
advantageous	routinely
message	immeasurable
decorative	adventurous
reactive	practice
fortunately	dishonesty
definitely	police
dependable	immaturity
terrible	funnily

Some responses are listed here. There are others. Accept all correctly spelled words.

affect	definitive
affection	deposable
affectionate	depose
affine	deposition
affinity	disposable
defect	dispose
defection	disposition
defective	fine
definable	finite
define	infect
definite ·	infection
definition	infective

infinite	refect
infinity	refection
pose	refinable
position	refine
positive	repose

6 Missing Letters

In this word game, students fill in pairs of letters in the same order to build complete words. In each word, the pair of letters is missing twice. Each complete word contains a suffix from Unit 6. More

Lesson 26

The Prefixes *ob-*, *anti-*, *contra-*, and *inter-*

Objectives

- **Prefixes:** Learn to recognize and spell words with *ob-*, *anti-*, *contra-*, and *inter-*.
- **Word Building:** Join morphemes to build whole words.
- **Using Meanings:** Select prefixes based on the definitions of words to be formed. Match words to definitions based on the meaning of prefixes.
- **Assimilative Prefixes:** Learn and practice spelling the assimilative forms of *ob-*.
- **Building and Using Words:** Build new words by removing and replacing prefixes. Use the new words in context.

For general information on prefixes, refer to page 8 in the introduction.

Lesson 26 — Prefixes

ob-, anti-, contra-, and *inter-*

1 Recognizing Prefixes

In each group of words below, underline the prefixes listed on the left.

ob, oc, of, op- — **toward; against**

| obtain | obvious | occur | offensive |
| observe | obstruction | occupy | opposite |

anti- — **against, opposing**

| antibiotic | antiseptic | antisocial | antifreeze |

contra- — **against**

| contrast | contradiction | contravene | contraband |

inter- — **between, among**

| interrupt | intervention | interview | international |

2 Word Building

Join the morphemes that follow to build whole words. Write the words on the lines provided. Remember to drop the silent *e* if necessary.

1. anti + trust __antitrust__
2. inter + fere __interfere__
3. of + fer + ing __offering__
4. ob + lige + ed __obliged__
5. inter + rog + ate __interrogate__
6. inter + miss + ion __intermission__
7. anti + climac + tic __anticlimactic__
8. oc + cas + ion + al __occasional__
9. contra + cept + ion __contraception__
10. un + ob + trus + ive __unobtrusive__

Lesson 26   117

---

1 Recognizing Prefixes

Read aloud the representative words listed for each prefix. Read the words in a normal speaking voice without stressing the prefixes. Instruct students to underline the prefix as you read each word.

Tell students that a few prefixes, such as *ob-*, change in predictable ways. Later in this lesson they will learn how to predict these changes.

Ask students to identify the different forms of *ob-* in the representative words. Point out that the pronunciation of this prefix and its variants changes according to the root that follows, e.g., *obtain* and *obvious; occur* and *occupy*.

Additional activities:

Have students work in small groups to generate as many words as they can that start with these prefixes. You may want to have them use a dictionary to find additional words.

Have students identify roots and suffixes that they have studied or recognize in the representative words.

2 Word Building

Students should drop the silent *e* in number 4.

Lesson 26   **125**

3 Looking at Meanings: *inter-, intra-,* and *intro-; anti-* and *ante-*

Knowing the meanings of *inter-* and *anti-* is important for correct spelling, as there are other prefixes that sound similar but are spelled differently. Encourage students to use a dictionary to verify the meaning of a word whenever necessary.

Part A: Two additional prefixes, *intra-* and *intro-* are introduced. They are not included in Exercise 1 because they are used in few words. The word *introduce,* however, is so common that you should make sure students can spell it correctly. If students make errors in selecting which prefix to add to which partial word, go over the meanings with them.

Additional activities:

Once students have written the word suggested by the definition and partial word given, have them underline the portion of the definition that led them to choose a certain prefix.

Have students use the words in sentences.

Part B: The additional prefix *ante-* is introduced. Students are required to match one of the words listed at the beginning of the exercise to the definitions given. If students make errors in matching words with definitions, go over the meanings with them.

Additional activities:

Once students have written the word suggested by the definition, have them underline the portion of the definition that relates to the prefix in the word they chose.

Have students use the words in sentences.

4 Recognizing Patterns: More Prefixes That Change

A few prefixes change when added to roots that begin with certain letters. Remember that these changes often account for double consonants near the beginning of words.

The Prefix *ob-*

Prefix	Changes to	Before	Examples
ob-	oc-	c	ob + casion = occasion
ob-	of-	f	ob + fend = offend
ob-	op-	p	ob + portunity = opportunity

Join the morphemes below, changing *ob-* if necessary.

1. ob + fer ____offer____
2. ob + ponent ____opponent____
3. ob + jection ____objection____
4. ob + fensive ____offensive____
5. ob + ligatory ____obligatory____
6. ob + position ____opposition____
7. ob + casional ____occasional____
8. ob + currence ____occurrence____

5 Changing Prefixes

Remove a prefix from each of the words below and replace it with one of the following prefixes. Then use the word you have created in a phrase or short sentence.

ob-   of-   op-   contra-   inter-

	New words	Phrases or sentences
1. *re*ject	object	_____
2. *pre*dict	contradict	_____
3. *re*marry	intermarry	_____
4. *de*fensive	offensive	_____
5. *sup*position	opposition	_____

4 Recognizing Patterns: More Prefixes That Change

In this exercise, students study another prefix that undergoes assimilative changes. You may want to review the ones that were included in Lessons 9 and 10. The same kinds of changes occur here as with *ad-, in-, con-, dis-,* and *ex-*. Remind students that the changes are regular and occur each time *ob-* comes before certain letters.

Only the more common assimilative forms are presented here.

Students should study the chart carefully before attempting to join the morphemes that follow them. You may want students to underline double consonants once they have built the words.

Students will not need to change the prefix in numbers 3 or 5.

Additional activities:

Have students use some of the words they build in original sentences.

Have students try to find words starting with *obc-, obf-,* or *obp-* in a dictionary. They will find few or none, depending on the dictionary they use.

5 Changing Prefixes

By removing one prefix and replacing it with another, students are using morphemes as practical building blocks of words. Remind students to use a dictionary if they are uncertain of a word.

The answers on the replica of the student page are examples. Accept any answer that forms a correctly spelled word.

When students are writing phrases and sentences, allow them to use any form of the word they have created.

Additional activity:

Have students use the original words in phrases or sentences.

Quizzes

Give a graded spelling quiz on the words in this lesson or other words that include these prefixes.

Sentences

Sentences for dictation are available at the back of this book.

Lesson 27

The Prefixes *auto-*, *sub-*, *super-*, and *trans-*

Objectives

- **Prefixes:** Learn to recognize and spell words with *auto-*, *sub-*, *super-*, and *trans-*.
- **Word Building:** Join morphemes to build whole words.
- **Creating and Using Words:** Create words with given prefixes and use the words in context.
- **Assimilative Prefixes:** Learn and practice spelling the assimilative forms of *sub-*.
- **Composing Sentences:** Write original sentences using selected words.
- **Using Meanings:** Select prefixes based on the definitions of words to be formed.
- **Recognizing Morphemes in Context:** Identify prefixes in context.

Lesson 27 — Prefixes

auto-, *sub-*, *super-*, and *trans-*

1 Recognizing Prefixes

In each group of words below, underline the prefixes listed on the left.

auto-, aut-	*self*		
	autograph	automation	autism
	automobile	autobiography	autopsy

sub-, sup-, suc-, suf-	*under; lesser*			
	submit	subway	support	success
	substandard	subconscious	supposed	suffering

super-, sur-	*superior, above; additional*		
	supervisor	superior	survivor
	supermarket	superficial	surcharge

trans-	*across*		
	transfer	transition	translator
	transportation	transatlantic	transaction

2 Word Building

Join the morphemes that follow to build whole words. Write the words on the lines provided. Remember to add, drop, or change letters if necessary.

1. auto + crat ___autocrat___
2. sup + ply + er ___supplier___
3. re + sur + face ___resurface___
4. sub + mar + ine ___submarine___
5. sub + norm + al ___subnormal___
6. super + flu + ous ___superfluous___
7. super + stit + ion ___superstition___
8. trans + fuse + ion ___transfusion___
9. auto + nom + ous ___autonomous___
10. sub + di + vise + ion ___subdivision___

120 Lesson 27

---

1 Recognizing Prefixes

Read aloud the representative words listed for each prefix. Read the words in a normal speaking voice without stressing the prefixes. Instruct students to underline the prefix as you read each word.

Point out the prefixes that have more than one meaning.

The prefix *auto-* comes from Greek. See if students can guess its origin. Have students identify the words that include Greek roots they have studied (*autograph* and *autobiography*). As with other Greek morphemes, the form that ends in *o* is used before morphemes that begin with a consonant.

Some prefixes have assimilative forms. When you come to *sub-*, ask students to identify the different forms in the representative words. Ask students why there is a double consonant near the beginning of words with the prefixes *sup-*, *suc-*, and *suf-*.

Point out that the pronunciation of *super-* changes in the word *superior*.

Additional activities:

Have students work in small groups to generate as many words as they can that start with these prefixes. You may want to have them use a dictionary to find additional words.

Have students identify roots and suffixes that they have studied or recognize in the representative words.

3 Using the Dictionary

Create a whole word starting with each prefix below. Do not use words included in Exercises 1 or 2. Use a dictionary if necessary. Then write a short phrase or sentence using your word.

	Words	Phrases or sentences
1. auto-	autonomy	_____
2. sub-	substitute	_____
3. super-	superimpose	_____
4. trans-	transcription	_____

4 Recognizing Patterns: More Prefixes That Change

A few prefixes change when added to roots that begin with certain letters. Remember that these changes often account for double consonants near the beginning of words.

The Prefix sub-

Prefix	Changes to	Before	Examples
sub-	suc-	c	sub + ceed = succeed
sub-	suf-	f	sub + ficient = sufficient
sub-	sup-	p	sub + ply = supply

Join the morphemes below, changing *sub-* if necessary.

1. sub + fix ___suffix___
2. sub + text ___subtext___
3. sub + focate ___suffocate___
4. sub + posed ___supposed___
5. sub + plier ___supplier___
6. sub + cessful ___successful___
7. sub + cession ___succession___
8. sub + stantial ___substantial___

Use two of the words you formed in original sentences.

_____

_____

Lesson 27   121

2 Word Building

Students should change the *y* to *i* in number 2 and drop the silent *e* in numbers 8 and 10. Note the shift in the accented syllable that occurs in *super flu ous* (number 6) and *auto no mous* (number 9) when the morphemes are joined.

3 Using the Dictionary

This exercise encourages students to use prefixes to build words of their choosing with the help of the dictionary when necessary. Allow them to use any form of the words they create in their phrases and sentences.

Additional activity for advanced students:

Challenge them to make two words for each prefix given and have them use both words in sentences.

4 Recognizing Patterns: More Prefixes That Change

This is the last assimilative prefix included in this book. Remind students that the changes are regular and occur each time *sub-* comes before certain letters. Only the more common assimilative forms are included.

Students should study the chart carefully before attempting to join the morphemes that follow it. You may want students to underline double consonants once they have built the words.

Students will not need to change the prefix in numbers 2 or 8.

Advanced students may enjoy trying to use two of the words they formed in a single sentence.

5 Looking at Meanings

Add one of the following prefixes to each partial word below to form a word that matches the definition given. Use a dictionary if necessary.

> auto-   sub-   super-   trans-

Definitions	Partial words	Whole words
1. can be carried across	portable	transportable
2. below the main heading	heading	subheading
3. superior to people	human	superhuman
4. self-operating	matic	automatic
5. plunge under	merge	submerge
6. oversee	vise	supervise
7. move over to a new place	plant	transplant
8. self-governing	nomous	autonomous

6 Recognizing Prefixes in Context

Underline the following prefixes in the sentences below.

> auto-   sub-   suf-   sup-   super-   sur-   trans-

1. Many suffragists were subjected to ridicule.
2. The superhighway construction involved several surveyors.
3. The supervisor was so supportive, it was a real transformation.
4. When I'm surrounded by people, I feel as though I'm suffocating.
5. It's not surprising that she automatically suppressed the bad news.
6. Ramón is supposed to get his automobile's transmission overhauled.

5 Looking at Meanings

Learning to relate the meanings of prefixes to the words in which they are used should help students to spell the prefixes correctly.

Additional activities:

Once they have written the word suggested by the definition and partial word given, have students underline the portion of the definition that led them to choose a certain prefix.

Have students use the words in sentences.

Have advanced students make up some examples of their own to try out on other students.

6 Recognizing Prefixes in Context

Tell students to underline in the sentences all of the prefixes in the given list and to read the sentences before they start underlining.

Additional activity:

Have students circle roots, suffixes, and other prefixes that they recognize in these sentences.

This kind of activity can be done using any printed material, such as newspapers, magazines, or ads.

Quizzes

Give a graded spelling quiz on the words in this lesson or other words that include these prefixes.

Sentences

Sentences for dictation are available at the back of this book.

Lesson 28

The Prefixes *multi-*, *poly-*, *mono-*, *uni-*, *bi-*, and *tri-*

Objectives

- **Prefixes:** Learn to recognize and spell words with *multi-*, *poly-*, *mono-*, *uni-*, *bi-*, and *tri-*.
- **Word Building:** Join morphemes to build whole words.
- **Completing Words in Context:** Build words to fit in context by adding prefixes to partial words.
- **Building and Using Words:** Select, reorder, and combine morphemes to build whole words. Use the words in context.
- **Number Prefixes:** Learn to identify and use prefixes that refer to numbers.
- **Composing Sentences:** Write original sentences using selected words.

Lesson 28 — Prefixes

multi-, poly-, mono-, uni-, bi-, and tri-

1 Recognizing Prefixes

In each group of words below, underline the prefixes listed on the left.

multi-	*much, many*			
	multiply	multitude	multicultural	multipurpose
poly-	*much, many*			
	polyester	polygamy	polytechnic	polyunsaturated
mono-, mon-	*one, alone*			
	monopoly	monotonous	monorail	monogram
uni-	*one*			
	uniform	united	unique	universe
bi-	*two*			
	bicycle	bisect	biweekly	bifocal
tri-	*three*			
	triple	triangle	tripod	triathlon

2 Word Building

Join the morphemes that follow to build whole words. Write the words on the lines provided. Remember to drop the silent *e* if necessary.

1. uni + son   unison
2. bi + ceps   biceps
3. tri + plane   triplane
4. multi + race + ial   multiracial
5. poly + syllab + ic   polysyllabic
6. mono + pol + ize   monopolize

Lesson 28   123

1 Recognizing Prefixes

Read aloud the representative words listed for each prefix. Read the words in a normal speaking voice without stressing the prefixes. Instruct students to underline the prefix as you read each word.

Point out the following:

The meanings of all these prefixes relate to numbers or quantity.

There are two forms of the prefix *mono-*. As with other Greek morphemes, the form that ends in *o* is used before morphemes that begin with a consonant.

The pronunciation of *poly-* changes in *polygamy*. The pronunciation of *mono-* changes in the words *monopoly* and *monotonous*. The pronunciation of *uni-* changes in the words *united* and *unique*. The pronunciation of *tri-* changes in the word *triple*.

2 Word Building

Students should drop the silent *e* in number 4.

Some of these words may be unfamiliar to students. Have them try to guess meanings based on the prefixes presented in this lesson, other morphemes they have studied, or related words they know.

3 Adding Prefixes to Make Complete Words

In this exercise, students must form complete words by filling in missing prefixes. Partial words and contexts are supplied, so that only one prefix should make sense in each blank.

Have students read a whole phrase or sentence before they fill in the blank and then reread it afterward.

If students have trouble doing this exercise, have them focus on the number or amount given in the context (e.g., *three* in number 1).

Students are asked to underline the word or words that helped them to select the correct prefix. The underlined words should all relate to numbers or quantities.

Additional activities:

Have students use their knowledge of numeric prefixes to tell you what words might mean the following:

- something with two horns (bicorn)
- something with three horns (tricorn)
- someone with one spouse (monogamist)
- someone with many spouses (polygamist)
- speaking only one language (monolingual)
- speaking three languages (trilingual)

Have students add as many different numerical prefixes as they can

3 Adding Prefixes to Make Complete Words

Each sentence below contains a clue to the meaning of the missing prefix. Write one of the following prefixes in each blank to build a word that makes sense in the sentence. Write the whole words on the lines provided. Then underline the word or words that were the clue.

poly-   mon-   uni-   bi-   tri-

Whole words

1. A __tri__angle has three sides.   __triangle__

2. The __uni__corn has one horn.   __unicorn__

3. The __bi__gamist had two wives.   __bigamist__

4. In a __mon__archy, there's one ruler.   __monarchy__

5. A __tri__mester is three months long.   __trimester__

6. A __poly__graph measures many things.   __polygraph__

7. An eyeglass for one eye is a __mon__ocle.   __monocle__

8. A __bi__lingual person speaks two languages.   __bilingual__

4 Jumbled Morphemes

Use the morphemes in each group below to create three different words. Choose two words from each group and use them in short phrases or sentences.

Phrases or sentences

1. cycle tri bi uni ist

   __bicycle__   _____

   __tricycle__   _____

   __unicyclist__

to the root words *sect, cycle, plane, weekly, monthly, form, lateral, linear, national, partite,* and *ped.*

4 Jumbled Morphemes

Allow students to use any form of the words they create in their phrases and sentences.

Remind students to use a dictionary if necessary and to proofread their work.

If students are using notebooks, they can write extra or longer sentences than space in the book allows for.

The answers on the replica of the student page are examples. Accept all correctly spelled words.

Be sure that students drop the silent *e* from *cycle* in number 1 and *tone* in number 2 when necessary.

2. ous tone mono ly y

__monotony_____   _____

__monotonous_____   _____

__monotonously_____

3. nat al multi ion ply

__multinational_____   _____

__nation_____   _____

__multiply_____

5 Number Prefixes

The prefixes in this lesson refer to numbers, either specifically (*uni-, bi-, tri-,* and *mono-*) or in general (*multi-* and *poly-*). Some other number prefixes are listed below. Use a dictionary or math text to find out their meanings, and fill in the blanks. Then write one word starting with each prefix. The first one is done for you.

Prefix	How many?	Whole words
1. quadr	four	quadruple
2. penta	five	pentagon
3. hexa	six	hexagonal
4. oct	eight	octopus
5. nona	nine	nonagenarian
6. deca	ten	decade
7. kilo	thousand	kilometer
8. mega	million	megaton

Now use two of your words in original sentences.

_____

_____

5 Number Prefixes

The purpose of this exercise is to make students aware that there are many numeric prefixes other than the ones presented in this lesson. Knowing numeric prefixes can help students both to spell and to understand new words with those prefixes.

The whole words on the replica of the student page are examples.

Encourage students to use a dictionary to find example words.

If you feel that this exercise is beyond the needs or capabilities of your students, let them skip it.

Advanced additional activity:

Have students try to figure out the following math problems, using numeric prefixes to represent numbers at first and then numerals below the numeric prefixes to check their work. Do the first one with them.

1. quadr x   uni =   quadr
   4   x   1   =   4

2. deca -   oct =   (bi)
   10   -   8   =   (2)

3. tri   x   bi =   (hexa)
   3   x   2   =   (6)

4. oct   ÷   bi =   (quadr)
   8   ÷   2   =   (4)

5. bi + tri + uni =   (hexa)
   2 + 3 + 1   =   (6)

6. kilo x kilo =   (mega)
   1,000 x 1,000 =   (1,000,000)

7. nona - hexa + penta = (oct)
   9   - 6   + 5   = (8)

8. uni   x kilo   =   (kilo)
   1   x 1,000   =   (1,000)

9. hexa ÷ bi   =   (tri)
   6   ÷ 2   =   (3)

10. quadr + hexa - penta = (penta)
    4   + 6   - 5   = (5)

Quizzes

Give a graded spelling quiz on the words in this lesson or other words that include these prefixes.

Sentences

Sentences for dictation are available at the back of this book.

Unit 7

Review of Lessons 26–28

Objectives

- **Prefixes:** Review prefixes studied in Unit 7.
- **Taking Words Apart:** Divide words into morphemes.
- **Assimilative Prefixes:** Review and practice the assimilative forms studied in Unit 7.
- **Changing Morphemes:** Remove and replace prefixes in given words to form new words.
- **Composing Sentences:** Write original sentences using selected words.
- **Word Building:** Add selected prefixes to roots to build whole words.
- **Creating Words in Sentences:** Build words to fit in context by reordering and combining morphemes.
- **Puzzle:** Review words from this unit by completing a crossword puzzle.

You may need to review some of the patterns for spelling prefixes before beginning this review, depending on how well students have managed with individual lessons. Remind them that they can refer to the lessons whenever necessary.

For detailed information about patterns and strategies, refer to the lesson notes for individual lessons.

Prefixes Presented in This Unit

anti-	mon-	op-	super-
aut-	mono-	poly-	sur-
auto-	multi-	sub-	trans-
bi-	ob-	suc-	tri-
contra-	oc-	suf-	uni-
inter-	of-	sup-	

1 Taking Words Apart

Divide the following words into morphemes and write each one under the correct heading. You may write either the original form of the prefix or the one used in the word. Remember to add or change letters if necessary.

	Prefixes	Roots	Suffixes	
1. obscurity	ob	scure	ity	
2. opponent	op/ob	pone	ent	
3. bimonthly	bi	month	ly	
4. monotony	mono	tone	y	
5. obligation	ob	lige	ate	ion
6. interracial	inter	race	ial	
7. supporter	sup/sub	port	er	
8. presuppose	pre sup/sub	pose		
9. subscription	sub	script	ion	
10. contradictory	contra	dict	ory	

---

1 Taking Words Apart

All of these words follow regular patterns. Encourage students to refer to the glossary or a dictionary to check any individual morphemes if necessary.

Remind students that they should write the original form of a root. If a silent *e* has been dropped, they should restore it. Both silent *e*'s should be restored in number 5.

If a word contains an assimilative form of a prefix, students may write either the original form of the prefix or the form that is used in the word.

Students who have difficulty should first identify the prefixes presented in this unit.

Note whether students divide the two suffixes in *obligation*. The number of blanks given should help them. Review those suffixes if necessary.

2 Reviewing Prefixes That Change

Part A. Fill in the blanks in the chart below.

Prefix	Changes to	Before	Example words
ob-	oc-	c	occurrence
ob-	of-	f	offer
ob-	op-	p	opposite
sub-	suc-	c	successful
sub-	suf-	f	sufficient
sub-	sup-	p	supporter

Part B. Write the correct form of the prefixes *ob-* or *sub-* in each blank in the following words. The words must make sense in the sentences.

1. Did you __SUC__cumb to that flu virus?

2. She __ob__tained the necessary papers.

3. No one __ob__jected to my leaving early.

4. Prefixes and __suf__fixes are morphemes.

5. He was __sub__jected to a full interrogation.

6. The news was __sup__pressed during the war.

7. The heat and humidity are quite __op__pressive.

8. The apartment is __oc__cupied by a family of eight.

3 Changing Prefixes

Remove the prefix from each of the words below and replace it with one of the following prefixes to form a new word.

   ante-   anti-   contra-   inter-   intro-

1. *sym*biotic __antibiotic__

2. *ad*diction __contradiction__

3. *sub*mission __intermission__

4. *re*view __interview__

5. *post*date __antedate__

6. *pro*duced __introduced__

Unit 7 Review   127

2 Reviewing Prefixes That Change

Review any parts of Lessons 26 and 27 before students begin this exercise if necessary.

Part A: Students fill in blanks in the chart of prefix changes and supply example words.

Part B: Students form complete words by filling in missing prefixes. The prefixes to fill in are *ob-*, *sub-*, or an appropriate variant form. Partial words and contexts are supplied, so only one prefix should make sense in each blank.

Have students read a whole sentence before they fill in the blank and then reread it afterward to be sure that it makes sense.

Students having trouble doing this exercise should ignore the contexts at first and just focus on finding a prefix that would fit in the blank. Refer them to the chart in Part A if they have problems with variant forms.

Additional activity:

Have students write another phrase or sentence for each word.

3 Changing Prefixes

The prefixes to be removed are italicized in each word.

Remind students to use a dictionary if they are uncertain of a word.

For most of these words, only one of the given prefixes can be substituted. Number 2 could be *contradiction* or *interdiction*. Accept any answer that forms a correctly spelled word.

Students are also asked to use two of their words in sentences. The exercise instructions are deliberately flexible about how many sentences should be written. Advanced students may enjoy trying to use both their words in a single sentence. If students need more room, encourage them to use their notebooks. Make sure that they proofread their own sentences.

Help them to correct misspellings by using what they already know. Errors in words not yet studied should not be treated negatively.

Additional activity:

Have students use two of the original words in sentences.

Unit 7 Review   135

Now use two of your words in original sentences.

_____

_____

4 Adding Prefixes to Roots

Different prefixes can be used with the same root. If the prefix listed at the top of the column can be used with the root on the left, write the word in the correct space. Check a dictionary if necessary. The first one is done for you.

	trans-	ob-/of-/op-	sub-/suf-/sup-
1. press	_____	oppress	suppress
2. fer	transfer	offer	suffer
3. fice	_____	office	suffice
4. ject	_____	object	subject
5. port	transport	_____	support
6. verse	transverse	obverse	_____

5 Creating Words in Sentences

Combine the morphemes under each blank to create words that make sense in the following sentences.

1. They hold ___international___ meetings ___biannually___.
   nat inter al ion   ann bi ly ual

2. He's ___obstinate___ about not wearing ___uniforms___.
   stin ate ob   form s uni

3. I'm ___surprised___ we don't need ___antifreeze___ in the car yet.
   ed prise sur   freeze anti

4. Her ___survival___ after that ___automobile___ accident is miraculous.
   vive al sur   mobile auto

5. Those curtains are so ___insubstantial___ they're almost ___transparent___.
   ial stant sub in   ent trans par

4 Adding Prefixes to Roots

In this exercise, students add prefixes as appropriate to given roots. Not all of the prefixes can be added to all of the roots.

Remind students to check words in a dictionary if necessary. Make sure that they proofread the words they write. Be sure that they use the appropriate form of the assimilative prefixes.

Additional activity:

Have students use some of the words they form in sentences. Encourage them to be ambitious in their writing.

5 Creating Words in Sentences

Remind students to read a whole sentence before starting to combine the morphemes to create words. After they've written words in the blanks, they should reread the sentence to be sure that it makes sense.

Make sure that students drop the silent *e* in *surprised* and *survival.*

6 Crossword Puzzle

Use the clues below to complete this crossword puzzle. Many of the answers contain prefixes from Unit 7.

T	R	A	N	S	P	O	R	T	A	T	I	O	N
R		N		O		F			T		N		E
A	U	T	O	M	O	T	I	V	E		C		I
N		I		E		E			H	U	G		
S	U	B	S	T	A	N	D	A	R	D		B	
A		I		H			U		R	O	B		
T		O		I			T		E		O		
L	A	T	I	N		P	R	O	D	U	C	E	R
A		I		G		O		M		I		H	
N		C		S		S		A		T	O	O	
T		S	U	B	S	T	I	T	U	T	E		
I	T		A		E		I			A	D		
C	O	N	T	R	A	D	I	C	T	I	O	N	S

Across

1. Means of traveling from place to place
8. Having to do with cars
9. A friendly squeeze
10. Of a quality below accepted measures; inferior
12. Steal from
13. Language that provided English with many morphemes
14. A person who manufactures things
15. Also
16. A person or thing that takes the place of another
18. He, she, or ____
20. Short for advertisement
21. Inconsistencies: That statement is full of ____.

Down

1. Across the ocean between America and Europe
2. Medicines that fight infections
3. Opposite of nothing
4. Many times
5. Consumed food
6. One-twelfth of a foot
7. Residential parts of a town or city
11. Able to operate by itself
12. Say out loud from memory
14. Put up in a public place: The notice was ____ on the bulletin board.
17. To block the way; prevent
19. Opposite of from
20. ____ apple a day

Unit 7 Review   129

---

6 Crossword Puzzle

Have students complete the crossword puzzle. Tell them that many of the answer words contain prefixes from Unit 7. The clues are mostly definitions that rely on the students' general knowledge.

Encourage them to use a dictionary if they wish. You might want them to work in pairs or small groups. If necessary, give them the following list of answer words and have them check off words as they use them.

Answer words:

ad	often
an	posted
antibiotics	producer
ate	recite
automatic	rob
automotive	something
bar	substandard
contradictions	substitute
hug	to
inch	too
it	transatlantic
Latin	transportation
neighborhoods	

Sentences

Sentences for dictation are available at the back of this book.

Unit 7 Test

We recommend that you test your students on the words from Unit 7 before going on. The following is a suggested list of words from Unit 7. You may want to substitute other words to meet the needs of your students.

Dictate each word and use it in a simple sentence. Students should be able to spell 90 percent of these words correctly.

reoccurring	superiority
obviously	unsuccessful
opposition	supportive
contradictory	subconsciously
antisocial	multiplication
interruption	polytechnic
autographed	monopolize
supervisory	universal
transitional	bicyclist
survival	tripled

Unit 7 Review   **137**

Lesson 29

The Roots *ceed, ceive, cide,* and *clude*

Objectives

- **Roots:** Learn to recognize and spell words with *ceed, ceive, cide,* and *clude.*
- **Word Building:** Join morphemes to build whole words. Select and combine morphemes to build at least 20 words.
- **Variant Forms:** Practice adding *-ion* and *-ive* to roots.
- **Homophones:** Write definitions of homophones. Practice using context to determine correct spellings.
- **Spelling *ceed* and *ceive:*** Memorize seven words with these roots.
- **Word Game:** Play a game to build words.

For general information on roots, refer to page 8 in the introduction.

---

1 Recognizing Roots

In each group of words below, underline the roots listed on the left.

ceed/cede, cess — **go**

exceed	recede	access
succeed	precede	excessive
proceed	concede	procession

ceive, cept — **take**

deceive	conceive	accept	receptive
receive	conceptual	except	deception
perceive	inconceivable	acceptance	perception

cide, cise — **kill; cut**

suicide	precise	incision
homicide	concise	excised
insecticide	decisive	imprecision

clude, clus — **close, shut**

include	exclude	seclusion
conclude	preclude	reclusive

2 Word Building

Join the morphemes that follow to build whole words. Write the words on the lines provided. Remember to drop the silent *e* if necessary.

1. pesti + cide   <u>pesticide</u>   4. in + cess + ant   <u>incessant</u>
2. ne + cess + ity   <u>necessity</u>   5. de + ceive + ing   <u>deceiving</u>
3. pre + cise + ly   <u>precisely</u>   6. ante + cede + ent   <u>antecedent</u>

130   Lesson 29

---

1 Recognizing Roots

Read aloud the representative words listed for each root. Read the words in a normal speaking voice without stressing the roots. Instruct students to underline the root as you read each word.

Point out the following:

All the roots in this lesson have variant forms: *cess* is a variant of *ceed* and *cede*; *cept* is a variant of *ceive*; *cise* is a variant of *cide*; and *clus* is a variant of *clude.* When you come to these roots, be sure students can identify the variant forms in the representative words.

The pronunciation of *cise* changes in the words *incision* and *imprecision.*

Students should recognize the other root in the word *insecticide* (*sect* meaning *cut,* which was studied in Lesson 16).

The root *cess* takes the suffix *-or* rather than *-er* (e.g., *successor, predecessor*).

The "*i* before *e* except after *c*" rule applies mainly to the root *ceive.* If students know that mnemonic, tell them it can help them to remember the spelling of words with that root.

Additional activities:

Have students work in small groups to generate as many words

---

7. ac + cess + ible __accessible__   9. in + con + clus + ive __inconclusive__

8. se + clude + ed __secluded__   10. mis + con + cept + ion __misconception__

3 Variant Forms

All the roots in this lesson have more than one form. The meaning of the roots doesn't change, even when the spelling and pronunciation do. Learning to recognize variant forms of roots can help you to develop spelling strategies.

Part A. Words with the root *ceed/cede, ceive,* and *clude* often have related words with the roots *cess, cept,* and *clus.* The suffixes *-ion* and *-ive* are usually added to the variant forms *cess, cept,* and *clus.* For each word listed below, write related words ending in *-ion* and *-ive.* Use a dictionary if necessary.

	Related nouns ending in *-ion*	Related adjectives ending in *-ive*
1. recede	recession	recessive
2. succeed	succession	successive
3. include	inclusion	inclusive
4. exclude	exclusion	exclusive
5. receive	reception	receptive
6. deceive	deception	deceptive
7. conclude	conclusion	conclusive
8. perceive	perception	perceptive

Part B. Words with the roots *cide* and *cise* often have a related form ending in *-ion.* Write the *-ion* form of the words below. Remember to add, drop, or change letters if necessary.

1. decide __decision__   3. precise __precision__

2. concise __concision__   4. excise __excision__

as they can that include these roots.

Have students identify prefixes and suffixes that they have studied or recognize in the representative words.

2 Word Building

Students should drop the silent *e* in numbers 5, 6, and 8.

3 Variant Forms

This exercise emphasizes the relationships among related forms of the same root. It also illustrates that a root may have different forms depending on how it is used in a sentence. Predicting the spelling of a word by associating it with a related word is an important strategy. If students are learning new words with these roots, they should pay particular attention to the sound the root makes in a word.

Part A: Students are asked to write the forms ending in *-ion* and *-ive* of words with the roots *ceed/cede, ceive,* and *clude.* The variant forms are used to form the related words.

Have students pronounce the new words before they write them. Encourage them to use a dictionary to check their spelling if necessary.

Additional activity:

Have students use all three forms of one of the words in sentences. You may want advanced students to use all three forms of more than one of the words.

Part B: Students are asked to write the form ending in *-ion* of words with the root *cide* and its variant form *cise.* Be sure students drop the silent *e* before adding the suffix.

Additional activity:

Have students use one pair of words (the given word and the related *-ion* form) in sentences. Challenge students to use both words in a single sentence.

4 Words in Context: A Strategy for Homophones

The words *access* and *excess*, *precede* and *proceed*, and *accept* and *except* are often pronounced alike. Students must learn to use context clues to predict accurately which spelling to use.

Part A: Encourage students to write their own definitions of the words. The definitions will vary.

You may want to discuss the meanings of the words with students before they continue with Part B. Having them use the words in short oral phrases will help you to judge how well they understand the words.

Part B: Tell students to read a whole sentence first to decide which word to select. After they've written words in the blanks, they should reread the sentence to be sure that it makes sense.

If students select a wrong word, review the definitions to help them understand why their chosen word does not fit.

5 The Roots *ceed* and *ceive*

Since there are only three words that have the root *ceed* (*succeed*, *exceed*, and *proceed*) and only four with the root *ceive* (*receive*, *deceive*, *perceive*, and *conceive*),

---

4 Words in Context: A Strategy for Homophones

The words *precede* and *proceed* sound almost alike, but they have different meanings. Two other pairs, *access* and *excess* and *accept* and *except* also sound alike but have different meanings.

Part A. Write a definition for each of these words. Use a dictionary if necessary.

access ___means or act of approaching; right to enter or make use of___

excess ___exceeding what is normal or sufficient; remainder___

precede ___to go before in time or order; to preface or introduce___

proceed ___to go forward or onward; to continue___

accept ___to receive; to admit to a group or place; to regard as true___

except ___with the exclusion of; unless; otherwise than___

Part B. Fill in the blanks in the following sentences with one of the words below the blank. The word must make sense in the sentence.

1. I ironed all the clothes ___except___ Willie's.
   accept/except

2. He had been on a long trip the ___preceding___ year.
   preceding/proceeding

3. Was the winner there to ___accept___ her award?
   accept/except

4. The ___access___ road leading to the ball field is full of ruts.
   access/excess

5. Do you remember who ___preceded___ you on the list?
   preceded/proceeded

6. I can eat anything ___except___ nuts and dairy products.
   accept/except

7. Darlene ___proceeded___ to give directions to the stranger.
   preceded/proceeded

8. Delia cut off the ___excess___ material before she hemmed the curtains.
   access/excess

132   Lesson 29

---

students should memorize them.

Point out to students that they will also be learning to spell words built from these seven root words, such as *exceedingly* and *receiver*. An exception to note is that *procedure* has only one *e*, despite being formed from *proceed*.

If students have trouble memorizing the spellings, help them to devise mnemonics for remembering the three *ceed* words and the four *ceive* words. One student devised the following: He proceeded to exceed the speed limit, so he succeeded in getting fined.

Additional activity:

Have students use all seven words in phrases or sentences. Remind students that many other words can be formed from the seven basic words by adding prefixes and suffixes. Challenge advanced students to use as many of the words as they can in a single sentence.

5 **The Roots *ceed* and *ceive***

The roots *ceed* and *ceive* present special spelling problems. *Ceed* sounds like *cede*. *Ceive* is hard to spell because *ei* is an unusual vowel pattern in English.

Sometimes, the easiest way to remember a spelling is to memorize it. There are only seven common words that contain the roots *ceed* or *ceive*, so you should try to memorize them. The seven words are all in Exercise 1.

The three words that have the root *ceed*:

exceed   _succeed_   _proceed_

The four words that have the root *ceive*:

deceive   _receive_   _perceive_   _conceive_

6 **Challenge Word Building**

On a separate piece of paper, combine the morphemes below to build at least 20 words. Use as few or as many morphemes as you need for each word. Use a dictionary if you are unsure of a word.

Prefixes	Roots	Suffixes
con- in-	ceive/cept cise	-ion -ly
ex- pre-	clude/clus cess	-ive

7 **Word Pyramid**

Use the letters found in *cise* to complete the words below. Each word contains the letters *c, i, s,* and *e* at least once in any order. All of the words are used in this book.

C I S E

I N <u>S</u> <u>E</u> <u>C</u> T

<u>S</u> <u>E</u> <u>C</u> U R <u>I</u> T Y

<u>S</u> U F F <u>I</u> <u>C</u> <u>I</u> <u>E</u> N T

<u>S</u> <u>I</u> G N <u>I</u> F <u>I</u> <u>C</u> A N <u>C</u> <u>E</u>

<u>I</u> N <u>C</u> O N <u>C</u> L U <u>S</u> <u>I</u> V <u>E</u> L Y

Lesson 29   133

---

exclusively   precept
inception   preceptive
inceptive   preceptively
incise   precise
incision   precisely
incisive   precision
incisively   preclude
include   preclusion
inclusion   preclusive
inclusive   preclusively
inclusively

Additional activities:

Have students compare their lists and develop a master list of all the words they form.

Have students use some of the words they build in sentences.

7 **Word Pyramid**

In this word game, students build complete words by filling in the letters *c, i, s,* and *e*. The letters can be in any order, and some will be used more than once in some words. All of the answer words are from lessons in this book.

Remember that word games are intended to be fun. Students may want to work in pairs or small groups. If they find this game confusing or frustrating, let them skip it.

Quizzes

Give a graded spelling quiz on the words in this lesson or other words that include these roots.

Sentences

Sentences for dictation are available at the back of this book.

---

6 **Challenge Word Building**

Emphasize that students can use as few or as many morphemes as needed for a particular word. More than one suffix can be added to build some of the words.

Encourage students to use a dictionary if necessary.

Have students check to be sure that they have added, dropped, or changed letters when necessary.

Possible responses are listed here.

There may be others. Accept all correctly spelled words.

cession	conclusion
conceive	conclusive
concept	conclusively
conception	except
conceptive	exception
conceptively	excess
concession	excessive
concessive	excessively
concessively	excise
concise	excision
concision	exclude
concisely	exclusion
conclude	exclusive

Lesson 30

The Roots *cur, dict, duce,* and *fer*

Objectives

- **Roots:** Learn to recognize and spell words with *cur, dict, duce,* and *fer*.
- **Word Building:** Join morphemes to build whole words.
- **Patterns:** Review and practice Doubling Pattern 2 for adding suffixes.
  Learn that in words with the roots *fer* and *cur*, /ənt/, /əns/, and /ənsē/ are usually spelled *-ent/-ence/-ency.*
- **Composing Sentences:** Write original sentences using selected words.
- **Variant Forms:** Practice spelling words with variant forms of *duce*.
- **Completing Words in Context:** Build words to fit in context by adding roots to partial words.
- **Creating Words in Sentences:** Build words to fit in context by reordering and combining morphemes.

1 Recognizing Roots

Read aloud the representative words listed for each root. Read the words in a normal speaking voice without stressing the roots. Instruct students to underline the root as you read each word.

Roots provide the core or central meaning of a word. Note that the spelling of a root may change when certain suffixes are added. These changes generally follow the patterns reviewed in Lesson 3.

Point out the following:

The *r* in the root *cur* is doubled before suffixes that start with a vowel.

The roots *dict* and *duct* take the suffix *-or* rather than *-er* (e.g., *predictor, conductor*).

The root *duct* is a variant form of the root *duce*. When you come to *duce*, be sure students can identify the variant form in the representative words.

The accented syllable changes in words with the root *fer*, which affects the doubling of the *r*. This problem is addressed in Exercise 3.

Additional activities:

Have students work in small groups to generate as many words as they can that include these roots.

Lesson 30   Roots
cur, dict, duce, and *fer*

1 Recognizing Roots

In each group of words below, underline the roots listed on the left.

cur	**run**		
	current	cursive	recurring
	curriculum	excursion	occurrence

dict	**say, speak**		
	dictate	verdict	addictive
	dictionary	predictable	contradictory

duce, duct	**lead**		
	produce	introduce	reduce
	product	introduction	conductor

fer	**carry, bring**		
	offer	different	referral
	transfer	preferred	conference

2 Word Building

Join the morphemes that follow to build whole words. Write the words on the lines provided. Remember to drop the silent *e* if necessary.

1. con + cur   concur
2. in + duce   induce
3. e + duc + ate   educate
4. in + fer + ence   inference
5. vin + dict + ive   vindictive
6. de + duct + ible   deductible
7. re + duct + ion   reduction
8. dif + fer + ent + ial   differential
9. pro + duct + ive + ity   productivity
10. un + pre + dict + able   unpredictable

134   Lesson 30

3 Reviewing Doubling Pattern 2

If a word has more than one syllable, look at the last one. If the last syllable has one vowel, ends in one consonant, and is accented, double the final consonant before adding a suffix that begins with a vowel.

Part A. When Doubling Pattern 2 is used with words that contain the root *fer,* it is more difficult to decide if the *r* should be doubled. That is because the accent sometimes shifts to a different syllable when a suffix is added.

Mark the accented syllable in the following words with an accent mark (´). Pronounce each word first. Then answer the questions that follow.

> con fer   con fer ral   con fer ence

1. In which two words is the second syllable accented? ___confer and conferral___

2. In which word does the accent shift when the suffix is added? ___conference___

3. In which word is the *r* doubled when the suffix is added? ___conferral___

4. In which word is the *r* not doubled when the suffix is added? ___conference___

Fill in the blanks in this pattern.

Pattern: When a suffix is added to a word with the root *fer,* the *r* is doubled if the accent stays on the ___second___ syllable. The *r* is not doubled if the accent shifts to the ___first___ syllable.

Part B. Add the suffixes to the words below. Remember to pronounce the word with the suffix added to determine if the accent shifts. Use a dictionary if necessary.

1. occur + ing ___occurring___
2. refer + ence ___reference___
3. prefer + ing ___preferring___
4. prefer + able ___preferable___
5. prefer + ence ___preference___
6. refer + al ___referral___
7. offer + ed ___offered___
8. recur + ent ___recurrent___
9. infer + ence ___interference___
10. transfer + ing ___transferring___

Lesson 30   135

Ask students to identify any prefixes or suffixes that they recognize in the representative words. Point out how many morphemes they can recognize now compared with earlier in the book.

2 Word Building

In number 3, the root *duce* is presented without the *e.* Some students might be confused by the indication of a soft *c* if this were presented *e + duce + ate.*

Students should drop the silent *e* in number 9.

3 Reviewing Doubling Pattern 2

The roots *cur* and *fer* offer an opportunity to review doubling final consonants when adding suffixes that begin with a vowel. Before starting this exercise, review Doubling Pattern 2 from Lesson 3 if necessary.

The root *fer* presents particular difficulty because the accent sometimes shifts from one syllable to another when suffixes are added, but these shifts in accent are not consistent. For example, the accent stays on the root in *referral* but shifts to the prefix in *reference.* It is this shift in accent that signals whether or not the final *r* is doubled.

Unfortunately, some students, particularly those with certain learning disabilities, have a great deal of trouble identifying the accented syllable. If a student cannot hear the stress, this strategy is not going to be helpful. We recommend that you emphasize that the student must recognize these words as ones that will have to be memorized or checked in the dictionary.

Part A: Make sure that students understand that the *r* is doubled when the accent stays on the root *fer* and that *r* is not doubled when the accent shifts to the prefix.

Part B: Emphasize that students should pronounce the word with the suffix added before writing it. It is the addition of the suffix that causes the accent to shift in such pairs as *prefer* and *preference.*

If students make errors when building these words, note which aspect of the doubling pattern is causing them difficulty and review it with them.

4 The Suffixes -ence and -ent

This exercise gives students another strategy for choosing how to spell the schwa in words that end with the suffixes /əns/ and /ənt/. When added to words with the roots *cur* and *fer*, these suffixes are spelled *-ence* and *-ent*.

The position of the blanks should help students to realize that there is no form of *confer* and *prefer* ending in *-ent*. Students should use a dictionary to check the words they build. If students have difficulty with doubling the *r* at the end of the root, review Exercise 3.

5 Variant Forms

This exercise emphasizes the relationships among related forms of the same root. It will help students realize that they may be able to spell a word if they can analyze it.

Encourage students to use a dictionary to check spellings as well as to look for additional related words. Show students that they can find other forms of a word both in main entries and in the related-words part of an entry. They can also check to see if words are, in fact, related.

The answers on the replica of the student page are examples. Accept all correctly spelled words.

Additional activities:

Have students compare the words they write and develop a master list.

Have students use some of their words in sentences.

6 Adding Roots to Make Complete Words

Write one of the following roots in each blank below to make a whole word. The word must make sense in the phrase or sentence. Remember to drop the silent *e* if necessary. Then write the whole word on the right.

cur   dict   duce/duct   fer

Whole words

1. a foreign ___cur___rency — currency
2. an e___duc___ational program — educational
3. There is a big dif___fer___ence. — difference
4. the intro___duct___ion to the book — introduction
5. a monthly payroll de___duct___ion — deduction
6. They in___cur___red large expenses. — incurred
7. under the juris___dict___ion of the city — jurisdiction
8. He was penalized for miscon___duct___. — misconduct

7 Creating Words in Sentences

Combine the morphemes under each blank to create words that make sense in the following sentences. Remember to add or drop letters if necessary.

1. A ___dictionary___ is a useful ___reference___ book.
   ary ion dict   ence re fer

2. The police ___deduced___ who ___abducted___ the child.
   duce de ed   ab ed duct

3. The company will ___reduce___ ___production___ next year.
   duce re   duct ion pro

4. The announcer ___referred___ to the ___unpredictable___ weather.
   fer ed re   dict un able pre

5. He likes to ___contradict___ his father just to be ___different___.
   dict contra   dif ent fer

Lesson 30   137

6 Adding Roots to Make Complete Words

In this exercise, students must form complete words by filling in missing roots. Affixes and contexts are supplied, so that only one root should make sense in each blank.

Seeing words with roots missing helps students to understand that it is the root that gives a word its essential meaning.

Have students read a whole phrase or sentence before they fill in the blank and then reread it afterward to be sure that it makes sense.

Students having trouble doing this exercise should ignore the contexts at first and just focus on a root that would fit in the blank.

Be sure that students drop the silent *e* from the root in number 2.

Have students write another phrase or sentence for each word.

7 Creating Words in Sentences

Remind students to read a whole sentence before starting to combine the morphemes to create a word. After they've written words in the blanks, they should reread the sentence to be sure that it makes sense.

Note whether students double the *r* correctly in number 4 and be sure that they don't double it in numbers 1 and 5. Students should drop the silent *e* in number 2, *deduced.*

Quizzes

Give a graded spelling quiz on the words in this lesson or other words that include these roots.

Sentences

Sentences for dictation are available at the back of this book.

The Roots *gress, ject, lect, mit,* and *mote*

Objectives

- **Roots:** Learn to recognize and spell words with *gress, ject, lect, mit,* and *mote*.
- **Word Building:** Join morphemes to build whole words.
- **Variant Forms:** Practice spelling words with the variant form of *mit*.
- **Pattern Review:** Review and Practice Doubling Pattern 2 for adding suffixes.
- **Composing Sentences:** Write original sentences using selected words.
- **Related Words:** Identify nouns in context and write related verbs.
- **Building and Using Words:** Remove and replace roots in given words and use the new words in context.

1 Recognizing Roots

Read aloud the representative words listed for each root. Read the words in a normal speaking voice without stressing the roots. Instruct students to underline the root as you read each word.

Point out the following:

The roots *gress, ject,* and *lect* take the suffix *-or* rather than *-er* (e.g., *aggressor, projector, collector*).

Although the English spelling is the same, *lect* meaning *read* is a different Latin root from *lect* meaning *gather* or *choose*.

When *-ion* is added to words ending in *ss,* /shən/ is spelled *ssion* (e.g., *digression, transgression, admission, transmission*). Refer to Lesson 7, Exercise 5 if necessary.

Miss is a variant form of the root *mit*. When you come to *mit*, be sure students can identify the variant form in the representative words.

Additional activities:

Have students work in small groups to generate as many words as they can that include these roots.

Ask students to identify any prefixes or suffixes that they have studied or recognize in the representative words.

Lesson 31 — Roots

gress, ject, lect, mit, and *mote*

1 Recognizing Roots

In each group of words below, underline the roots listed on the left.

gress	go, step		
	progress	regressive	digression
	congress	aggressive	transgression

ject	throw		
	eject	dejected	objection
	project	rejection	conjecture

lect	gather; choose;		read
	collect	election	lectern
	recollection	selected	lecturer

mit, miss	send; let go		
	admit	emit	permit
	admission	transmission	permissive

mote	move		
	motion	remote	promotion
	unemotional	locomotive	automotive

2 Word Building

Join the morphemes that follow to build whole words. Write the words on the lines provided. Remember to add or drop letters if necessary.

1. neg + lect   neglect
2. ag + gress + ion   aggression
3. pro + gress + ive   progressive
4. inter + mit + ent   intermittent

138   Lesson 31

2 Word Building

Students should double the final consonant of the root in numbers 4 and 6. Review the doubling patterns if necessary. Students should also drop the silent *e* in numbers 7 and 8.

Additional activity:

Have students identify any assimilative prefixes they recognize in these words.

3 The Root *mit*

One of the strategies presented in Lesson 7 for determining the spelling of /shən/ was that when a root ends in *t*, /shən/ will probably be spelled *-tion*. The root *mit* is an exception to this generalization. As is often the case, *-ion* is added to the variant form *miss*, resulting in the *ssion* spelling of /shən/. This exercise draws students' attention to this and gives them practice in spelling words with this form.

Part A: Students are asked to write the related noun form ending in *mission* for verbs ending in *mit.* Encourage them to use a dictionary if necessary. Be sure that they pronounce the nouns before writing them.

Students are asked to use one pair of words in a sentence. Using different forms of the same word in context helps students to develop the concept of related words. Make sure that they proofread their own sentences.

Additional activity:

Have students find other related words that use the *miss* form of the root. Suggest that they try the suffixes *-ive* and *-ible* to get them started.

Part B: If students are still having trouble with Doubling Pattern 2, review it before they begin this part of the exercise. The only word in which the *t* is not doubled is *commitment.*

Students are asked to use two of the new words in sentences. Allow them to use any form of the related words. If they need more room, encourage them to use their notebooks.

Note also that the root *mit* can take both *-ant/-ance* and *-ent/-ence* (*admittance* and *intermittent*).

4. Related Words

In each phrase or sentence below, underline the word ending in -ion. Then on the lines provided, write the verb ending in *gress, lect, ject,* or *mit* that is related to the word you underlined. The first one is done for you.

Related verbs

1. transmission fluid — transmit
2. presidential election — elect
3. What is your projection? — project
4. The admission price is high. — admit
5. the progression from A to Z — progress
6. I have no objection to her visit. — object
7. an interesting collection of tapes — collect
8. A small transgression will be forgiven. — transgress

5. Changing Roots

Remove the root from each word below and replace it with one of the following roots. Write the new word on the line provided. Then use the word you have created in a phrase or sentence.

gress   ject   lect   mit/miss   mote

	New words	Phrases or sentences
1. pro*mote*	progress	_____
2. re*gress*ion	rejection	_____
3. e*mot*ion	election	_____
4. sub*ject*ive	submissive	_____
5. *miss*ive	motive	_____

140   Lesson 31

---

4. Related Words

In this exercise, students are asked to write the related verb form of words ending in -ion. They should read the phrases and sentences first to identify the word ending in -ion before deciding what the related verb is. Apart from words with the root *miss,* they can form the verbs by removing the final suffix from the word without changing any other letters.

Additional activity:

Have students use some of the verbs they write in original sentences.

5. Changing Roots

The root to be removed and replaced is italicized in each word.

Remind students to use a dictionary if they are uncertain of a word.

The answers on the replica of the student page are examples.

Accept any answer that forms a correctly spelled word.

Additional activity:

Have students use the original words in phrases or sentences.

Quizzes

Give a graded spelling quiz on the words in this lesson or other words that include these roots.

Sentences

Sentences for dictation are available at the back of this book.

The Roots *form, pel, pend, plore,* and *pute*

Objectives

- **Roots:** Learn to recognize and spell words with *form, pel, pend, plore,* and *pute.*
- **Word Building:** Join morphemes to build whole words. Select, reorder, and combine morphemes to build whole words.
- **Variant Forms:** Practice spelling words with variant forms of *pel* and *pense.*
- **Completing Words in Context:** Build words to fit in context by adding roots to partial words.
- **Creating and Using Words:** Create words and use them in context.

1 Recognizing Roots

Read aloud the representative words listed for each root. Read the words in a normal speaking voice without stressing the roots. Instruct students to underline the root as you read each word.

Point out the following:

Pulse and *pense* are variant forms of the roots *pel* and *pend.* When you come to *pel* and *pend,* be sure students can identify the variant forms in the representative words.

The root *pel* follows Doubling Pattern 2. The *l* is usually doubled

---

Lesson 32

Roots
form, pel, pend, plore, and *pute*

1 Recognizing Roots
In each group of words below, underline the roots listed on the left.

form	*shape*		
	formal	conform	reform
	uniform	transformer	information

pel, pulse	*push, drive*		
	expel	repellent	impulse
	compel	expulsion	propulsive

pend, pense	*hang; weigh; pay*		
	suspense	dependent	indispensable
	suspended	pendulum	compensation

plore	*cry, wail*		
	implore	explore	imploring
	deplore	unexplored	deplorable

pute	*think, reckon; arrange*		
	dispute	imputed	deputy
	computer	reputation	disreputable

2 Word Building
Join the morphemes that follow to build whole words. Write the words on the lines provided. Remember to add, drop, or change letters if necessary.

1. pro + pel + er ___propeller___   3. sus + pense + ion ___suspension___

2. ap + pend + ix ___appendix___   4. per + form + ance ___performance___

Lesson 32   141

---

when suffixes beginning with a vowel are added (*repellent*).

Have students listen carefully to the sound made by the *du* in *pendulum.* Remind them that it is the same sound as that in *gradual* and *individual.*

Additional activities:

Have students explore the meanings of some of these representative words and discuss how the present meaning has emerged. Students can recognize more than

one morpheme in many words, such as *uniform* and *expel.*

Ask students to identify any prefixes or suffixes that they have studied or recognize in the representative words.

2 Word Building

Be sure that students double the final consonant of the root in numbers 1 and 6 and that they drop the silent *e* in numbers 3 and 7–9.

3 Variant Forms

This exercise emphasizes the relationships among related forms of the same root. Predicting the spelling of a word by associating it with a related word is an important strategy.

Encourage students to use a dictionary if necessary.

The answers on the replica of the student page are examples. Accept all correctly spelled words.

Additional activity:

Have students compare the words they write and develop a master list.

4 Adding Roots to Make Complete Words

In this exercise, students must form complete words by filling in missing roots. Affixes and contexts are supplied, so that one root should make the most sense in each blank.

Have students read a whole phrase or sentence before they fill in the blank and then reread it afterward.

Students having trouble doing this exercise should ignore the contexts at first and just focus on the words that have missing roots.

Be sure that students drop the silent *e* from the root in numbers 1–3.

Additional activity:

Ask students to write another phrase or sentence for each word.

5 Creating and Using Words

From each root listed below, create two words by adding prefixes or suffixes or both. Then use each word you form in a phrase or short sentence.

	Words	Phrases or sentences
1. pend	dependable	_____
	expenditure	_____
2. plore	exploration	_____
	implore	_____
3. pel	repellently	_____
	propel	_____
4. form	informal	_____
	uninformed	_____

6 Jumbled Morphemes

Combine the morphemes in each group below to create four different words. Use as few or as many morphemes as you need for each word. Remember to drop the silent *e* if necessary. Write the words on the lines provided.

1. de in pend ly ent ence

   depend   independence
   independent   dependently

2. dis ed pute in pense able

   disputed   disputable
   indispensable   dispense

3. re able pute form ation

   reformation   reputable
   reputation   formation

5 Creating and Using Words

Remind students to use the glossary if necessary and to use more than one affix for some of the words. Encourage them to be adventurous in creating words.

Creating two words for each root emphasizes the consistency of the spelling of the root.

The answers on the replica of the student page are examples. Accept all correctly spelled words.

6 Jumbled Morphemes

In this exercise, students are required to build four words from a group of morphemes that are not in correct order. Not every morpheme will be used in each word.

Encourage students to use a dictionary if they are uncertain of a word. Be sure that they drop the silent *e* from the root when necessary.

The answers on the replica of the student page are examples. Accept all correctly spelled words.

Additional activities:

Have students compare their answers and develop a master list of words that can be formed from these morphemes.

Have students write original sentences using some of the words they formed.

Quizzes

Give a graded spelling quiz on the words in this lesson or other words that include these roots.

Sentences

Sentences for dictation are available at the back of this book.

Lesson 33

The Roots *reg*, *rupt*, *scribe*, *sist*, and *spire*

Objectives

- **Roots:** Learn to recognize and spell words with *reg*, *rupt*, *scribe*, *sist*, and *spire*.
- **Word Building:** Join morphemes to build whole words.
- **Variant Forms:** Practice spelling words with the variant form of *scribe*.
- **Patterns:** Learn that in words with the root *sist*, /∂nt/, /∂ns/, and /∂nsē/ are usually spelled -*ent*/-*ence*/-*ency*. Learn two common exceptions to the pattern.
- **Building and Using Words:** Build words by adding roots to partial words. Use the whole words in context.
- **Word Game:** Play a game to build words.

1 Recognizing Roots

Read aloud the representative words listed for each root. Read the words in a normal speaking voice without stressing the roots. Instruct students to underline the root as you read each word.

Point out the following:

Rect and *script* are variant forms of the roots *reg* and *scribe*. When you come to *reg* and *scribe*, be sure students can identify the variant forms in the representative words.

Lesson 33 — Roots

reg, rupt, scribe, sist, and *spire*

1 Recognizing Roots

In each group of words below, underline the roots listed on the left.

reg, rect	**guide, rule**			
	regular	regimen	irregular	incorrect
	regulate	deregulation	direction	correction

rupt	**break**		
	rupture	disruptive	abruptly
	interrupt	corruption	eruption

scribe, script	**write**		
	inscribe	subscribe	scripture
	describe	subscription	transcript

sist	**cause to stand, place; stop**		
	persist	desist	consistent
	consistency	resistance	irresistible

spire	**breathe**		
	inspire	transpire	spirit
	conspiracy	aspiration	respiration

2 Word Building

Join the morphemes that follow to build whole words. Write the words on the lines provided. Remember to drop the silent *e* if necessary.

1. pre + scribe __prescribe__
2. bank + rupt __bankrupt__
3. sub + sist + ence __subsistence__
4. non + de + script __nondescript__

144   Lesson 33

The *g* in *reg* is hard in some words (*regular, regulate, irregular*) and soft when followed by an *e* or *i* (*regimen*).

The sound of the *t* at the end of roots changes to /ch/ if the suffix -*ure* is added (*rupture, scripture*).

When the silent *e* is dropped from the root *spire* (as in *conspiracy, aspiration, spirit, respiration*), the pronunciation of the root changes.

The root *rect* takes the suffix -*or* rather than -*er* (e.g., *director*).

Additional activities:

Have students work in small groups to generate as many words as they can that include these roots.

Ask students to identify any prefixes or suffixes that they have studied or recognize in the representative words.

5. reg + i + ment ___regiment___   8. inter + rupt + ion ___interruption___

6. in + sist + ent ___insistent___   9. mis + di + rect + ed ___misdirected___

7. spire + ite + ual ___spiritual___   10. in + de + scribe + able ___indescribable___

3 Variant Forms

Words with the root *scribe* often have related words with the root *script*. Beside each word below, write two related words using the root *script*. Use a dictionary if necessary. Remember that the variant form of the root is often used when *-ion* is added to a word.

1. describe ___description___ ___nondescript___

2. prescribe ___prescriptive___ ___prescription___

3. transcribe ___transcript___ ___transcription___

4 Pattern Awareness

Most words with the root *sist* are followed by *-ent*, *-ence*, or *-ency*. Add the suffixes indicated at the top of each column below to the words on the left.

	-ent	**-ence/-ency**
1. insist	insistent	insistence
2. exist	existent	existence
3. persist	persistent	persistence
4. consist	consistent	consistency

There are two common exceptions to this pattern that you should memorize. *Assist* and *resist* are followed by *-ant* and *-ance*. Add *-ant* and *-ance* to the words below.

	-ant	**-ance**
5. assist	assistant	assistance
6. resist	resistant	resistance

Lesson 33   145

2 Word Building

Be sure that students drop both silent *e's* in number 7 and the one in number 10.

3 Variant Forms

This exercise emphasizes the relationships among related forms of the same root. If students are learning new words with these roots, they should pay particular attention to the sound the root makes in a word.

Encourage students to use a dictionary if necessary.

The answers on the replica of the student page are examples. Accept all correctly spelled words.

Additional activity:

Have students compare the words they write and develop a master list.

4 Pattern Awareness

Although most words with the root *sist* take the suffixes *-ent/ -ence/-ency,* there are two common exceptions, *assist* and *resist.* Students may need to develop a mnemonic to help them to remember these exceptions.

Point out that *exist* is a combination of the morphemes *ex + sist.* The first *s* of the root is dropped since the prefix *ex* ends with the same sound. The same is true for *expire.*

Additional activity:

Have students use *assistant* and *assistance* and/or *resistant* and *resistance* in sentences. This may help them to remember these two exceptions.

---

5 **Adding Roots to Make Complete Words**

Write one of the following roots in each blank below to make a whole word. Remember to drop the silent *e* if necessary. Then use the word in a phrase or short sentence.

rect   rupt   scribe   sist   spire

Phrases or sentences

1. cor__rupt__ed _____

2. di__rect__ory _____

3. tran__sist__or _____

4. sub__scrib__er _____

5. con__spir__acy _____

6. as__sist__ance _____

7. indi__rect__ly _____

8. unin__spir__ing _____

6 **Missing Links**

Add a morpheme from this lesson that will link each pair below. The missing link will form the end of the first word and the beginning of the second word. The number of blanks indicates how many letters are in each missing link.

1. in __s i s t__ er

2. dis __r u p t__ ure

3. di __r e c t__ angle

4. cor __r e c t__ ified

5. con __s c r i p t__ ure

6. tran __s c r i p t__ writer

5 **Adding Roots to Make Complete Words**

In this exercise, students must form complete words by filling in missing roots. Be sure that students drop the silent *e* from the end of the root when necessary.

Only one answer is possible for most of the words. Number 1 could be *corrected* or *corrupted*. Accept all correctly spelled words.

When students are writing phrases and sentences, allow them to use any form of the words they have created.

6 **Missing Links**

In this word game, students form two unrelated words by writing a missing root in the blanks. The root that is filled in will form the end of the first word and the beginning of the second: *insist* and *sister*. All of the missing roots are from this lesson. The number of blanks indicates the number of letters in the missing root.

Remember that word games are intended to be fun. Students may want to work in pairs or small groups. If they find this game confusing or frustrating, let them skip it.

Quizzes

Give a graded spelling quiz on the words in this lesson or other words that include these roots.

Sentences

Sentences for dictation are available at the back of this book.

Lesson 34

The Roots *sume, tract, turb,* and *vide*

Objectives

- **Roots:** Learn to recognize and spell words with *sume, tract, turb,* and *vide.*
- **Word Building:** Join morphemes to build whole words.
- **Variant Forms:** Add *-ion* to variant forms.
- **Creating Words in Sentences:** Build words to fit in context by reordering and combining morphemes.
- **Using Meanings:** Select roots based on the definitions of words to be formed.
- **Building and Using Words:** Build new words by removing and replacing roots. Use the new words in context.

1 Recognizing Roots

Read aloud the representative words listed for each root. Read the words in a normal speaking voice without stressing the roots. Instruct students to underline the root as you read each word.

Point out the following:

Sumpt and *vise* are variant forms of the roots *sume* and *vide.* When you come to *sume* and *vide,* be sure students can identify the variant forms in the representative words.

The roots *tract* and *vise* take the suffix *-or* rather than *-er* (e.g.,

---

Lesson 34

Roots

sume, tract, turb, and *vide*

1 Recognizing Roots

In each group of words below, underline the roots listed on the left.

sume, sumpt	*take; take up*		
	assume	presumably	consumer
	resume	presumption	assumption

tract	*draw, pull*		
	tractor	subtract	attract
	traction	contracted	distraction

turb	*confuse, agitate*		
	turbine	disturb	perturb
	turbulent	disturbance	unperturbed

vide, vise	*see*			
	vision	video	revise	evidence
	invisible	provide	television	provision

2 Word Building

Join the morphemes that follow to build whole words. Write the words on the lines provided. Remember to drop the silent *e* if necessary.

1. abs + tract ___abstract___
2. con + sume ___consume___
3. turb + o + jet ___turbojet___
4. sumpt + uous ___sumptuous___
5. ad + vise + ory ___advisory___
6. super + vise + or ___supervisor___
7. un + at + tract + ive ___unattractive___
8. un + dis + turb + ed ___undisturbed___
9. im + pro + vide + ent ___improvident___
10. sub + con + tract + or ___subcontractor___

---

tractor, supervisor). The word *advisor* is also commonly spelled *adviser,* but this is an exception.

Additional activities:

Have students work in small groups to generate as many words as they can that include these roots.

Ask students to identify any prefixes or suffixes that they have studied or recognize in the representative words.

2 Word Building

Be sure that students drop the silent *e* in numbers 5, 6, and 9.

3 Variant Forms

This exercise emphasizes the relationships among related forms of the same root.

Encourage students to use a dictionary if necessary. Remind them to pronounce the nouns ending in *-ion* and to proofread the words they write.

Additional activity:

Have students use pairs of words (the verb and the noun) in sentences.

4 Creating Words in Sentences

In this exercise, students reorder and combine morphemes to create words that make sense in a given sentence.

Remind students to read a whole sentence before starting to combine the morphemes to create words. After they've written words in the blanks, they should reread the sentence to be sure that it makes sense.

Be sure that students drop the silent *e* in numbers 1, 2, 4, 5, and 8.

5 Looking at Meanings

Add one of the following roots to each partial word below. The word you create must fit the definition on the left. Use a dictionary if you are unsure of a word.

sume	tract	turb	vise

Definitions	Partial words	Words with roots added
1. to interrupt or bother	dis	disturb
2. to give counsel	ad	advise
3. someone who comes to see you	itor	visitor
4. to take up again	re	resume
5. to draw towards someone	at	attract

6 Changing Roots

Remove the root from each of the words below and replace it with one of the following roots. Then use the word you have created in a phrase or sentence.

sume/sumpt	tract	turb	vide/vise

	New words	Phrases or sentences
1. pre*fer*	presume	_____
2. ex*pend*	extract	_____
3. re*spire*	revise	_____
4. dis*pose*	disturb	_____
5. pro*gress*	provide	_____
6. de*mote*	devise	_____
7. con*fusion*	consumption	_____
8. sub*mission*	subtraction	_____

Lesson 34   149

---

5 Looking at Meanings

Learning to relate the meanings of roots to the words in which they are used should help students to spell the roots correctly.

Be sure that students drop the silent *e* from *vise* in number 3.

Additional activities:

Once students have written the word suggested by the definition and partial word given, have them underline the portion of the definition that led them to choose a certain root.

Have students use the words in sentences.

6 Changing Roots

The root to be replaced is italicized in each word.

Remind students to use a dictionary if they are uncertain of a word.

The answers on the replica of the student page are examples.

Accept any answer that forms a correctly spelled word.

When students are writing phrases and sentences, allow them to use any form of the words they have created.

Additional activity:

Have students use the original word in a phrase or sentence.

For advanced students:

See how many different words students can build from any of the given words by removing and replacing one affix at a time. They can find additional affixes in the glossary.

Quizzes

Give a graded spelling quiz on the words in this lesson or other words that include these roots.

Sentences

Sentences for dictation are available at the back of this book.

Review of
Lessons 29–34

Objectives

- **Roots:** Review roots studied in Unit 8.
- **Related Words:** Write nouns related to verbs in context.
- **Patterns:** Review Doubling Pattern 2 for adding suffixes. Practice spelling /ənt/, /əns/, and /ənsē/ at the end of words.
- **Word Building:** Add *-ion* to roots to build new words. Add *ceed* or *ceive* to prefixes. Select and combine morphemes to build at least 20 words.
- **Word Game:** Play a game to build words.

You may need to review some of the patterns for adding and spelling roots before beginning this review, depending on how well students have managed with individual lessons. Remind them that they can refer to the lessons whenever necessary.

For detailed information about patterns and strategies, refer to the lesson notes for individual lessons.

1 Variant Forms

In this exercise students write the singular or plural noun form of a verb given in the context of a sentence. The target verb is italicized.

Roots Presented in This Unit ····························

cede	dict	mote	scribe
ceed	duce	pel	script
ceive	duct	pend	sist
cept	fer	pense	spire
cess	form	plore	sume
cide	gress	pulse	sumpt
cise	ject	pute	sumpt
clude	lect	rect	tract
clus	miss	reg	vide
cur	mit	rupt	vise

1 Variant Forms

Some roots have variant forms. Knowing the variant form can help you to spell related words. In each of the following sentences, a verb form is italicized. Complete the sentence by writing the noun form of the same root in the blank provided. The first one is done for you.

1. You *deceived* me, and I dislike any form of __deception__ .

2. If you *subscribe* to that new magazine, why not cancel your other __subscription__ ?

3. I won't *permit* you to watch that movie even if your friends have __permission__ .

4. If you *introduce* the speaker, I'll take care of the other __introductions__ .

5. Bread, eggs, and milk were *provided,* but we had to buy the other __provisions__ .

6. A bridge that's *suspended* over water or a gorge is a __suspension__ bridge.

7. She *succeeded* in winning the tournament, so we celebrated her __success__ .

8. The driver *concluded* that he had room, but his __conclusion__ proved wrong.

Remind students to read a whole sentence before writing the noun in the blank. They should reread the sentence afterward to be sure that it makes sense. Make sure that the sentences are mechanically correct, i.e. that students use the plural form of the noun when appropriate.

2 **Doubling Pattern 2**

This is a review of the roots presented in Lessons 29–34 for which the final consonant is often doubled according to Doubling Pattern 2. Review that pattern before beginning this exercise if necessary.

Part A: Be sure that students underline only the three letters of the roots listed at the beginning of the exercise. They may be tempted to underline the *ff* in *different* or the *cc* in *occurring*. You may want them to circle the doubled consonants where they occur before the suffixes. Ask students to explain why they occur in these words.

3 **Adding Roots and Suffixes**

Part A: Students add the suffix -ion to the given roots. This includes practice in using variant forms of roots correctly and in applying the strategies for spelling /shən/ at the end of a word.

Remind students to add, drop, or change letters when necessary. If students have trouble with any of these words, review the particular root causing them difficulty.

Part B. Add the roots *ceed* or *ceive* to the following prefixes. Write the whole words on the lines provided.

1. pro __proceed__   5. per __perceive__

2. ex __exceed__   6. con __conceive__

3. suc __succeed__   7. de __deceive__

4. re __receive__

Remember that these are the only *ceed* and *ceive* words, so memorizing the spellings is the best strategy.

4 **Practicing a Pattern: /ənt/, /əns/, and /ənsē/**
Several roots in this unit can have the suffixes *-ant/-ance/-ancy* or *-ent/-ence/-ency* added to them. For each root on the left, check the correct column to show which suffixes can be added. Then write an example of the root with one of the suffixes added. Use a dictionary and remember to add, drop, or change letters if necessary.

	-ant/-ance/-ancy	-ent/-ence/-ency	Example words
1. differ		√	differences
2. repel		√	repellent
3. recur		√	recurrence
4. insist		√	insistent
5. incess	√		incessantly
6. inform	√		informant
7. accept	√		acceptance
8. disturb	√		disturbance
9. intermit		√	intermittently
10. depend		√	independent
11. precede		√	precedence

152   Unit 8 Review

Part B: Students add the roots *ceed* or *ceive* to the given prefixes. Every *ceed* and *ceive* word is included.

Additional activity:

Have students use words from Part A or Part B in sentences.

4 **Practicing a Pattern: /ənt/, /əns/, and /ənsē/**

In this exercise, roots that take the suffixes *-ant/-ance/-ancy* or *-ent/-ence/-ency* are reviewed. Once students have completed the chart, they can use it for reference when necessary.

Encourage students to use a dictionary to help determine which suffixes can be added to the roots if they are not sure. Remind them that the pronunciation will not help them to spell these suffixes. Point out that learning which root words take which set of suffixes will provide another strategy for predicting the spelling of the schwa sound in these words.

Be sure that students double the final consonant when necessary in numbers 2, 3, and 9 and that they drop the silent *e* in number 11.

Students' example words will vary from those given on the replica of the student page.

Additional activities:

Have students use some of their example words in sentences.

Have students compare their example words and develop a master list.

5 **Challenge Word Building**

Emphasize that students can use as few or as many morphemes as needed for a particular word. For instance, the roots *miss, scribe,* and *script* are whole words.

Remind students to use a dictionary if necessary. Have them check to be sure that they have added, dropped, or changed letters when necessary.

5 Challenge Word Building

On a separate piece of paper, combine the morphemes below to build at least 20 words. Use as few or as many morphemes as you need for each word. Use a dictionary if you are unsure of a word.

Prefixes		Roots	Suffixes	
con-	re-	ceive/cept	-able	-ion
de-	sub-	mit/miss	-ible	-ive
per-		scribe/script	-er	

6 Missing Letters

A pair of letters has been omitted twice from each word below. The second time the letters are used they are reversed. Fill in the missing letters to make whole words. Each of the answers has a root from Unit 8. Study the example before you begin.

Example: __d__ __e__ ject __e__ __d__

1. p __r__ __e__ f __e__ __r__
2. __v__ __i__ ndict __i__ __v__ e
3. un __d__ __i__ v __i__ __d__ ed
4. transm __i__ __s__ __s__ __i__ on
5. rep __e__ __l__ __l__ __e__ nt
6. __d__ __e__ plor __e__ __d__
7. subm __i__ __s__ __s__ __i__ ve
8. prop __e__ __l__ __l__ __e__ r
9. __s__ __e__ c __e__ __s__ sion
10. __r__ __u__ pt __u__ __r__ e
11. p __e__ __r__ spi __r__ __e__
12. in __d__ __i__ v __i__ __d__ ual

6 Missing Letters

In this word game, students fill in pairs of letters to build complete words. In each word, the pair of letters is missing twice, but the second time it is used, the order of the letters is reversed. Each complete word contains a root from Unit 8. More than one word may be formed for some of the items. Accept any correctly spelled word, even if it does not contain a root from Unit 8.

Sentences

Sentences for dictation are available at the back of this book.

Unit 8 Test

We recommend that you test your students on the words from Unit 8 before going on to the text review. The following is a suggested list of words from Unit 8. You may want to substitute other words to meet the needs of your students.

Dictate each word and use it in a simple sentence. Students should be able to spell 90 percent of these words correctly.

Some responses are listed here. There are others. Accept all correctly spelled words.

conceivable	deception	perceiver	remiss
conceive	deceptive	perception	remission
conceiver	describable	perceptive	remit
concept	describe	permissible	remitter
conception	describer	permission	scribe
conceptive	description	permissive	script
conscribe	descriptive	permit	submission
conscript	miss	permitter	submissive
conscription	mission	receivable	submit
deceivable	missive	receive	subscribe
deceive	perceivable	receiver	subscriber
deceiver	perceive	reception	subscription
		receptive	

succeed	permission
excessively	emotional
receivership	compelling
deceptive	independent
undecided	deploring
precision	reputable
including	irregularity
conclusive	interruption
recurrent	transcription
unpredictable	persistence
producer	inspiration
introduction	consumerism
transferral	contractual
progressive	disturbances
objectionable	visibly

Text Review

Objectives

- **Patterns:** Review and practice patterns for adding suffixes. Review patterns for spelling words with Greek morphemes and practice using combining forms. Practice spelling the schwa when adding selected suffixes to roots. Practice spelling /shən/, /shəl/, and /shəs/ at the end of words.
- **Word Building:** Build words by adding selected morphemes to given morphemes. Select and combine morphemes to build whole words.
- **Composing Sentences:** Write original sentences using selected words.

You may want students to keep track of the words they have to look up while working on the text review. If not already there, these words could be added to the list of personal spelling problems that students have been keeping in their notebooks.

You may need to review some of the more difficult patterns for adding and spelling morphemes before beginning this review. Remind them that they can refer to the lessons whenever necessary.

For detailed information about patterns and strategies, refer to the lesson notes for individual lessons.

Units 1-8 — Text Review

1 Patterns for Adding Suffixes
Part A. Fill in the blanks to complete the following sentences.

1. The silent *e* at the end of a root is dropped when a suffix that starts with a __vowel__ is added.
2. If a word has one syllable, one vowel, and ends in one consonant, __double__ the final consonant before adding an ending that begins with a vowel.
3. If the last syllable of a word has one vowel, ends in one consonant, and is __accented__, double the final consonant before adding an ending that begins with a vowel.
4. When adding a suffix to a word that ends in a consonant plus *y*, change the *y* to __i__, unless the suffix begins with __i__.

Part B. Join the morphemes that follow to build whole words. Remember to follow the patterns above.

1. ply + able ___pliable___
2. slip + ery ___slippery___
3. happy + ly ___happily___
4. in + vent + or ___inventor___
5. pre + fer + ed ___preferred___
6. re + cur + ing ___recurring___
7. ad + mit + ance ___admittance___
8. as + sume + ing ___assuming___
9. com + pel + ing ___compelling___
10. con + fer + ence ___conference___
11. im + prove + ment ___improvement___
12. ap + ply + cate + ion ___application___

2 Greek Morphemes
Part A. Fill in the blanks to complete the following sentences.

1. In words from Greek, /f/ is usually spelled __ph__.
2. In words from Greek, /k/ is usually spelled __ch__.
3. Greek words sometimes begin with a silent __p__.

154   Text Review

---

1 Patterns for Adding Suffixes

Review any part of Lesson 3 before beginning this exercise if necessary. Students should be comfortable with using all these patterns by now.

Part A: Students complete sentences stating patterns for adding suffixes.

Part B: Students join morphemes to build words. Dropping the silent *e* is necessary in numbers 8 and 12. Changing *y* to *i* is necessary in numbers 1, 3, and 12. Doubling the final consonant of the root before adding the suffix is necessary in numbers 2, 5, 6, 7, and 9. No changes are necessary in numbers 4, 10, and 11.

Additional activity:

Have students use some of the words they build in sentences.

Part B. Many Greek morphemes function as combining forms. Combine the following morphemes to make 12 different words, and write them on the lines provided.

astro	geo	logy	photo	tele
bio	gram	meter	psycho	thermo
chrono	graph	phono/phone	techno	

astrology	photograph	geology
biology	telegram	thermometer
chronology	telephone	technology
telephoto	psychology	phonology

3 Adding Prefixes, Roots, or Suffixes to Make Complete Words

Part A. Add a root to each prefix or suffix below to create a word. Write the whole word on the right.

1. de ___decide___
2. ex ___explore___
3. re ___resist___
4. in ___inspire___
5. im ___immerse___

6. di ___diverge___
7. ial ___residential___
8. ious ___curious___
9. ance ___significance___
10. ion ___rejection___

Part B. Add at least one prefix and one suffix to each root below to create a word. Remember to add, change, or drop letters if necessary.

1. gress ___progressive___
2. pense ___suspension___
3. quest ___unquestionable___
4. plete ___completely___
5. spire ___respiration___

6. sign ___designer___
7. ject ___objectively___
8. mit ___remittance___
9. quire ___inquiry___
10. pel ___compelled___

2 Greek Morphemes

Review any parts of Lessons 19–21 before beginning this exercise if necessary.

Part A: Students complete sentences stating patterns that are helpful for correctly spelling words of Greek origin.

Part B: Remind students that many Greek morphemes function as combining forms. In this part of the exercise, students combine Greek morphemes in a variety of ways to make words.

Make sure that students use the correct form of *phono* when combining morphemes.

Answers given on the replica of the student page are examples. Accept all correctly spelled words.

Additional activity:

Have students use some of the words they build in sentences.

3 Adding Prefixes, Roots, or Suffixes to Make Complete Words

Part A: Students form complete words by filling in missing roots. Prefixes or suffixes are supplied. Encourage students to use the glossary to find appropriate roots if necessary.

Many roots make sense in each blank. Answers given on the replica of the student page are examples. Accept all correctly spelled words.

Part B: Students add prefixes and suffixes to the given roots to form complete words. Encourage students to be adventurous in adding affixes. They can add more than one prefix and more than one suffix to many roots. Remind them to use the glossary to find appropriate affixes if necessary.

Many affixes make sense with each root. Answers given on the replica of the student page are examples. Accept all correctly spelled words.

Additional activities:

Have students compare their answers and develop a master list of words.

Have students use some of their words in sentences.

Challenge students to use as many of their words as possible in a single sentence.

4 Spelling the Schwa Sound

Add one of the following suffixes to each word below. Write the new words on the lines provided. Remember to add, drop, or change letters and use a dictionary if necessary.

-ant   -ent   -able   -ate   -ery/-ary/-ory/-ry
-ance/-ancy -ence/-ency -ible   -ite

1. refer _____reference_____   10. expect _____expectant_____
2. assist _____assistant_____   11. passion_____passionate_____
3. brave _____bravery_____   12. defend _____defendable_____
4. insist _____insistence_____   13. oppose_____opposite_____
5. apply _____appliance_____   14. emerge _____emergency_____
6. digest _____digestible_____   15. indulge _____indulgent_____
7. ignore _____ignorant_____   16. consider _____considerate_____
8. reduce _____reducible_____   17. moment _____momentary_____
9. appear _____appearance_____   18. describe_____describable_____

5 Spelling /shən/, /shəl/, and /shəs/

Add one of the following suffixes to each root below and write the new words on the lines provided. Remember to add, drop, or change letters if necessary.

-ion   -ial   -ious

1. race _____racial_____   7. benefit _____beneficial_____
2. caut _____cautious_____   8. essence _____essential_____
3. relax _____relaxation_____   9. finance _____financial_____
4. infect _____infectious_____   10. convert _____conversion_____
5. office _____official_____   11. educate _____education_____
6. revise _____revision_____   12. persuade _____persuasion_____

156   Text Review

4 Spelling the Schwa Sound

This exercise incorporates some of the most difficult spelling problems addressed in this book. Review any parts of Lessons 6, 8, and 23 before beginning if necessary.

Students add to given root words suffixes beginning with vowels that are often pronounced as schwas. Remind them to use a dictionary to check their spelling and to add, drop, or change letters whenever necessary.

Several of these suffixes can be added to some of the root words given, e.g., *considerable* and *considerate*. Answers given on the replica of the student page are examples. Accept all correctly spelled words.

5 Spelling /shən/, /shəl/, and /shəs/

This exercise incorporates other difficult spelling problems addressed in this book. Review any parts of Lessons 7 and 22 before beginning if necessary.

Students add the suffixes -*ion*, -*ial*, or -*ious* to given root words. Remind them to add, drop, or change letters when necessary. Tell them to pronounce the words before they write them and to use a dictionary to check their spelling if they are unsure of a word.

Remind students that the variant form of a root is often used in related words, especially when forming nouns ending in -*ion*.

More than one of these suffixes can be added to some of the root words given. Answers given on the replica of the student page are examples. Accept all correctly spelled words.

6 Writing Sentences

Use three words from Exercise 4 and three words from Exercise 5 in original sentences.

_____

_____

_____

_____

_____

7 Word Building

For each root on the left, build four words using any of the prefixes and suffixes given.

1. pose   -able   -al   de-   dis-   -ion   -ite   pro-   re-   sup-

    disposable   proposal   supposition   reposition

2. cede/ceed   -ent   pre-   pro-   re-   sub-/suc-   -ure

    precede   procedure   succeed   precedent

3. verse   ad-   al-   con-   -ible   -ion   -ly   re-   trans-

    reversal   reversible   conversion   adversely

4. scribe/script   con-   de-   -ion   pre-   pro-   sub-

    description   prescription   subscribe   conscript

6 Writing Sentences

The exercise instructions are deliberately flexible about how many sentences should be written. Encourage students to be adventurous in their writing. By now many of them should be able to use several words in a single sentence, and others may be able to write a short paragraph incorporating their words.

If students need more room, encourage them to use their notebooks. Make sure that they proofread their sentences.

If students ask how to spell a word they have not studied, encourage them to look it up in the dictionary.

7 Word Building

Students add prefixes and suffixes to the roots given on the left to build four words for each root. Encourage students to be adventurous in adding affixes. They can add more than one prefix and more than one suffix to many roots.

Be sure that students drop the silent _e_ from _pose, cede, verse,_ and _scribe_ when necessary and use the variant form of the root if appropriate.

Many affixes make sense with each root. Answers given on the replica of the student page are examples. Accept all correctly spelled words.

Additional activities:

Have students compare their answers and develop a master list of words.

Have students use some of their words in sentences.

Challenge students to use as many of their words as possible in a single sentence.

Quizzes

Give a graded spelling quiz on the words in this book or other words that include the same morphemes. Be sure to include any morphemes that your students have found particularly difficult.

Sentences for Dictation

Lesson 4

1. Bus drivers are usually trained to drive carefully and safely.
2. I really look forward to seeing Beverly because she's so friendly and cheerful.
3. Let's eat quickly when we get to the mall and then do the shopping afterward.
4. Howard tries to be helpful, but he works too hastily and carelessly.
5. Her coworkers would be grateful if she talked quietly, but it's pointless to ask.
6. Edward dressed so hurriedly that his sweater is on backward.

Lesson 5

1. Friendship often leads to the greatest happiness.
2. There's a movement in our neighborhood to help fight homelessness.
3. His granddaughter's companionship and thoughtfulness mean a lot to him.
4. Can the government forbid shipments of arms to other countries?
5. Carefulness and good workmanship were stressed during the apprenticeship.
6. What's the likelihood of a department store having curtains with those measurements?

Lesson 6

1. If you loosen the seatbelt, it will be easier to fasten.
2. Our bosses insist on having the newest machinery in the factory.
3. The radio announcer warned listeners that a winter storm advisory was in effect.
4. The doctor at the clinic told my mother she needs minor surgery.
5. Look in the phone directory to get the library's number.
6. You have just seen the fastest runner in history set a new record.

Lesson 7

1. Maria's car failed the emissions test at its last inspection.
2. My grandparents, who are Russian, often tell about their immigration to this country.
3. As a mark of devotion, we always have a big Mother's Day celebration.
4. Luis wants to be an electrician or a laboratory technician.
5. After a brief discussion, they headed in the direction of the television store.
6. She questioned my reaction to the politician's views, so I explained my objections.

Lesson 8

1. Clarence is intelligent, but he's easily influenced by others.
2. Recently there have been frequent unpleasant and violent world events.
3. I was hesitant about offering assistance, since Vincent was reluctant to ask for it.
4. One significant consequence of modern medicine is longer life expectancy.
5. The patients can ring for the nurse if there's an emergency.
6. Residents in our apartment building are impatient because repairs are needed urgently.

Unit 2 Review

1. The musician makes weekly appearances on two different shows.
2. It's inconvenient to have to do laundry and shop for groceries daily.
3. The darkness in the basement led to all the confusion down there.
4. The residents show great appreciation for any lively entertainment.
5. The floor at the brewery is often slippery, so the primary concern is safety.
6. The actor was careful not to let the audience know where the machinery was hidden.

Lesson 9

1. According to Gary, it's unnecessary to use unleaded gas in the old truck.
2. Is it cool to go around with your shoelaces untied and your shirt unbuttoned?
3. The deadline for applications is approaching, but Tina's is still incomplete.
4. Apart from the immediate family, no one knew that my father was unemployed.
5. It was impossible to accustom the newly adopted kitten to living indoors.
6. My grandmother thinks that modern appliances are unimportant and unimpressive.

Lesson 10

1. Voting in local or national elections is not complicated.
2. Members of Congress disagreed on what to do about the trade deficit.
3. Her unconventional and permissive perspective on education deserves attention.
4. My parents decided to get divorced after efforts to resolve their differences failed.
5. Congratulations on persuading Lila to overcome her difficult dilemma.
6. Such exceptional dishonesty and corruption are despised by everyone.

Lesson 11

1. The preview for the movie was mistakenly released too early.
2. The couple reluctantly postponed their wedding plans, but refused to wait much longer.
3. The electrician is preparing to replace some unsafe wiring.
4. The employment agent said that the company has progressive production methods.
5. We urgently need protection against redevelopment in our neighborhood.
6. I promised my aunt I'd remember to pick up coffee, red beans, and cherry preserves.

Unit 3 Review

1. It's important to remind children not to go far afield when unaccompanied.
2. That outfit would be irresistible, except that it's definitely too expensive.
3. Susan found it depressing to be compared constantly to her younger cousin.
4. Let's make an effort to collect and distribute discarded clothes.
5. Mary got involved in some illegal business by mistake, but she quit immediately.
6. Perhaps one consequence of Nancy's disease is that she'll accept more assistance.

Lesson 12

1. According to these papers, Tom has a recent police record.
2. Martin Luther King, Jr., was central in early civil rights activism.
3. Around 10 percent of the people at work were infected by that flu virus.
4. I have to concentrate to remember exactly what the new security precautions are.
5. Until an effective cure is found, AIDS will remain incurable.
6. Some of the unsatisfactory flavorings are artificially manufactured.

Lesson 13

1. The finalists in the competition were profiled in the local newspaper.
2. Florence finally quit her job as a filing clerk at the oil refinery.
3. The company was profoundly affected by the unfounded rumors about its finances.
4. Tony gave the customer a refund because the fish fillets had definitely gone bad.
5. I'm fundamentally confused about what to do after I finish school.
6. The owner refuses to believe that the building's foundations have shifted.

Lesson 14

1. The kids waited patiently in line for rides at the amusement park.
2. Amanda's passionate nature really emerged during the argument.
3. We were commended for supplying duplicates of the forms so efficiently.
4. I was told I needed a recommendation when I applied for that job.
5. Musicians often get immersed in a different lifestyle.
6. Customers can be impatient and demanding if we can't supply an appliance immediately.

Lesson 15

1. Mr. Porter's opponent proved to be a complete impostor.
2. You're supposed to be supporting the Portland Trail Blazers.
3. His spirits have improved since the support group started.
4. We're in a tough position according to reports on job opportunities.
5. Our car was impounded, so we've been using public transportation.
6. Some people disapprove of disposable diapers because they pose problems in landfills.

Lesson 16

1. Conservative politicians questioned the requested extension of the subsidy.
2. He pretended not to understand my query about the job requirements.
3. Neva is trying to preserve her sanity despite being completely overextended.
4. Jesse was intent on reserving seats for the big game on Saturday.
5. In the meat section where Roberta works, they're required to sanitize everything.
6. The doctors requested that I stay in the hospital for intensive observation.

Lesson 17

1. Two of the witnesses testified that the accused had a history of substance abuse.
2. The maintenance crew I work on is constantly busy with an assortment of jobs.
3. The tenant resorted to not paying rent to make the landlord pay attention.
4. The testimony contains detailed information about the design of the appliance.
5. Constance obtained a significant amount of money from some distant relative.
6. Carmen protested the difficult circumstances she had to work in at the bakery.

Lesson 18

1. The controversial convention was about AIDS education and prevention.
2. We have divergent ideas about what attracts adventurous tourists.
3. George diverted the teacher's attention by drawing him into a conversation.
4. Several new kinds of textiles have been invented this century.
5. Good verbal skills are useful in many contexts.
6. When he inverted the words in the sentence, he reversed the meaning.

Unit 4 Review

1. The students were required to reenact a historical event in class.
2. Francine refuses to buy candy because it contains a substantial amount of sugar.
3. According to Ricardo, he's completely cured despite the infection after the surgery.
4. The way Hank replied to the question revealed his attention to detail.
5. All the residents intend to sign the petition protesting the closing of the school.
6. Manufacturers in all sectors are trying to conserve energy and cut costs.

Lesson 19

1. The program notes for the play are full of grammatical errors.
2. Phil keeps the thermostat turned low and wears thermal underwear and socks.
3. The entertainer's biography was made into a funny television program.
4. People use the telephone in emergencies now, but they used to send telegrams.
5. I'll photocopy that diagram for you if you would like.
6. The photographer used a telephoto lens for that photo.

Lesson 20

1. It seems logical to have a biopsy of any tumor.
2. The price of motorcycles is astronomically high.
3. Catalogs and other junk mail generate a lot of paper for recycling.
4. Reva is taking biology, geology, and astronomy at school this semester.
5. Astronauts need to have nitrogen and oxygen in the Space Shuttle.
6. The biography of the Democratic presidential candidate will be published soon.

Lesson 21

1. The diameter of that round mirror is almost a meter.
2. Our recreation center offers classes ranging from aerobics to mechanics.
3. Developing technology makes cars continually more aerodynamic.
4. Christina has chronic flu symptoms, but the thermometer doesn't indicate a fever.
5. Our lab technician's favorite television programs are psychodramas.
6. If we synchronize our visits to the optometrist, we can ride over there together.

Unit 5 Review

1. Our aerobics teacher uses all sorts of new techniques.
2. The geography of the area makes it illogical to build an airport.
3. A mechanic telephoned from the shop to say your bicycle is fixed.
4. Do you think Christopher's psychological problems could be genetic?
5. Let's get a professional photographer to take the wedding photographs.
6. It would be better if the events on that television program were in chronological order.

Lesson 22

1. Global warming is actually a controversial theory.
2. Those identical twins are usually quite comical.
3. It's essential and logical to build muscles gradually.
4. My brother's outrageous behavior sometimes makes me anxious.
5. Personally, I'm curious about that famous martial arts master.
6. We'll need additional chairs for the special family dinner on Memorial Day.

Lesson 23

1. My favorite uncle is definitely a remarkable man.
2. Unfortunately, we had to redecorate the living room because of water damage.
3. After graduating, Nate went into his family's profitable sausage-making business.
4. Lisa didn't think it was possible to carry the packages such a considerable distance.
5. The shortage of available housing has reached incredible and desperate levels.
6. I'm saving for a personal stereo with collapsible earphones and rechargeable batteries.

Lesson 24

1. The tourists were unrealistic about how much they could see in one day.
2. The course on dealing with alcoholism in the family was genuinely constructive.
3. Jackie criticized the organization at the meeting but apologized later.
4. Geraldine's a creative cook and often manages to use alternative ingredients.
5. Ali is optimistic that the medicine will help him get out of intensive care soon.
6. Sasha routinely buys inexpensive clothes and always looks gorgeous.

Lesson 25

1. Was it noticeable that I had difficulty during the band practice?
2. We were all hungry and thirsty after so much activity.
3. It was a pleasure going out with such mature and witty people.
4. Janice is optimistic about having more leisure time in the future.
5. It's a certainty that the festivities will be postponed if it's a rainy day.
6. People get exposure to different cultures by having friends of other nationalities.

Unit 6 Review

1. It's encouraging that so much nutritious food is naturally delicious.
2. The lecturer maintained that capitalism and communism are opposite ideologies.
3. Betty eventually got the message to go to the service counter in the electronics store.
4. It's unbelievable that my grandfather's financial information was kept so confidential.
5. The artist realizes that it's possible to finish the picture if the deadline is reasonable.
6. The new sofa is especially comfortable and is covered with attractive material.

Lesson 26

1. The man who interrupted the speaker so often was obviously antisocial.
2. Henry obtained more antibiotic ointment for the first aid kit.
3. Estella is preoccupied with preparing for her job interview.
4. Willie felt an obligation to contradict that statement because he opposes it.
5. New technology is occasionally introduced at the company where I work.
6. What a contrast when one friend offers to help and another friend simply interferes.

Lesson 27

1. I'd shop at the supermarket if I could reach it by public transportation.
2. The substitute teacher has the support of the parents.
3. The survivors of the accident were transferred successfully to the hospital.
4. The supervisor will automatically ask if there are sufficient supplies for the transaction.
5. Luther succeeded in getting the actress to autograph a copy of her autobiography.
6. The superior personal stereos supposedly have auto reverse.

Lesson 28

1. The school has a unique multicultural program.
2. Wilma suffered multiple fractures in the bicycle accident.
3. Nina is bilingual in Spanish and English, but her mother is actually trilingual.
4. The uniforms are made of a cotton and polyester blend and are monogrammed.
5. Joe monopolized the floor space with his tripod and other camera equipment.
6. The audience was united in agreeing that the speeches were uniformly monotonous.

Unit 7 Review

1. That substandard supplier automatically adds a surcharge for transportation.
2. Simple observation gives only a superficial understanding of how automobiles work.
3. Is there international support for multilateral peace-keeping forces?
4. The transition from regular glasses to bifocals is occasionally difficult.
5. That new antiseptic cream is supposedly superior to any now offered.
6. Mr. Wong had a successful triple-bypass operation and is not suffering ill effects.

Lesson 29

1. During a recession both employees and supervisors have to accept wage freezes.
2. The reclusive couple succeeded in finding a secluded house to rent.
3. The committee decided that precise directions for using the pesticide were necessary.
4. That driver had been caught exceeding the speed limit the preceding month.
5. You have to concede that everyone does not have equal access to exclusive schools.
6. Until the last page of the book, I was deceived into concluding that the victim had committed suicide.

Lesson 30

1. The current educational system has predictable problems.
2. A preferable system would introduce alternative curriculums.
3. The travel agent has offered a reduction in the cost of the excursion.
4. She always preferred to shop around for the best products at reduced prices.
5. It's currently impossible to predict how fresh the produce at the market will be.
6. Transferring the products to different stores is a frequent occurrence.

Lesson 31

1. I can pick up the car after the transmission and emissions have been checked.
2. Marcus was dejected at the recollection of his ex-girlfriend's rejection of his ring.
3. Carlo admitted that he was aggressively going after a promotion on the production line.
4. Despite Stella's objections, her parents won't permit her to live in a remote area.
5. Progress made on the recycling project includes selecting a collection agency.
6. The candidates are emotional about the forthcoming congressional elections.

Lesson 32

1. They disputed whether the expensive tickets for the performance were overpriced or not.
2. The support group explored the issue of co-dependency and shared information.
3. Depending on how successfully you learn computer skills, your job may be transformed.
4. The nurse was compelled to keep the patient in suspense until after exploratory surgery.
5. After Cathy bought the sweater on impulse, she decided it was a deplorable color.
6. That store reputedly sells dependable products at inexpensive prices.

Lesson 33

1. Our regular subscription to the newspaper expired last month.
2. An incorrect amount of flour can give bread an irregular consistency.
3. Ramón was describing an irresistible movie when we were interrupted.
4. The hero of the story persisted in resisting the conspiracies against him.
5. We had a spirited conversation about the need to follow directions consistently.
6. The supervisor's abrupt resignation disrupted our work schedules.

Lesson 34

1. Presumably the video store has that movie, provided it's not already rented out.
2. Evidently the farmer made the assumption that the tractor had invisible defects.
3. We were distracted by the disturbance in the street, but we gradually resumed work.
4. I'm perturbed by the lack of traction on my tires and assume I need a new set.
5. That car looks attractive in the television ads, but the gas consumption is high.
6. The carpenter revised the contract, subtracting a month from the deadline date.

Unit 8 Review

1. The customer evidently needs assistance in using the store directory.
2. New federal regulations presumably reduce the possibility of corruption in banking.
3. My aunt referred me to a progressive doctor who prescribed different drugs.
4. The book includes a description of the process of setting up an independent business.
5. After an emotional acceptance speech, the television producer received the award.
6. The lawyer predicted that his client would decide to settle the dispute out of court.

Glossary of Morphemes

Prefixes

a-
  without; on, in; in a state of

ad-, ac-, af-, al-, ap-, as-, at-
  toward, to, near, or in

anti-
  against, opposing

auto-, aut-
  self

bi-
  two

con-, col-, com-, cor-
  with, together

contra-
  against

de-
  reverse, remove, reduce

di-
  separation, twoness

dis-, dif-
  absence; opposite;
  reverse, remove

ex-, ef-, e-
  out of, from

in-, im-
  in

in-, im-, il-, ir-
  not

inter-
  between, among

intra-
  inside, within

intro-
  in, inward

mis-
  wrongly, badly

mono-, mon-
  one, alone

multi-
  much, many

ob-, oc-, of-, op-
  toward; against

per-
  through; thoroughly

poly-
  much, many

post-
  after, later; behind

pre-
  before

pro-
  forth, forward

re-
  back, again, anew

sub-, sup-, suc-, suf-
  under; lesser

super-, sur-
  superior, above; additional

trans-
  across

tri-
  three

un-
  not, opposite of;
  reverse an action

uni-
  one

Roots

act
  do

aero, aer
  air, of aircraft

astro, ast
  star, constellation

bio
  life

ceed/cede, cess
  go

ceive, cept
  take

cent
  one hundred; center

chrono, chron
  time

cide, cise
  kill; cut

clude, clus
  close, shut

cord
  heart

crat, cracy
  representative or
  form of government, power

cur
  run

cure
  care

cyclo, cycle
circle, wheel

dict
say, speak

duce, duct
lead

fact, fect, fit, fic(t)
make, do

fer
carry, bring

file
line, thread; draw a line

fine
end

form
shape

found, fund
bottom; pour

fuse
pour; melt

gen
something produced; producer

geo
earth

gram
write, draw

graph
write, draw

gress
go, step

ject
throw

lect
gather; choose; read

log(ue), logy
word, speech; study of

mand, mend
entrust; order

mechan
machine

merge, merse
plunge, immerse, dip

metro, metr, meter
measure

mit, miss
send; let go

mote
move

muse
gaze, ponder; source of artistic inspiration

pass, pat
endure, suffer

pel, pulse
push, drive

pend, pense
hang; weigh; pay

phono, phone, phon
sound

photo
light

plore
cry, wail

ply
fold together; fill

pone, pose, post, pound
put, place

port
carry

prove
test

psycho, psych
mind, soul

pute
think, reckon; arrange

quest, quer, quire
seek, ask

reg, rect
guide, rule

rupt
break

sane
healthy

scribe, script
write

sect
cut

serve
keep, save; guard

side
sit, settle

sign
mark, sign

sist
cause to stand, place; stop

sort
chance, lot; go out

spire
breathe

stance, stant
stand

sume, sumpt
take; take up

tail
cut

techno, techn
art, skill, science

tele
distant

ten, tain
hold

tend, tent, tense
stretch

test
witness

text
weave, construct

thermo, therm
heat

tour
turn, around

tract
draw, pull

turb
confuse, agitate

vent
come, arrive

verb
word

vert, verge, verse
turn, bend, incline

vide, vise
see

Suffixes

-able
able to, capable of, liable to

-age
action or result of an action;
collection; state

-al
relating to, characterized by

-ance, -ancy
state or quality of; action

-ant
inclined to; being in a
state of; someone who

-ate
cause, make; state, condition;
someone who

-en
made of; cause to be or have;
become

-ence, -ency
state or quality of; action

-ent
inclined to; being in a state of;
someone who

-er
more

-er, -or
someone who; something that

-ery, -ary, -ory, -ry
place where; collection,
condition, or practice of

-est
most

-ful
full of

-hood
state, quality, or condition of

-ial
relating to, characterized by

-ian
person who; of, relating to,
belonging to

-ible
able to, capable of, liable to

-ic
relating to, characterized by

-ice
state or quality of

-ine
of, pertaining to; chemical
substance

-ion
act, result, state of

-ious
full of, characterized by

-ism
act, condition, doctrine, or
practice of

-ist
someone who

-ite
quality of; follower or resident
of; mineral product

-ive
performing or tending toward
an action

-ize
cause to be or become

-less
without, lacking

-ly
in the manner of

-ment
state, act, or process of

-ness
state, quality, condition, or
degree of

-ous
full of, characterized by

-ship
state, quality, or
condition of; skill

-ty, -ity
state or quality of

-ure
act, process; function or body
performing a function

-ward
direction

-y
characterized by